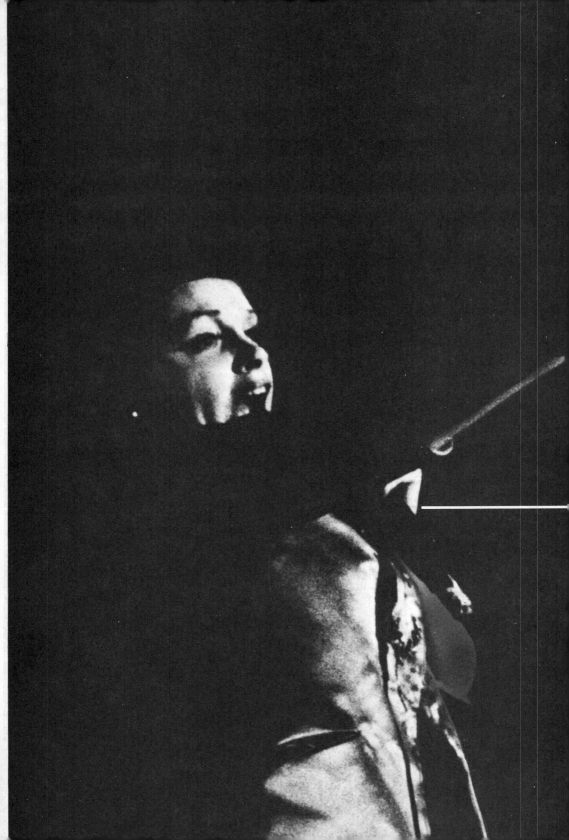

The Great
American
Popular
Singers

Henry Pleasants

SIMON AND SCHUSTER
New York

Published by Simon and Schuster
A Division of Simon & Schuster, Inc.
Simon & Schuster Building
Rockefeller Center
1230 Avenue of the Americas
New York, New York 10020

SIMON AND SCHUSTER and colophon are registered trademarks of
Simon & Schuster, Inc.

Designed by Edith Fowler

Manufactured in the United States of America

10 9 8 7 6 5 4 3 2 1
10 9 8 7 6 5 4 3 2 1 Pbk.

Library of Congress Cataloging in Publication Data

Pleasants, Henry.
    The great American popular singers.

    Reprint. Originally published: New York: Simon and Schuster, 1974.
    Includes index.
    1. Singers—United States—Biography. 2. Music,
Popular (Songs, etc.)—United States—History and
criticism. I. Title.
[ML400.P647 1985]   784.5′0092′2 [B]   84-20251
ISBN: 0-671-54098-X
ISBN: 0-671-54099-8 Pbk.

BY HENRY PLEASANTS

VIENNA'S GOLDEN YEARS OF MUSIC
  selected, translated and edited
  from the collected works of Eduard Hanslick (1950)

THE AGONY OF MODERN MUSIC (1955)

THE MUSICAL JOURNEYS OF LOUIS SPOHR
  selected, translated and edited
  from Louis Spohr's Selbstbiographie (1961)

DEATH OF A MUSIC?
  The Decline of the European Tradition
  and the Rise of Jazz (1961)

THE MUSICAL WORLD OF ROBERT SCHUMANN
  selected, translated and edited from
  the critical writings of Robert Schumann (1965)

THE GREAT SINGERS
  From the Dawn of Opera to Our Own Time (1967)

SERIOUS MUSIC—AND ALL THAT JAZZ!
  An Adventure in Music Criticism (1969)

THE GREAT SINGERS (revised and updated)
  From Jenny Lind and Caruso to Callas and Pavarotti (1981)

ACKNOWLEDGMENTS

I am indebted to William E. Anderson, Herbert R. Mayes, Dr. William B. Ober and my aunt, Maria W. Smith, who read all the chapters in draft and offered many valuable corrections, suggestions, observations, etc., and to Chris Ellis, Dick Haymes, Max Jones, Paul Oliver, George T. Simon and Lee Wiley, who read certain chapters in which their expertise was most helpful. I also wish to express my appreciation to Alan Eichler, Stuart Triff and Lucille Sack for providing me with tapes of Peggy Lee, Ethel Merman and Barbra Streisand respectively, and to William Lerner, of Music Masters, who was always ready to locate and supply out-of-the-way records. I am especially grateful to *Stereo Review, Down Beat* and the Country Music Foundation and Library for making available to me most of the pictures that appear in these pages. I have Lester Glassner at CBS Records and Jack Bradley at the New York Jazz Museum to thank for the photos of Ethel Waters with Eubie Blake and of Bing Crosby with the Rhythm Boys. John Kobal, of London, graciously provided photos of Fannie Brice, Eddie Cantor, Ruth Etting, George Jessel and Al Jolson. My thanks also to the Rodgers and Hammerstein Record Collection of the New York Public Library, Research Division. I gratefully acknowledge, as so often before, the assistance, cooperation and support of my collaborators at Simon and Schuster, in this case Strome Lamon, Edith Fowler, Gerry Sachs and Sophie Sorkin.

I learned much in conversation and correspondence with knowledgeable friends and acquaintances, and from the courtesy of singers who permitted me to observe them on stage and in rehearsal, among them Morgan Ames, Ernie Anderson, Pearl Bailey, Tony Bennett, John Bunch, Willis Conover, Bo Diddley, Billy Eckstine, Jack Elliott, Chris Ellis, Edward Esmond, Sergio Franchi, Hugo Friedhofer, John Garvey, Norman Granz, Dick Haymes, Jon Hendricks, Jack Jones, Max Jones, Howard Keel, Gene Lees, Mundell Lowe, Johnny Mandel, Phil Moore, Dan Morgenstern, Claude Nobs, Paul Oliver, Lou Rawls, Rex Reed, Peter Reilly, Arthur Schwartz, Charles Suber, Sarah Vaughan, Ian Whitcomb, Alec Wilder, Lee Wiley, Andy Williams and Hank Williams, Jr.

I am grateful also to the authors of the many books on individual singers upon which I have drawn in the pertinent chapters.

My thanks, above all, to the singers themselves. For twenty years, and especially during the three years I devoted to this book, they have given me, on stage and screen, and on records, countless hours of treasurable musical and vocal delight. I can only hope that the book itself will convey some notion of what their art has meant to me—and to millions the world over!

CONTENTS

8 | CONTENTS

ILLUSTRATIONS

PREFACE

In considering a paperback reissue of *The Great American Popular Singers*, a decade after its original hardcover publication, one is immediately confronted with a question: to what extent should it be updated to take account of what has happened in popular singing in the intervening years?

Rereading this book ten years after its publication, I am struck by the way in which it seems to embrace, define, assess and enclose an epoch. That epoch ended in the mid-fifties with the emergence, memorably heralded by Elvis Presley, of a new Afro-American (and sometimes British) idiom, a blend of country & western and rhythm & blues variously labeled "rock" and "pop."

I am always distressed when I hear this book referred to as being about "pop" singers. It isn't. It is about "popular" singers. "Pop" was not a term much used—if at all—in association with the singers discussed here, with the possible exception of Presley, and I find it an indignity to apply it to, say, Bing Crosby, Billie Holiday, Frank Sinatra, Peggy Lee, B. B. King or Ella Fitzgerald. "Popular" is dismissive enough as an adjective for artists of such taste and attainment, but it is inescapable as a term distinguishing them from "classical" singers. "Jazz," too, is a dismissive term, convenient for those reluctant to acknowledge or unable to appreciate the superlative artistry of its greatest practitioners. But it is embedded in the vernacular, and we have to live with it.

Thus, in considering any updating, and in reflecting upon what I have heard of the singers who have come—and gone—in the past ten to fifteen years, I incline to the view that these later singers, "pop" singers if you like, belong to a different world and to a different book, to be written by a different author.

I am reminded here of something I wrote some years ago, reviewing a concert by a "folk" singer, then at the height of a brilliant career, at the Royal Festival Hall in London. I left, I said, before the encores, "aware, as never before, that my age gap was showing." Nor was it, nor is it, just an age gap. It is also a gap of musical upbringing, musical experience, musical expectation and musical predilection. As one reared on European or "classical" music, especially opera and art song, I was able to submit the American popular singers who are the subjects of this book to the criteria obtaining for an essentially European or "classical" approach to singing, and to find that in many important respects they were superior to "classical" singers, their art reinvoking—unwittingly—the objectives, criteria and devices of the Italian vocal masters of the seventeenth and early eighteenth centuries, and enriched by exposure to, and absorption of, the African musical elements that distinguish our American popular music from its European antecedents.

I can say the same of the songwriters whose music they have sung and of the arrangers who have provided their instrumental backings, including improvisatory pianists and head arrangements. I would like here to pay my tribute to the late Alec Wilder, my friend and only slightly older contemporary, whose book, *American Popular Song: The Great Innovators, 1900–1950* (1972), was a counterpart to my own. Alec and I shared the predilection to look beyond the superficial idiomatic differences between American "popular" music and European-oriented "classical" music and to explore and expose the more fundamental common roots. His choice of dates suggests that he, too, felt that he was embracing, defining and assessing an epoch that had run its course.

The best of the newer singers are excellent in their way, most notably, at the moment, Michael Jackson. But their way is not mine. To my ears—and eyes—they are too frenetic, too given to bizarre costuming and lighting. The decibel count is too high, the dynamics too obviously controlled by an engineer at a console. Where the older singers used the microphone as a means of singing *to* you instead of *at* you, they shout into it, mostly unintelligibly, competing with too obtrusive and too dominant instrumental and vocal backing. And I find what they sing to be of more social than musical significance or substance. There is excellence in what the best of them accomplish, but the criteria are not mine. I leave its definition and assessment to others closer to the idiom and the scene than I, at my age and with my background, have found it possible or congenial to be.

And so, I prefer to leave this book as it was, and is. I do, however, take this opportunity to say that I could wish, in retrospect, to have given a chapter instead of casual references, to the vocal art of Fred Astaire, whom I have come to regard not as a dancer who sang, but as a singer whose dancing was a choreographic extension of his singing, just as I think—and, fortunately, said—that Louis Armstrong was a singer whose trumpet playing was an instrumental extension of his vocal predilections.

I wish that I might have written more about Mabel Mercer, whom I had not heard in a room at the time of writing. She was one of those singers whose art is not adequately projected on record, as is true, too, of the more recent "room singer," Steve Ross. I could wish, too, that Gladys Knight had sung and recorded more often without the Pips. As a soloist she has given me great pleasure. And I would like to record my admiration of the vocalism of Jack Jones and Glen Campbell.

It remains to note that some of the singers discussed in these pages are no longer with us, most notably and sadly: Bing Crosby, Louis Armstrong, Elvis Presley, Ethel Waters, Mabel Mercer and Ethel Merman. I owe to them all, as well as to those still living, memorable and treasureable experiences of the singer as a great artist.

Introduction

In calling this book *The Great American Popular Singers* I am governed by the terminological and categorical conventions of our time. Musical society today is dichotomous, one part of it identified with a European idiom we think of as Serious or Classical, the other with an Afro-American idiom we think of as Popular. The singers I shall be writing about have worked, and many are still working, in the Afro-American idiom.

They have not necessarily been the most popular of all popular singers. But they have been, in my view, the most accomplished, the most innovative and the most influential. All of them are classified, or categorized, by common terminological usage as "popular singers." The inevitable derogatory connotations implicit in the term have inhibited, I believe, a just appreciation of their stature and achievements as singers and as artists.

It might seem at first glance that what distinguishes the popular singer from the classical singer is primarily the music he sings, namely, popular music, as opposed to opera, oratorio and art song, mostly sung in foreign languages. This is certainly a factor. I do not find it, however, in terms of vocal art, a significant factor. Before an Afro-American idiom became dominant in popular music throughout a great part of the world, beginning in the early years of this century, opera, oratorio and concert singers sang popular music and sang it well. Much of the music in the classical singer's repertoire today, moreover—music that we now categorize as serious—was, in its day, as popular as the most popular songs of Irving Berlin, George Gershwin and Cole Porter.

Decisive for the distinction now drawn between the classical and the popular singer, *as singers*, is, I suspect, not so much what the popular singer sings as the way he sings it. It is a way incompatible with the requirements and conventions of opera, oratorio and art song. Many classical singers have sung the same songs the popular singers sing without losing their status as classical singers. But few would argue that they have sung them as well. There is an idiomatic gap that they cannot, as a rule, bridge. "As almost any music lover knows," wrote Morgan Ames in *High Fidelity*, making an exception for Leontyne Price's *Right as Rain* album, "the best thing to do with pop albums by opera singers is to use them for place mats at wakes."

What distinguishes the popular singer most fundamentally from the classical singer is, in my opinion, the relationship of his singing to language. Therein lies the secret of his artistry. Therein, too, lies the root of society's reluctance to take him seriously, to accept him as an artist. Because the best of the popular singers have mined so fruitfully the music of language, and of American English at that, they are felt to be, somehow, unmusical, or at least less musical than those who may sustain a ravishing melodic flight at the expense of textual intelligibility.

One cannot discuss the musicality of their singing without reference to the basic problem of the relationship of music to language. Even for those of us who think of music as the lyrical extension of speech, there is always the question Does music become more musical the further it develops beyond the rudimentary melodic inflections and oratorical rhythms and emphases of speech? For those who would agree that it may, there remains another daunting question: At what point will it have progressed so far as to have lost contact with its roots in speech and begin to be less musical?

It is not, certainly, a mere matter of words or intelligible text. Music exists and flourishes without words. Many songs are written as melodies first, the words added later. Many melodies have served for a variety of texts, including texts in a variety of languages. Most of us enjoy songs in texts we do not understand, not excluding English as it is usually sung by classical singers. The riddle of which comes first, the words or the music, remains as insoluble as that of the chicken and the egg.

But questions remain: To what extent are we to regard the musical instrument as a vocal substitute? How far will a melody without words—its contours, its inflections, its dynamic structure, its rhythmic character, its rhetorical implications—reflect an origin in the melody of language? To what extent will it be drawing its melodic nourishment from a linguistic root?

Preoccupation with these questions, witting and unwitting, has been reflected in the fluctuations of practice and taste among musicians and music lovers over the centuries. It should not be forgotten that Italian opera was originally a reaction against the melodic artificiality of sixteenth-century polyphony, an attempt to redirect vocal music toward the melodic and dramatic properties of the Italian language. The question of the relationship between music and language is what the ensuing controversy over the *prima pratica* and the *seconda pratica* (the old school and the new school) was all about. As Monteverdi put it—and he was a master of both:

> The *prima pratica* considers the harmony not commanded, but commanding, not the servant but the mistress of the words. *Seconda pratica* considers harmony not commanding but commanded, and makes the words the mistress of the harmony.

The operas of Caccini, Monteverdi and Cavalli were essentially *recitative*, the melodic line dictated by the requirements of rhetorical prosody, rather at the expense of the self-contained tune or aria. The devices of embellishment and ornamentation—trills, turns, *appoggiature*, mordents, slurs, *portamenti*, roulades, cadenzas, etcetera—later to become the clichés of exhibitionistic vocal virtuosity and acrobatics, originated as expressive effects designed to emphasize and supplement the contours and cadences of speech. As such they were taken over into instrumental music and subsequently abused by both instrumentalists and singers as mere ornamentation. They were ultimately anathematized as trivial and vainglorious, in the second half of the nineteenth century, by Wagner, Schumann, Bülow and others, not without reason, and have survived only as relics in a largely outdated repertoire, and then only in sterile, slightly ridiculous form.

The recitative character of early Italian opera gave way to a public preference for tune and vocal display. The art of the singer tended to merge with the art of the instrumentalist, and to be judged by instrumental criteria. Melody superseded melodic substance in a rhetorical context. Voice became more important than text, and singers became more concerned with sound than with sense. They were further burdened by requirements, often more athletic than musical, of extraordinary range both above and below the vocal norm. Vocal production itself came to reflect the singer's problem of making himself heard above large orchestras in large auditoriums.

First Gluck, then Wagner and, in his later works, Verdi, were aware of the artistic loss implicit in the divorce of singer from language. Each opposed the trend in his own way, Wagner the most dogmatically. His music dramas, in theory, represented a return to the rhetorical and recitative ideals of the earliest Italian operas. Music was again to be the handmaiden of language. His reform, however, was distorted by the size and assertiveness of his orchestra. The singer could again be a talker, but too often he had to raise his voice. He had to contend not just with the German language, but with Wagner's outlandish German. The effort went astray, not because theory and concept were wrong, but because the singer lost out to the orchestra, and because even the orchestra was denied its heritage of song and dance.

European music, with the abandonment of tonality in the aftermath of Wagnerian and Straussian transcendentalism and the bawling operatic passions of Italian verismo, had reached a stage of intellectualization where mere song addressed to a lay public in congenial and readily assimilable melody and rhythm seemed incompatible with what were reckoned to be the objectives and aspirations of high art. It was left to the jazz musician and the popular singer, uninhibited by artistic pretension and avant-garde fashion, to remind us that music begins with speech.

All language is intrinsically musical. Some languages are more conspicuously melodic, or mellifluous, than others, just as among individuals speaking the same language some will speak it more musically than others. An experienced listener can identify languages simply by their melodic and rhythmic characteristics and by the way speakers produce their voices. Within a single language he can identify regional characteristics—he need not know a word of the language. He reacts to musical phenomena, just as an experienced listener can identify a certain composer from a few measures without knowing the particular composition.

American English is the youngest of the Western languages, a vital, inventive, obstreperous, irreverent, irrepressible and irresponsible newcomer, spawned from the haphazard mixture of races and nationalities that has colored every other aspect of American life. Its lyricism, as reflected in song, owes much to the Irish, the Scots and the Welsh, whose modes of speech are the most musical of the Anglican dialects; to the Jews, whose Yiddish is among the most musical of the German dialects, and to the Italians, whose contribution to American song from their native musicality is symbolized in the art of Frank Sinatra, Perry Como, Buddy Greco, Morgana King and Al Martino as well as in that of others whose Italian origin has been obscured by anglicized names (Tony Bennett, Vic Damone, Frankie Laine, Dean Martin and many more). It owes most of all to the black American, whose African heritage not only has given us the blues, ragtime, jazz, gospel song, rhythm-and-blues and soul, but who also, through his melodic contribution to the white speech of the South and Southwest, has richly influenced the indigenous musical styles once called hillbilly and now more respectfully designated country-and-western, or simply country. A possibly significant number of fine singers have had some American Indian blood (Mildred Bailey, Chuck Berry, Johnny Cash, Lena Horne, Waylon Jennings, Loretta Lynn, Johnnie Ray, Kay Starr and Lee Wiley), but it seems unlikely that their singing has been influenced by Indian languages, although an Indian heritage may well have contributed to their musicality.

A combination of circumstances, as unforeseen as it was unprecedented, conspired in the 1920s to revolutionize, first in America, later elsewhere, both popular song and popular singing. Popular music had been absorbing and reflecting black influences for nearly a century. There was always an interchange, a process of imitation and counterimitation, or parody. Blacks originally imitated—or parodied—the manners and speech of their white masters. The imperfect result was thought by whites to be so amusing—and so charming—

Buddy Greco   Al Martino   Frankie Laine   Vic Damone

that they parodied the imitation for their own amusement. The phenomenon of imitation breeding imitation is documented in the century-long history of the minstrel show. First, whites blacked their faces to imitate blacks imitating whites. Then blacks followed suit in their own minstrel shows, blacking their already black faces to imitate whites imitating blacks.

This naive, unselfconscious give-and-take bore fruit in the work of many popular singers of the 1920s and before. A kind of song and a kind of singing, most vividly and most memorably represented by Sophie Tucker and Al Jolson, were enormously popular. One winces today when recalling that the songs were called "coon songs" and the style of singing "coon shouting." By the 1920s the more common designation was "blues," which did not mean, then, the classic twelve-bar form associated with the term today. It was simply a jazzy or bluesy popular song evolving from the slow transition from ragtime to jazz. Another term, thanks to Al Jolson, was "mammy songs." What is important to remember is that these songs were written by both black and white songwriters and sung by both black and white singers.

Until the 1920s the mutuality of black and white influences, while evident in the public performance of many artists, both black and white, was inhibited by segregation. There was not one entertainment world, but two, with the black modeled upon the white. The T.O.B.A. (Theater Owners' Booking Agency—the initials were interpreted by some of the performers as standing for Tough on Black Artists—or Black Asses) was a black counterpart of the Keith Circuit. So extensive had black vaudeville become by 1920 that *Billboard*, in its issue of October 30, counted 112 theaters for blacks playing vaudeville, roadshows and pictures, 39 bands and orchestras, 12 booking agencies, 170 vaudeville and burlesque acts representing more than 500 partners or associates in their respective acts.

Two developments conspired, at the onset of the 1920s, to moderate the effects of segregation and to accelerate the blending of black and white in an Afro-American idiom. One was the breakthrough of black artists into the white entertainment world, heralded by the success with white audiences on Broadway of Sissle and Blake's *Shuffle Along* in 1921. The other was recording, hitherto an exclusively white domain.

The key date, in recording, was February 1920, when Perry

Bradford, numbered with Lovie Austin, Shelton Brooks, W. C. Handy, and Clarence and Spencer Williams, among the early black "blues" composers, persuaded Fred Hager, of the General Phonograph Corporation, to let a black singer, Mamie Smith (not related to Bessie), instead of Sophie Tucker, record his "That Thing Called Love" and "You Can't Keep a Good Man Down" for the Okeh label. The record sold well, and a subsequent recording, again by Mamie Smith, of Bradford's "Crazy Blues" sold even better.

A market among blacks for black records had been discovered. Other labels and other singers were quick to follow suit in the production of what came to be known as race records. Of the many singers who made them, only Bessie Smith and Ethel Waters are remembered today by any but specialists and old-timers. But there were other fine artists among them—Clara Smith, Mamie Smith, Trixie Smith (none of them related to Bessie), Mae Barnes, Lucille Bogan, Bernice Edwards, Lucille Hegamin, Rosa Henderson, Alberta Hunter, Sara Martin, Florence Mills, Gertrude Saunders, Edith Wilson and many more.

A considerable number of their records from the early 1920s have been reissued on LP in the past few years. They are helpful not only as a reminder of singers and styles of a bygone era, but even more importantly as a point of reference in assessing the mixture of black and white in both material and performance. Compared with a Bessie Smith, a Ma Rainey or an Ida Cox, for example, all of whom hailed from the more primitive rural Southern carnival, circus and medicine show circuits, the others sound citified. They worked closer, even in songs they thought of as blues, to the popular white styles of the time, granting that the white styles were already more or less tinged with black. One hears echoes of white popular singers in their enunciation and melodic cadences, suggestions of Nora Bayes, Vaughn De Leath, Bee Palmer, Sophie Tucker and Al Jolson. But the distinctive coloration—melodic, rhythmic and linguistic—was black.

Race records they may have been, directed at the black consumer and styled to his tastes. But white singers and white instrumentalists, Al Jolson and Sophie Tucker among them, heard the records, or even the singers themselves, in black vaudeville or in the black nightclubs of New York's Harlem and Chicago's South Side, and were influenced in turn.

Nora Bayes

Vaughn De Leath

Of equal moment for the evolution of a new approach to popular singing was radio. By 1920, amateur receivers were numerous. On November 2 of that year, Dr. Frank Conrad's Station KDKA in East Pittsburgh broadcast the returns of the Harding-Cox Presidential election. A month later, when Vaughn De Leath sang two recitals of popular songs over the De Forest Radiophone from the World Tower Building in New York, she received scores of letters from sailors and wireless operators thanking her for the entertainment.

There is no need here to go further into the history of radio broadcasting as it exploded, especially in the United States, in the ensuing decade. It will suffice to note that by late 1922 there were, in the United States, some 3,000,000 sets being serviced by more than 200 transmitters, and that by 1925 radio was an $800,000,000-a-year industry. It is pertinent to distinguish, however, between singing styles on records, as required by the recording procedures of the time, and singing styles on the radio. Recording, still in its relatively primitive pre-electrical phase, and so unresponsive to softer sounds and delicate shadings that clarinets were commonly substituted for violins in orchestral accompaniments, offered few inducements to subtleties of vocal production and phrase. Radio, which did not involve the cutting of an impression on wax, did.

The implications were plain in a *Billboard* article on the microphone in the issue of April 1, 1922, headed "New Radio Rules." The reference was to staff behavior during broadcasts, and the article described "a new and very sensitive instrument which catches the buzzing and whispering usually heard in the background. Someone even has said that the new instrument will record the swish of a powder puff as it passes over the nose of some fair lady."

The "new" instrument was not really so new. David E. Hughes had invented the carbon microphone in 1878. What was new was its sensitivity. What was important was not its ability to record the swish of a powder puff, but its ability to pick up the lightest pressure of a singer's breath upon his vocal cords for transmission to listeners in their homes hundreds and thousands of miles away, or, as employed in a P.A. system, to thousands of listeners in large auditoriums. No longer would singers have to pitch their voices to reach the ticket holder in the last row of the gallery. They could *speak* to you without raising their voices, wherever you were. It is here that the story of the modern popular singer, in one vital aspect, begins.

The impact of the microphone upon vocal technique and upon the articulation of song and text would have been immense in any case. That the coming of radio just happened to coincide with a growing awareness and acceptance of a new Afro-American musical idiom compounded and intensified the repercussions. Radio made it possible for the singer to address the listener with an unprecedented intimacy. Jazz, using the term in its widest and loosest sense, made it possible for him to articulate his message with an unprecedented immediacy. The microphone liberated him from the burden of making himself heard over considerable distances in public places. Jazz liberated him from the precise pitches and more or less arithmetically calculated rhythms of European music, permitting him to order the words within a phrase in a manner closer to the natural melody and the natural rhythm of speech.

This latter emancipation the popular singer owes to the black American. It has everything to do with the fact that so many of the finest American popular singers have been black. At the root of the phenomenon is the black singer's predilection for oral and improvisatory communication, for narrative balladry, exhortatory evangelism and lyrical exaltation. Exposed to European music in North, Central and South America and the Caribbean Islands, the black singer found its systematically determined scales and its—to him—stereotyped and anemic rhythms inhibitive and restrictive, its elaborate harmonic organization irrelevant.

He could see no artistic virtue in moving cleanly from, say, C to E, when his intuition sensed melodic and rhetorical substance in uncharted pitches between the authorized notes. So, while accepting the European diatonic major and minor modes, and a European four-beats-to-the-bar rhythm, he bent the notes and shifted the rhythmic accentuation to suit his communicative purpose, achieving a rhetorical eloquence previously unknown in Western music.

Many of the characteristics of popular singing, as it has evolved from the coincidence of radio and Afro-American musicality, are bewildering, even repulsive, to the European-oriented ear. The conversational character of the melodic utterance, rendered the more conspicuous by a vernacular text distinctly enunciated, is felt as a violation of traditional concepts of sustained vocal line. The popular singer's habit of singing on and through certain consonants is at variance with the European tendency to think of the voice in instrumental terms.

Even the popular singer's vocal production seems too casual, too relaxed, too easy. The slurs, the notes attacked on a tangent, so to speak, then eased onto pitch, the sliding cadences, the melodic deviations and the occasional verbal ad-libbing and "scatting"—all these may strike the lover of classical music as somehow vulgar and sloppy. The mischief seems to be compounded by the popular singer's habit of body-swaying and finger-popping, regarded by the European-oriented listener as evidence of primitive rhythmic inflexibility, but, in fact, essential to the popular singer in giving him an explicit beat to steal from (rubato).

I know how the classical singer and the classical music lover feel on the subject. Trained as a classical singer, I was a newspaper music critic in the days when Bing Crosby's records were beginning to sell in the millions, and I heartily shared the distaste for crooning, as it was then called, common among most people closely associated with classical music. It seemed, when heard from our point of view, to be saccharine, lugubrious, callow, maudlin, musically slovenly, lacking in vocal virility and incisiveness, short of range—in brief, just something tasteless for schoolgirls to become excited about. Then came the young Sinatra, and our worst fears seemed to have been realized.

I remember these unaccommodating reactions now when I listen with pleasure and admiration to the records of these two singers, including records made back in the days when I rejected them so confidently. What I hear now is a wonderfully relaxed, intimate vocal communication, a feeling for rhythm, phrase and line rarely matched by classical singers, and a smooth, often lovely, almost always pleasing vocal tone, unblemished by forcing or by conspicuous differences in character and color between one register and another, not to speak of what is accomplished in the handling of text!

I was reacting, in the 1930s, as one totally identified with classical, or European, music, especially with opera. My judgments reflected the conventional attitudes and prejudices of the time, and indeed of today. I knew nothing of vocal history beyond what could be heard on records, and I readily assumed that the criteria of my own time and community were absolute. I react today, forty years later, as an historian, and I react according to what I have learned of

Ruth Etting, with composer Harold Arlen (at the piano) and lyricist Ted Koehler

Irving Berlin and George Jessel

nearly four centuries of Western vocal evolution and of vocal practices and conventions of other civilizations. There will be occasion to
go further into what I see as the virtues—and some of the shortcomings, too—of the great popular singers, in discussing them individually, and to note specifically the many striking parallels with
earlier European and non-European procedure.

This introduction may serve, I hope, to identify some of the
considerations governing my selection of singers. There will be some
surprise, I know, and probably some indignation, too, that I slight
such undeniably popular singers as Deanna Durbin, Nelson Eddy,
Allan Jones, Mario Lanza, Jeanette MacDonald, Grace Moore, John
Charles Thomas and Lawrence Tibbett. I have heard and admired
them all. But within the context of my purpose they have all been,
idiomatically, Europeans—opera singers or operetta singers singing in
an operatic manner. Even in popular music their singing has rarely,
and then only faintly, reflected the Afro-American idiom which is my
principal concern. It seems pertinent to note that this essentially
operatic style of singing, this manner of vocal production and vocal
articulation, has all but vanished, in popular music, from the musical
theater, the moving-picture musical, the television spectacular, radio
and records.

Even in my discussion of those working in the Afro-American
idiom there are bound to be omissions disturbing to some. It is
impossible for anyone who has not spent some time with the subject
to imagine the number of singers involved. Although most people
concerned with popular music, if asked to name twenty great singers,
could doubtless do so, it is unlikely that any two lists would be
identical. Any selector would be astonished at the famous names,
slipped from his own memory, that would turn up in other people's
lists. The total revealed by, say, twenty such lists would, I am sure, be
a revelation.

The fact is—I, at least, accept it as a fact—that we have been
living through a golden age of American song, so close to us and so
much a part of us that we have taken it for granted. We similarly
took for granted a golden age of songwriting as represented by Harold
Arlen, Irving Berlin, George Gershwin, Jerome Kern, Cole Porter,
Richard Rodgers, Arthur Schwartz, Vincent Youmans and many
more, now, at last, duly acknowledged, with authoritative and appreciative insight and scholarship, in Alec Wilder's *The American*

Popular Song—The Great Innovators 1900–1950. Some day in the not too distant future, one hopes, a corresponding acknowledgment will be made of the composer-arrangers who have played such a major role in the work of many of the great singers I shall be discussing. The gold in golden ages, it would seem, glistens only at a considerable distance in time, especially in America, and when the gold is American.

In *The Great Singers: From the Dawn of Opera to Our Own Time* I was covering three hundred and fifty years of operatic history, and from a thousand or so possible choices I selected seventy-odd. In this book I shall be covering only fifty years, but a wider range of categories: blues, jazz, popular song, swing, theater, films, country, gospel, rhythm-and-blues, soul, and others. Again, there is an embarrassment of riches. I have carded well over five hundred singers. Most of the names would be familiar to most readers. All of them would be familiar to some.

In making my selections I have looked, as I did in *The Great Singers,* not necessarily for my own personal favorites in any specific category, but rather for those who seem most vividly to have influenced or reflected that category. Some choices must be obvious— Mahalia Jackson in gospel singing, for example, or Hank Williams in country. In other areas the choices are neither so obvious nor so simple.

I should, however, acknowledge and account for my passing over the many singers active today in the area familiarly categorized as "folk." I have no wish to give offense either to the individual singers or to their many sincere admirers by naming names. I shall say only that I have heard them all, certainly most of them, in person, on records or on television, and that I find them, as singers—with the exception of Odetta and Nina Simone, both of them admirable, highly accomplished musicians and vocalists—amateurs ingenuously celebrating their amateurism.

For the rest, I can only hope that even those who will not share the opinions governing my selections may yet endorse my objective in identifying and saluting the art of the popular singer. The best of them—and some who have not been quite the best—may, in singing for their supper, have harvested a feast. But their familiar designation and dismissal as mere entertainers has discouraged a just appreciation of their artistic accomplishment.

Odetta
Nina Simone

BOTH PHOTOS: COLUMBIA RECORDS/STEREO REVIEW

The Art of the
American Popular Singer

If "The Art of the American Popular Singer," as heading or concept, appears to many as a contradiction in terms, the reason may be that the best of the American popular singers have exemplified so happily the old adage: "Art is that which disguises art." They have made what they do appear too inevitable, too easy.

With classical singers the art is often all too obvious. Even with the greatest, the effect of their apparently easy surmounting of difficulties tends to be vitiated by the familiarity of the difficulties, thanks to the revealing inadequacies of less accomplished singers.

Nothing that I shall say in appreciation of the art of the American popular singer should be construed as a disparagement of classical singers. They do things, vocally and musically, that popular singers cannot do. They sing music that even the best of the popular singers cannot sing, or, to put it in better perspective, they work in a musical idiom, essentially European, whose criteria and conventions nowadays are in certain respects incompatible with the objectives of American popular song. Conversely, the popular singer does things, primarily in matters of phrasing, shading, rhythm, enunciation, accentuation and even vocal production, that lie beyond the capabilities and the predilections of most classical singers. It is not a question of superiority or inferiority. It is a question of musical idiom.

This question of idiom introduces the first of many paradoxes implicit in the common view of the popular singer as entertainer rather than as artist. For it is precisely in idiomatic terms that the popular singer is often closer than the classical singer to the *older, original* objectives and conventions of European singing. His enunciation is superior. His embellishments are richer in invention and variety, and are more imaginatively, more expressively employed. His rhythmic perceptions are keener, more subtle, especially his exploitation of the tensions inherent in *tempo rubato* (in the original, literal sense of "time stolen"). He is more resourceful, and stylistically more secure, in melodic deviation, elaboration and variation.

These are all matters upon which great stress was laid in the seventeenth and eighteenth centuries, and in which the classical singer, as recently as a century or a century and a half ago, was as expert as the popular singer is today. That was before his individual creative impulses, privileges and responsibilities were curbed by the increasing primacy of composer and orchestra, obliging him to stick to the written notes and the prescribed rhythms, usually under conductorial, always under critical, supervision and scrutiny.

The art of the American popular singer is closer than that of the contemporary classical singer, even in Italian opera, to the art of those who established the esthetic objectives, the techniques, the terminology and the appropriate criteria of Western singing in Italy in the seventeenth and eighteenth centuries. These are the objectives, techniques and criteria commonly and conventionally represented by the term *bel canto,* or beautiful song (or singing).

In *The Great Singers* I defined the term as referring to

> a mellifluous kind of singing aimed at an agreeable, well-rounded tone, an even scale from bottom to top, an unbroken legato, a nicety of intonation and an eloquence of phrase and cadence, a purity of vowels and a disciplined avoidance of shouting, nasality, harsh or open sounds, disjointed registers, undue vehemence and any other evidence of vulgarity, or of bad or negligent schooling.

These general criteria are acknowledged, if not always adhered to, by both classical and popular singers. All have to do, essentially, with *sound* and *line.*

Where the popular singer comes closer than the classical singer to the earliest Italian models is in his acceptance of song as a lyrical extension of speech. He is more concerned than is the classical singer with text, both with its meaning and with the melodic and rhythmical manner in which it might be spoken. One popular singer praising another is likely to refer to his "reading of the text, or lyric." It is not a formulation I have ever heard, or would expect to hear, from the mouth of a classical singer.

Italian opera, as I have pointed out in the Introduction, was a reaction against the melodic artificiality of sixteenth-century polyphony, in which the dynamics of prosody had been sacrificed to the blandishments of multiple-voiced euphony. It was an attempt to redirect vocal music, monodically rather than polyphonically, toward the melodic, rhythmic and dramatic properties of the Italian language.

What is so astonishing about the evocation of a bygone era in the art of the American popular singer is not that the objectives, the devices and the criteria are similar—excepting the trill, which the popular singer does not use—but that they are identical. It is astonishing because, as used by the popular singer, they neither represent, nor are they derived from, any historical continuity. The devices, or most of them, disappeared from European vocalism in the course of the nineteenth century, victims of misuse, abuse, overindulgence, prejudice and the whims of musical fashion. They have, to be sure, been rediscovered and trotted out in recent years in the revival of old *bel canto* operas. But those who use them do so without the immediacy, the invention and the stylistic security of the original singers.

The American popular singer, in his use of them, has certainly not been guided by the work of classical vocalists, or by consultation with musicologists. Most popular singers are anything but historians. They do not, as a rule, even know the traditional Italian terms for the devices they use. But there the devices all are, especially the *appoggiatura*, the mordent, the turn, the slur, the *portamento* and the *rubato*, exactly as they existed in early seventeenth- and eighteenth-century practice, employed in the same way and for the same purpose: to heighten and elaborate the expression of oral, vocal, linguistic communication. One can only assume that they are somehow fundamental and eternal, that their abuse and subsequent banishment from European music were symptoms of Europe's musical decadence.

The same may be true of the popular singer's role as the primary musician. His place in the hierarchy of his own musical society is certainly closer to that of the seventeenth- or eighteenth-century vocal virtuoso than is that of the latter's twentieth-century counterpart. The popular singer is the center of attention. The song, the arrangement, the recording, the setting, the lighting are built around him. He has interpretive privileges denied the classical singer, who is inhibited by the priorities accorded the composer and the conductor, and by the vigilance of critics safeguarding those priorities. He also bears commensurate responsibilities.

When Andy Williams appeared at the Royal Albert Hall in London in May of 1968, with a studio orchestra of forty, I attended each of the three rehearsals, and was stunned by the contrast with conventional classical music rehearsal procedure. Jack Elliott, a conductor and arranger long associated with Andy in Hollywood, was preparing the orchestra in arrangements of some twenty songs, the arrangements all made expressly and expensively for Andy Williams. But Elliott wasn't running the show. Andy was running it. He ran it quietly, purposefully and effectively.

He sang very little. He knew the songs. Elliott knew how he would sing them. Andy wanted to be sure that the orchestra knew the arrangements and could play them at the tempi he wanted, in the style he wanted, and with accents and colors where and as he wanted them. So he listened, mostly. When he had something to say, he said it, sometimes to the conductor, sometimes to an individual musician. It could have been, I reflected, the great Pacchierotti, with Bertoni as his house composer-conductor, rehearsing a production for the King's Theater in London in 1778!

All this runs counter to contemporary concepts in classical music of a proper apportioning of privilege and responsibility as between composer and performer, and as between conductor, as composer-surrogate, and soloist. Even those who concede the legitimacy of the parallels will argue that Western music in Europe, in the nineteenth century, outgrew this predominance of the solo performer.

That is the fashionable view, a reflection of what I am tempted to call the Cult of the Composer. "The progress of musical art," says Joseph Machlis in his The Enjoyment of Music, "demanded the

victory over improvisation. The composer ultimately established his right to choose the notes, the performer being limited to playing, or, at most, interpreting them."

This was a weighty argument in an epoch that produced the great European composers from Mozart to Mahler and the great European conductors from Mendelssohn to Furtwängler and Toscanini, but their like have not been around for a while, and we are left, in classical music, with performers crippled creatively by the discipline of composer theology and the dictation of conductor autocracy. The popular singer, while he may suffer from prejudicial categorization, is free of traditional and institutional inhibition.

In European, or classical, music, today, all singers sing all music in essentially the same way. They differ one from another only in the extent to which they approach or surpass a norm, or ideal, of performance, commonly accepted and commonly understood. No two performances of the same song or aria by different singers are exactly alike. But when compared with the variants of a popular song as sung by, say, Louis Armstrong, Bing Crosby, Ella Fitzgerald, Peggy Lee and Frank Sinatra, the distinctions are slight, if not superficial.

The popular singer is not only allowed to take liberties denied the classical singer; he is expected, even required, to do so, just as the opera singer was expected to do so in the seventeenth and eighteenth centuries. The song, even the best song—and American popular music has been rich in fine songs—is not looked upon as an imperishable or immutable masterpiece, nor the composer's written or printed symbols as holy writ. To the popular singer it is raw material, a point of departure. He may drop notes or add them, introduce *appoggiatura*, slurs, slides, riffs, codas and cadenzas, change note values to accord with his rhythmic reading of the text, and so on, just as singers did in the heyday of Italian opera.

The popular singer's identification with a contemporary rather than with a traditional, inherited repertoire has been an important factor in preserving his privilege of doing with songs as he sees fit, of shaping or reshaping them in his own image. But it has also been a factor in blinding the classical-music public to the artistic validity of his musical and vocal procedures and accomplishments. A popular singer may be able to bring to bear upon a song by Harold Arlen, Irving Berlin or Cole Porter all the devices prized in Monteverdi's time, but this will not achieve for him equal status as an artist with the classical singer who brings none of these to bear, or very few, upon a song by Schubert, Schumann or Brahms, or upon an aria by Bellini or Verdi, although many might concede that the popular singer's was the more creative performance.

Another equally troublesome factor contributing to the popular singer's inferior status vis-à-vis the classical singer is the popular singer's uncontested inferiority in terms of forceful vocal utterance. This brings us inevitably and importantly to the microphone. Among those persons identified with classical music, and with opera in particular, the most persistent and pervasive prejudice against the popular singer has been his apparent dependence upon the mike, a dependence thought of as a demonstration of vocal infirmity, inadequacy or impotence.

It is nothing of the sort. The mike does not *make* the popular singer's voice. It can add nothing but volume to what is already there in his throat and head. It is a listener, an electronically activated ear, and nothing more than that. As such, however, because it "hears" so well, it is merciless in its exposure of blemishes, particularly when one works as close to it as the popular singer does. But it can also detect and amplify virtues, delicate refinements of melodic line and vocal inflection, minute shadings and subtleties of enunciation and phrase, that would be inaudible without its electronic assistance. The mike amplifies both good habits and bad, which is why the best of the popular singers sing so well, and *talk* so well when they sing. Working with so candid an ally, they must.

The microphone has also been employed, of course, in classical music. It is used in recording, on radio and television, and on the moving-picture sound track. It is used in outdoor performance and in large auditoriums where even a Caruso or a Ruffo might have had difficulty in making himself heard. But this is a long way from the use of the mike in the sense that it is used by the popular singer.

The classical singer, confronted by a mike, does not change his style or his technique. He sings as loudly, as forcefully and as high as ever, as indeed he must. He knows no other way to sing. All his training and routine have been directed toward developing these capacities, and the music he sings requires it, opera particularly. The sound engineer makes the adjustment. It is not the singer who exploits the mike, as the popular singer does. It is the mike, as regulated by a sound engineer, that exploits the classical singer.

The popular singer's accomplishment has been not only the mastery of the microphone's fiendish exactions, but also his appreciation of its potential as a vocal and musical auxiliary, as a kind of supplemental larynx. With the help of the mike the popular singer has restored to singing some of the charm and intimacy, and much of the virtuosity, too, that was lost in Western music when the emphasis swung from the rhetorical to the lyrical, and then to the melodramatic and the transcendental, in the nineteenth century.

Something is lost, to be sure, and I, opera-bred as I am, must be the first to acknowledge it. Missing are the suspense of assaults upon the upper and lower extremes of the vocal range, the ringing triumph and exultant defiance of the high note courageously challenged, superbly attacked and demonstratively sustained. To an opera buff, the popular singer seems a weakling, doing lazily and physically cheaply what comes all too easily.

The popular singer's voice has not been schooled to produce the big sound, the dramatic outbursts, the plangent, full-throated top notes of the opera singer. Since projection, in terms of volume, is taken care of by the microphone, the popular singer may take things more casually, applying less weight of breath upon the vocal cords. The microphone has made such schooling superfluous, even self-defeating. It can make any voice sound big, and when any voice can sound big, there is no competitive advantage in singing loud and high, a fact that some recent soul singers have yet to learn.

There are shortcomings, however, in the traditional European approach, too. The vogue of the high note has encouraged attitudes and achievements suggestive of athleticism rather than esthetics. It has produced singers, past and present, more matador than troubadour. What such singers did, and still do, can be accomplished artistically, and serve an artistic purpose. But in opera, particularly, the border between singing and shouting, between art and vulgarity, can be thin, and it is frequently violated. An ever more assertive orchestra and a rising standard pitch have compounded the opera singer's vocal problems. He has to sing louder and higher than is comfortable, convenient or healthy, in order to be heard.

He has to sing higher, too, because he is stuck—granting rare exceptions—with the original key, now, in older music, a full semitone higher than it was at the time of composition. (The so-called classical pitch of the eighteenth and early nineteenth centuries was

A=422—vibrations per second—and is assumed to have varied between A=415 and A=430. The internationally established standard pitch today, responsive to a general preference for more brilliant instrumental tone, is A=440, and in orchestral practice tends to be slightly higher. The difference from the older pitch is roughly a semitone.) There may be, and sometimes are, sound musical reasons for ruling out transposition, but the commonest reason, if not always acknowledged, is that transposition in opera is felt to be an admission of vocal inadequacy, with an inference of loss of face. The popular singer has no such inhibitions. One asks about an opera singer: "How's his top?" All the composer or arranger wants to know about a popular singer is: "Where's his top—or bottom?"

The popular singer wants an arrangement pitched where his work with melody and text will not be compromised by unseemly exertion. He wants to talk, to phrase conversationally, easily and intimately. He wants to tell you what is on his mind or in his heart, not to show you what a great voice he has, or what tremendous things he can do with it. He chooses keys, or tonalities, accordingly.

It seems pertinent to note in this connection that in the seventeenth and eighteenth centuries, too, arias were pitched to suit the individual singer's convenience, and that transposition was common when the same arias were sung by other singers, or even by the same singer as he or she grew older. "Time," wrote G. B. Shaw of Adelina Patti, "has transposed Patti a minor third down." The mean vocal range covered by the written notes, moreover, was usually modest, rarely exceeding an octave and a half. Singers added to it, above or below, at their own discretion and at their own risk.

These two facts, namely that the popular singer need not cultivate a big, powerful tone nor school it to survive taxingly high tessiture, and that he is free to choose congenial tonalities, have profoundly affected the way he sings, as compared with the way the classical singer sings. The release from the requirement of a big tone and a concern for distinct, musical enunciation have encouraged him to cultivate a lighter, more "forward" vocal production.

They have also encouraged a different attitude toward the articulation of consonants. Classical singers tend to slight them, finding them disruptive to the flow of tone and to a fluent legato. This is characteristic of the classical singer's policy of favoring tone over text. It probably also reflects the fact that the Italian language,

Sarah Vaughan with pianist Jimmie Jones and trumpeter Clifford Brown

the mother tongue of *bel canto*, has so few words ending with consonants. Popular singers sing on and through the consonants, especially *ms*, *ns*, *ngs* and *ls*, without any interruption of melodic line or inhibition of legato. They also employ the *coup de glotte*, or glottis stroke, to set off words beginning with vowels, especially the vowel *e* as in ever and ending.

The popular singer's concern for text and for lyrical enunciation has also affected his rhythmic procedures. He calculates his rhythmic progress in terms of four- or eight-measure episodes rather than in terms of so many beats to the measure, subdivided arithmetically, as in classical music. Within these four- or eight-measure episodes he distributes syllables at his own oratorical and rhetorical discretion, taking a bit of time from one, giving it to another.

Caccini, the principal innovative figure in the reform that led to the birth of Italian opera, must certainly have had something of this kind in mind when he wrote of "the noble manner of singing which is used without tying the man's self to the ordinary measure of time, making often the value of the notes less by half, and sometimes more, according to the conceit of the words." Domenico Corri, a pupil of Porpora, the greatest vocal teacher of the eighteenth century, put it more bluntly, a century later, when he wrote that "hours [that is, a rigid observance of time] are for slaves."

Paradoxical as it may seem, the popular singer, in order to benefit from his rhythmic freedom, requires, as does the jazz instrumentalist, firm, although not rigid, rhythmic support. With whatever type of instrumental backing he may work, a congenial rhythm section is indispensable. When such singers as Ella Fitzgerald, Tony Bennett and Frank Sinatra appear with symphony orchestras, as they do from time to time, they have their own rhythm section behind them, usually piano, drums, double bass and sometimes rhythm guitar. Even when they work with the big jazz bands, they may prefer their own rhythm section.

When a nightclub, television or recording program is being prepared, rehearsal usually begins with rhythm section alone. In modern recording, the singer may tape a song with nothing but the rhythm section, the instrumental backing being dubbed in afterward and subsequently "mixed." None of this, it should be emphasized, is to help the singer to "keep time." Quite the contrary. It supports the singer's own rhythmic procedure.

Beginning with the early crooners—Gene Austin, Russ Columbo, Bing Crosby, Little Jack Little, Whispering Jack Smith and Rudy Vallee—a by-product of both their concern for enunciation and the privilege of choosing congenial tonalities has been a lowering of pitch, especially in female voices.

Vocal production, with the best popular singers, proceeds naturally, almost imperceptibly, from speech, and the pitch of speech is normally lower than the pitch of song. The term "to raise the voice in song," or in anger, for that matter, refers not only to volume, but also to pitch. The opera-oriented ear experiences many surprises in the investigation of the ranges of popular singers.

Bing Crosby, for example, sings down to a low F or E, which is basso territory in opera, without sounding like a basso. The same is true of Frank Sinatra, whose range is that of an opera bass-baritone, but who does not sound like one. Among the women, not only Ella Fitzgerald but also Pearl Bailey, Lena Horne, Peggy Lee, Dinah Shore and Sarah Vaughan, among many others, sing lower than opera contraltos without sounding like baritones, as opera contraltos usually do when they carry a weighty tone down into the vocal cellar.

Many popular singers have as wide a range as the average opera singer, *i.e.*, about two octaves. Sometimes, as with Ella and Sarah, it is wider. But it begins lower, and it ends lower at the upper end of the range. An upward extension is often achieved, as in Ella's case, and Sarah's, too, by recourse to falsetto, a type of vocal production not usually associated with female voices. It was formerly much cultivated by male singers, especially tenors, in both operatic arias and songs, but it has gone out of fashion, in opera, at least, in the past fifty years, probably because of the apparent suggestion of both artifice and effeminacy. There is less contrast between the normal and the "false" voice in females, which is why its employment by such singers as Ella and Sarah has passed largely unnoticed.

Sarah Vaughan, who sings easily down to a contralto low D, ascends to a pure and accurate high C. I have heard Cleo Laine, the greatly and justly admired English jazz singer, produce a G above high C without discernible effort. Her natural range is that of a contralto, giving her an overall compass of well over three octaves. And I have heard Aura Lully, the Romanian jazz singer featured a year or so ago with Duke Ellington, sing up to the B flat above Cleo Laine's high G. This puts her in a class with Lucrezia Agujari, known

COLUMBIA RECORDS/STEREO REVIEW

Tony Bennett

Dick Haymes   JOHN KOBAL COLLECTION   Jack Jones   RCA RECORDS/STEREO REVIEW

indelicately as La Bastardella, who so astonished Mozart when he heard her in Parma in 1770, and who almost certainly had recourse to falsetto.

Falsetto is common among male singers in the country, gospel and rhythm-and-blues categories. They sing habitually and confidently in the area between an opera tenor's high B flat and high E flat, as, indeed, flamenco tenors do. Rossini and Bellini wrote extensively for tenors in that range. The vocalism of country and, especially, of gospel and rhythm-and-blues and soul singers, moving fluently from head voice to falsetto and back, would seem to offer a clue as to how the tenors of that time coped with such requirements.

The general trend among popular singers has been not only toward a lower pitching of the voice, excluding the upward extensions in falsetto, but also toward lower-pitched voices. I cannot think offhand of a prominent female popular singer whom I could categorize, in operatic or operetta terms, as a soprano. Tenors survive among the men, but not many. One thinks immediately of Tony Bennett and Andy Williams. Tony, particularly, who studied with an opera singer, works easily in an operatic tenor's range, including even a reliable high C. But the majority are high baritones (Vic Damone and Jack Jones), baritones (Dick Haymes and the young Frank Sinatra), and bass-baritones (Billy Eckstine is an outstanding example).

An area in which the popular singer is commonly reckoned inferior to the classical singer is that of virtuosity. It is true that popular singers do not dazzle their listeners with rapid scales, arpeggios, roulades, trills and *staccati*, but they have their own virtuosic devices, notably the type of singing known as "scatting," *i.e.*, free improvisation on syllables, often nonsensical, raised to an extraordinary level of accomplishment and invention by such singers as Louis Armstrong, Ella Fitzgerald, Cleo Laine, Anita O'Day and Sarah Vaughan. In melismatic ornamentation, too, the popular singers, especially in the rhythm-and-blues, gospel and soul categories, tend to be both more virtuosic and more imaginative than their classical counterparts.

Quite aside from considerations of vocalism, it is, I believe, no insignificant coincidence that so many popular singers have made careers as actors. The conventions governing their deportment on the stage, whether in nightclubs or in concert, require a far more his-

Fred Astaire
Frank Sinatra, Bing Crosby and Dean Martin

ABOVE: STEREO REVIEW   BELOW: REPRISE RECORDS

trionic performance than is expected, or even permitted, of classical singers. The latter are accustomed to stand like wooden Indians in the bend of the piano and "let the composer speak for himself," which is one reason why the solo song recital is virtually extinct. The popular singer is expected to lend the composer a hand and "sell the song."

But beyond the play of posture and gesture and facial expression and the ability to get on and off the stage without looking like an undertaker on duty, the popular singer's concern with the lyrical elucidation of text brings him, even as a singer, close to the actor's art. For a Bing Crosby, a Dean Martin and a Frank Sinatra, or for a Doris Day and a Barbra Streisand, the gap between singing and acting is narrower than that which faces the classical singer moving from the studio to the opera house.

It works both ways. Many actors, suddenly required to sing, as Rex Harrison was in *My Fair Lady*, sing better than most singers, simply because they understand language, prosody, phrasing, pacing and building. Fred Astaire is another example of an artist (primarily a dancer) who has sung more persuasively than most singers sing. The same may be said of Marlene Dietrich, Walter Huston and Lee Marvin.

I should like, in conclusion, to remark one more, possibly significant, difference between the classical and the popular singer. Classical singers are as a rule, and especially nowadays, musically educated—more or less. They are likely to be university graduates. They read music. They count time. Many read well at sight. Of the popular singers treated in the following chapters, most have not gone beyond high school. Some never got that far. Most have had no formal musical education. Many could not at first, some still cannot, read music.

I would not go so far as to attribute their accomplishments as artists to lack of education. Their creativity has been natural and unique. But the absence of formal schooling and the requirement of developing their professional skills competitively before a paying public may have been to their advantage as innovators, securing and nourishing the blessings that were theirs by endowment. They learned from one another, from the instrumentalists and the composer-arrangers with whom they have worked, and from the public.

Who else, come to think of it, could have taught them?

1

Al Jolson

He needed applause the way a diabetic needs insulin. He was kind, sentimental and charitable to a fault. He was arrogant and surly. He was a braggart. He was crude and untutored. As a human being he left much to be desired. But he was the greatest entertainer the world has ever known.

Thus Pearl Sieben in *The Immortal Jolson*. Not alone among the great artists of his own or any other time, Al Jolson was insecure. And his was the kind of insecurity for which success, even in the unprecedented degree to which he achieved and enjoyed it, offers only an ephemeral—and addictive—alleviation. It has to be repeated, regularly and often. Eddie Cantor, in *Take My Life*, remembers him after the triumph of the moving-picture biography *The Jolson Story*, in 1946:

Still he was insecure. We were neighbors in Palm Springs. We walked together, talked together, ate together, and I knew him better than I had ever known him through the years. What amazed me was that this great personality had never learned how to live. He couldn't; there was something chemically wrong. The minute the curtain rang down, he died.

49

George Jessel, in *This Way, Miss*, picks up the refrain:

> He was only content while singing and acknowledging applause; the rest of the time he was champing at the bit while getting ready to go—and if he was not on, he was disconsolate. . . . He was cruel most times. . . . But God, what a great artist he was!

Those who know Jolson only from his later records and from the sound tracks of *The Jolson Story* (1946) and *Jolson Sings Again* (1949) may find it difficult to accept the superlatives expended unanimously not only by his older fans but also, and especially, by his professional contemporaries. It is not just that the light, bright, breezy, rather high baritone had become, by the 1940s, a somber bass, or that the melodic, rhythmic and elocutionary devices that had worked so freshly and so infectiously in the 1910s and 1920s had become mannerisms and clichés, unimproved by exaggeration. It is rather that they did not know Jolson in his prime, working his personal magic on a live audience.

One of his most successful pictures was *The Singing Fool* (1929). A more appropriate, if probably less merchandisable, title might have been *The Singing Suitor*. Whereas for most people courtship leads, ideally, to wedded bliss, for Jolson it led inexorably to the next courtship. He was married four times. But with women, says Pearl Sieben, "he was like a penniless urchin standing before the candy counter. He wanted what he couldn't have, and once he had tasted it, he wasn't interested."

The love of his life was an audience—any audience, just as long as it was physically present. For every audience was new, and every show meant a new challenge and a new conquest. His much quoted and often repeated "Wait a minute, wait a minute! You ain't heard nothin' yet!" might just as well have been: "Wait a minute, wait a minute, folks, I ain't finished with you yet!" It was the despairing cry of a victorious suitor intent on further indulgence in the delights of conquest. He could never bear to see an audience escape his fervent embrace.

Fervent it was. He created a sensation early in his vaudeville career by jumping into theater aisles in order to work closer to the audience. Or he would call to the technical crew, "Bring up the house lights!" then go to the edge of the stage, sit down, with his legs dangling into the pit, loosen his collar and tie, declare that "this is just like playing pinochle," and go into a routine of songs and patter. When playing *The Whirl of Society* on Broadway in 1912, in the early days of his stardom, he made the Shuberts rip out an entire row of seats in the middle of the house and put in a runway, à la burlesque. Gilbert Seldes, in *The Seven Lively Arts*, recalled Jolson at work on a runway:

> This galvanic little figure, leaping on it and shouting—yet always essentially dancing and singing—was the concentration of our national health and gaiety. In "Row, Row, Row," he would bounce upon the runway, propel himself by imaginary oars over the heads of the audience, draw equally imaginary slivers from the seat of his trousers, and infuse into the song something wild and roaring and insanely funny.

He is remembered most vividly by old-timers for his Sunday-night concerts for show people at the Winter Garden, which he inaugurated on April 2, 1911. Here, according to Eddie Cantor, was Jolson at his best, a real one-man show:

> Oh, there were some other people occasionally on the stage: a line of dancing girls, enough of a company to keep things going while Jolie took a glass of water or mopped his brow off stage. But he was the show, and many's the night he'd look at the audience about a quarter of eleven and say, "The girls are waiting backstage and they have some songs and dances, but they've worked pretty hard tonight, let's let them go home, huh? I'll stay here as long as you want, but let the poor kids go home, huh?" And he'd send everybody home while he stood there maybe another hour, singing, clowning, giving the audience the time of its life—and having the time of his own!

By the customs and conventions of the theater, just before and just after World War I, Jolson's easy familiarity with an audience was brash, if not brazen. To some it seemed presumptuous. Theater folk, even in vaudeville, were expected to keep their place behind the footlights and to treat the paying public with deference. Jolson was defying both tradition and commonly accepted precepts of what constituted good theater manners. By moving into the audience he was, in a sense, crashing the party, usurping the privileged status of those whom he was being paid to entertain. In stripping off collar and tie in the presence of the guests he was compounding the impudence by boorish behavior.

Jolson, in the century's second decade, was anticipating the relaxation of social protocol and standards of decorum that would be characteristic of the jazz age. Older critics, and probably some older members of the public, too, did not like it. Gordon Whyte, reviewing *Bombo* in *Billboard*, in the issue of October 22, 1921, said: "When this writer first saw Al Jolson he was a vaudeville artist. This was shortly after he terminated his career as a minstrel. He is a vaudeville artist today—a peerless one. . . . He has his public, and it supports him in everything he chooses to do." Two months later, *Billboard's* senior theater critic, Patterson James, would write:

It would not make the slightest bit of difference what you or I said about Al Jolson. He is as firmly established as an institution (for about one-third the population of New York) as Avenue B. . . . But as far as I am concerned, a little of Jolson goes a long way. He is an excellent performer in some ways. He projects a song unerringly. An audience has no terrors for him, because he sits on its knee and pats its cheek. . . . He also whistles well.

But he is going to meet the great tragedy of his life as an actor when he encounters an audience which will insist that he refrain from addressing them as "folks," which will decline to be put on a footing of personal social intimacy, and which will demand that he work at his business of entertaining not by using them, but by using the stage and his own wits for material.

He once planted his feet in the footlight trough, spoke at the audience as if it were the other half of a two-man talking act, and he has never gotten away from it. It is not talent which has landed him where he is. It is a realization of the fact that the man elevated on a platform has all the best of the people sitting beneath him. His small stock of ability has been capitalized with the cynical assurance of a successful clothing salesman. If he can get his finger in the buttonhole of your coat lapel, you buy the pants. That is all there is to it. . . . If you like Jolson's methods and his material, you will enjoy *Bombo*. I don't and I didn't.

There was undoubtedly rather more than a bit of "What Makes Sammy Run?" in Al Jolson. And why not? His was a typical American rags-to-riches story, rendered none the less attractive by the fact that he was born Asa Yoelson in Srednicke, Russian Lithuania, son of a rabbi who fled to America in 1890, did menial work in New York, saved enough money to pay steerage passage for the family, and finally settled with them, as rabbi of a small synagogue, in Washington, D.C. It was in the streets of Washington, as Pearl Sieben puts it, that "Al Jolson was born at the age of eight," singing with his brother Harry for congressmen and senators in front of the Hotel Raleigh. He spent what he earned on going to the theater.

It was the only life, much to the distress of his Orthodox father, that he would ever know, or want to know. First as a boy soprano, then, during his change of voice, as a whistler, eventually as a young baritone, he served a long and fruitful apprenticeship in bars, circuses, burlesque, minstrel shows and vaudeville. He enters musical and theater history as an end man with Lew Dockstader's Minstrels at the Fifth Avenue Theater in New York in 1909, when he was twenty-three, and he enters in the time-honored fashion: by stealing the show from the star.

The spot before the finale was reserved for Lew Dockstader himself; but by the time Jolson had finished his own solo turn the audience was his. Sime Silverman, covering for Variety, wrote: "Haven't seen such a demonstration for a single act, or any act, for that matter, as given to Al Jolson." And he quoted Dockstader's rueful remark to the audience: "Well, folks, I knew the kid had it, but I guess I just didn't now how much he had. Maybe he should have followed me."

For the next two years Jolson was in vaudeville in New York, sometimes playing three houses simultaneously, racing from one to the other as he did two spots a day in each. Then the Shuberts put him on in La Belle Paree at the Winter Garden, March 20, 1911, and Jolson had arrived. In the same year he made the first of his two-hundred-odd phonograph records.

The burlesque, vaudeville and minstrel-show apprenticeship was both fortunate and fateful, an introduction not only to the rudiments and arts of showmanship, but also to ragtime and the coon song, the fashionable popular styles of the time. As a small boy, Jolson had first heard a real coon shouter in the person of Eddie Leonard at the

JOLSON BROS.
AL & HARRY, 1899.
MAYFLOWER BURLESQUE COMPANY.

Harry and Al Jolson
The young Jolson

Bijou Theater in Washington. Now, as a blackface comedian and entertainer in his own right, he could do his own shouting. This affinity for, and identification with, the coon song—after his success with "My Mammy," coon songs came to be known euphemistically as "mammy songs"—endured throughout his life. His way with the idiom would influence just about every popular singer who came after him, male and female, black and white.

In those early days, of course, everybody else was singing coon songs too, black artists as well as white. But no one sang them more ardently, more infectiously, than Al Jolson. In the records of no other singer of the time, with the possible exception of Sophie Tucker, can one identify so instructively the elements that would ultimately lead the American popular singer into a new concept of phrasing drawn from Afro-American example.

It is fashionable nowadays to sneer at any association of Al Jolson with jazz. That he should have made history with a picture called *The Jazz Singer* is thought of as an appalling joke, even more appalling than Paul Whiteman's figurative coronation as "the King of Jazz." This is to judge a man who was already thirty-four, possibly older, in 1920 by the jazz standards of those who, when Jolson was thirty-four, had not been born. It would seem also to assume that jazz began with Sidney Bechet, King Oliver and Louis Armstrong.

It is to think in terms of jazz, however defined, rather than in terms of an Afro-American idiom in whose evolution the jazz of Bechet, Oliver and Armstrong was only an episode, however glorious. It is also to think of jazz in terms of only those Afro-American musical styles and accomplishments that have seemed to reflect the most of Africa and the least of America—or Europe. It is to forget that, as LeRoi Jones has put it so amiably, "none of the African prisoners broke out into 'St. James Infirmary' the minute the first of them was herded off the ship."

Jolson never sounded like Bessie Smith, whom he probably heard, or like Charley Patton or Blind Lemon Jefferson, whom he would hardly have heard. But he could sound a lot like Ethel Waters. And Ethel Waters could, and often did, sound a lot like him. Neither of them was a grass-roots-primitive musical genius. They were at once products and representatives of that process of imitation and counterimitation—black imitating white, and white imitating black imitating white—through which, beginning with ragtime and even earlier, African musicality was entering the mainstream of Western music in America. Jolson's place, and his importance, as an American singer can be assessed reasonably only within this Afro-American frame of reference.

There were always in Jolson's singing, even in his prime, characteristics distressing to the fastidious, whether of classical or jazz persuasion. His phrasing was blemished by habitual scooping and swooping, upwards and downwards, over intervals so wide that the effect was closer to wailing than singing. An agreeable but unexceptional voice, while skillfully used, was erratically focused, subject to abrasive nasality on such words as *way, may, mine, time,* etcetera. His enunciation was extraordinarily distinct, but it was also appalling to all who treasured the king's English. He vitiated vowel sounds and tortured diphthongs. A word such as *you,* for example, might be pronounced as *yoo, yew, yuh* and *you* all within the space of a few measures. Words of more than one syllable were methodically dismembered. The word *melody,* for example, became *mel-o-dee.* Louis Armstrong always indulged in this device, and he may well have got it from Jolson.

His dynamics tended to be uniform, neither very loud nor very soft, and there was little variety of color or timbre. He would seem to have been more concerned with the textual substance of a song than with its melodic contours. He was more orator than vocalist, a characteristic demonstrated again and again in his excursions into straight declamation. It was almost as if he found the tune inhibiting.

Therein lay the secret of his greatness. Therein, too, lay the root of some of his musical and linguistic misdemeanors. He loved words, and his maltreatment of them was a kind of smothering with affection. He would embrace a word, squeeze it, hug it, press it to his heart, and release it reluctantly rather the worse for wear. He often put more intensity into words than they could contain, or milked them for more than they could yield.

From none of all this should it be inferred that he was unmusical. But as a musician he could find text and tune restrictive; hence the many whistling choruses, where he would break away from the tune and improvise and embellish, much as the jazz musician does. Sometimes he would throw in a few measures of vocalized imitation trombone. No. He was very musical. It was simply a matter of priorities, and he sorted them out according to his purposes.

Like all singers, he was better in some songs than others, and some songs suited him better than others. With conventional, sentimental ballads and with any kind of operetta-like material, he often sounded, early in his career, and before his voice began to darken, like a Jewish and rather slovenly John McCormack. In later years he sometimes sounded like the Bing Crosby who had begun by imitating him. The more conventionally he sang, the more conspicuous, the more dismaying, were his slurs, his nasality, his wayward treatment of vowels and diphthongs. He was always a strong performer with any song. But he would hardly be remembered today, or be reckoned a pathbreaker in popular singing, had he not hustled into Mammy's arms or followed the swallow back home.

It was in up-tempo coon songs that he was unique in his own time and prophetic of the future. Despite leaden rinky-tink instrumental backings, he could give a song tremendous bounce and drive. He was obviously trying to break away from the rhythmical straitjacket of 1–2–3–4, to free syllables from their adherence to prescribed note values and lay them out in something closer to the rhythms of speech. In his 1929 recording of "I'm Sitting on Top of the World," for example, he seems, briefly, to be distributing syllables at his own discretion over a four-measure span, achieving at least an approximation of the approach to phrasing advanced by Bing Crosby and perfected by Frank Sinatra. On the same record he also employs a Sinatra-like *rubato*, tarrying on "top" and stealing from "of the world."

This performance, one of his best on record, is by no means an isolated example. In many of his early recordings one can hear him working toward the conversational rhythmic freedom and melodic cadences of the black vaudeville singers of the time. Personal reminiscences of Jolson in the early stages of his career include many references to his dropping into clubs in Chicago, New York and elsewhere to listen to black performers. It is impossible to sort out precisely what he picked up from them. One looks for clues in the records of those black artists only to find that they had been listening to Jolson just as intently as he to them.

It would be easy to assume that his slurring was derived from Negro example. Certainly he slurred for the same reason they did: to achieve something closer to rhetorical, oral communication than strict adherence to pitch would yield, and to heighten accentuation.

But careful listening leads to the conclusion that his slurring was more cantoral, at least more Jewish, than Negroid. There was nothing contradictory or inconsistent in this. Eastern European Jew and Afro-American each had to make an accommodation to a Western European diatonic scale. Slurring was one way of getting beyond what the diatonic law would allow.

European musicians have slurred, too. But they have done it less habitually and more discreetly. When slurring is overdone in European music, or done unwittingly or unskillfully, it is called *scooping* or *sliding* or *schmiering,* and is counted a sin. Slurring by black singers rarely gives offense, probably because it occurs in a stylistically appropriate context. Jolson's slurring, because his vocal style was closer than the black American's to European tradition, was often offensive to the European-oriented ear. It also tended to be a special kind of slurring, particularly the skidding descending major third cadence associated, in my memory, at least, not only with Jolson but also with other Jewish singer-entertainers, notably Eddie Cantor and George Jessel. When black singers imitated it, as they often did in the 1920s, they sounded not black but show biz.

Others of Jolson's devices were obviously of black derivation. He liked to interpolate words and syllables, or repeat them, in the black gospel-song fashion, even throwing in the occasional "Glory hallelujah!" and "Yessuh!" His frequent mauling of vowels may have been imitative, although his actual enunciation was not black. By the end of the 1920s, he was even indulging in jazzy "boop-boop-a-doop" breaks.

His melodic deviations (on "California, Here I Come," for example) may have owed something to black example, but they were certainly inspired, too, simply by his own compulsion to get the text across, come hell or high water. They were neither very adventurous nor very imaginative by the standards of later singers—although when he whistled they were both—but they were appropriate and effective.

Jolson's identification with the black American may not have gone very deep, if it can be said to have had any depth at all. But musically, at least, it was perceptive and shrewd. He recognized and welcomed the vitality and, above all, the oratorical fervor of the black American's music, even though most of what he heard in his show-biz world was already diluted. Later white singers would have the

Fanny Brice
With Eddie Cantor

advantage of superior black models, especially black instrumentalists, of whom Jolson, in his formative years, could have had no inkling, if only because these instrumentalists themselves had not yet matured —or even been born.

Jolson remained until the very end the headliner he had always wanted to be. But he was essentially a phenomenon of the 1920s and earlier. His death, on October 23, 1950, was thought of as marking "the end of an era." This was putting it charitably. It marked rather the passing of the last remnant of an era that had already faded into history. Jolson, as a singer, had outlived his time. It was simply evidence of the extent of his former greatness that *The Jolson Story* and *Jolson Sings Again* could shore up his declining celebrity and add the better part of a decade to a reign he now had to share, and hardly equally, with Bing Crosby and the young Frank Sinatra.

His survival into the swing era had been an uphill and, eventually, a losing battle. Although he pioneered the talking picture, and made many of them, he was not cut out for the new technology. He detested radio, went on the air late and reluctantly, and, until after *The Jolson Story*, achieved only a moderate success. He simply could not work without an audience he could see and feel, even when he must have known that radio gave him an audience of millions rather than a mere couple of thousands. On radio he sang, all too obviously, to the studio audience. The radio audience sensed it and resented it. As Eddie Cantor put it: "The Crosbys treated radio as if it were an instrument of introduction to your living room. Jolie treated it like an imposter."

Nor could he ever come to terms with the microphone or learn how to make it work for him. His style of performance and projection and his technique of vocal production were geared to reaching the balcony. His methods were set. He could no more shift to a crooning style than could an opera singer. At the close of his last show for the Chevrolet Hour in 1932, he told the studio audience, "This radio business is not for Jolie." He grabbed the silent mike and threw it to the floor. "It's a sad day," he said, "when Jolie needs a mike to sing into." And then he sang to the studio audience without it. In ill-tempered moments he would speak of "weak-voiced singers that would fall down if they didn't have a mike to hold on to."

But given a live audience, he could always work the old magic, and World War II gave him a live audience. He was off to sing for the troops long before the U.S.O. tours were organized, first to the Caribbean, then to Alaska and the Aleutians, to Ireland, England, North Africa and Sicily. With his faithful accompanist, Harry Akst, he did four or five shows a day—and loved it. Told by a grateful commanding officer how much he had done for the troops, Jolson replied with disarming candor, "It's nuthin' compared with what they're doing for me!"

He returned to the States in 1943, in ill health. He guested with Bing Crosby on radio for Kraft Cheese, and cut the sound tracks for *The Jolson Story* and *Jolson Sings Again*, unhappy only that he had to leave the acting of himself to Larry Parks. With the outbreak of the Korean War he was off again to sing for the boys.

Dick Haymes met him at a filling station in Palm Springs shortly before his departure, and Jolson told him of his plans. Haymes, knowing that Jolson's doctors had advised him to take it easy, wondered why he should be undertaking such a journey.

"Well," said Jolson, "I can't earn any bread here!"

Al Jolson was not worried about bread. When he died, shortly after his return from Korea, he left an estate of $4,000,000. But to him an audience was the staff of life.

There were memorial services in both New York and Hollywood, with Eddie Cantor delivering the eulogy in New York and George Jessel in Hollywood. There were enormous crowds in both places, and Jessel was moved to observe, "Jolson turned them away again!"

Jolie would have liked that. What he would not have liked was being unable to call back for a second show those who were turned away!

2

Bessie Smith

Bessie Smith is known to musical history as the Empress of the Blues. She was an Empress, all right, imperial and imperious in her singing, in her appearance, in her demeanor, and in her cups.

She is, significantly, the only artist in the annals of Afro-American music upon whom the imperial mantle has fallen. There have been Kings of This and Queens of That, and Dukes, Counts and Earls. But there has been no other Empress or Emperor. One has to look to sports to find an equivalent acknowledgment of ultimate, unchallenged supremacy—to Babe Ruth, the Sultan of Swat.

As is true of all great rulers, Bessie Smith not only dominated her own time, but also influenced profoundly the times that came after her. She has been dead for thirty-seven years, and she appears greater at this distance than she did at the height of her reign. So much that we treasure in American music either stems from her or was illuminated by her genius. Louis Armstrong, Mildred Bailey, Billie Holiday, Mahalia Jackson, Jack Teagarden, Ethel Waters and many more—they all heard her, or heard her records. They never forgot what they heard. Nor was she inspiring and influential as a singer only. Jazz instrumentalists worked closely with singers in the 1920s, as they would again in the swing era. Among those who may be heard backing Bessie on records are Red Allen, Louis Armstrong, Chu Berry, Jimmy Harrison, Coleman Hawkins, Fletcher Henderson and Tommy Ladnier. Many others, including Sidney Bechet, worked with her on the road. Countless more were among her devoted admirers. What she owed to the instrumentalists, and what they owed to her, are impossible to determine. There was a give and take we are all the richer for.

Her influence was not acknowledged immediately. It was probably not fully understood. Nor is it appreciated justly to this day, if only because it is the devices of her art that have survived rather than the music which they ennobled. The material most congenial to her was too rough, too uncompromising, too homespun. She was, in certain respects, an anachronism, defiantly black and rural Southern, not only in a white world but also in a black society aspiring to white conventions of urbanity. She was not too late on the scene to address her own people in their own language, and to achieve both fame and fortune. But she was late enough to learn what it means to go out of fashion without resources adaptable to new styles.

She made her first recording on February 16, 1923, and the progress of her career thereafter can be traced generally, her recording career precisely. Where she was, or when, prior to 1923 is something else again, including the date, if not the place, of her birth. The place was Chattanooga, Tennessee. The date is given variously as 1894, 1895, 1897, 1898 and 1900.

Frank Walker, her record producer at Columbia, thought 1900 most likely. Both Paul Oliver and Carman Moore, in their biographies of Bessie, opt for 1898. The tombstone placed on her grave in the Mount Lawn Cemetery, Sharon Hill, a suburb of Philadelphia, by Janis Joplin and a Philadelphia nurse, Mrs. Juanita Green, in the summer of 1970, gives her birth date as 1895. Chris Albertson, in *Bessie*, has noted April 15, 1894, as the date given on her application for a marriage license in 1923. This is also the date suggested by Dan Morgenstern in a *Down Beat* profile. According to George Hoefer, in his essay on Bessie for Nat Hentoff and Nat Shapiro's *The Jazz Makers*, "most reports at the time of her death in 1937 described her as being between 45 and 50." My own calculations suggest a date closer to 1890.

Ethel Waters, at the outset of her career, appeared on the same bill with Bessie in a black theater at 91 Decatur Street, Atlanta,

Georgia, as recounted in Ethel's autobiography, *His Eye Is on the Sparrow*. The story is much quoted for the light it throws on Bessie's character and behavior, and for its reflection of the antagonism felt by Southern blacks for their Northern brethren. It also provides, it seems to me, a clue to Bessie's age:

> Bessie was a heavy-set, dark woman, and very nice-looking. Along with Ma Rainey she was undisputed tops as a blues singer. When she came to Atlanta she'd heard a good deal about my low, sweet, and then new way of singing blues. Bessie's shouting brought worship wherever she worked. She was getting $50 to $75 a week, big money for our kind of vaudeville. The money thrown to her brought this to a couple of hundred dollars a week. Bessie, like an opera singer, carried her own claque with her. These plants in the audience were paid to throw up coins and bills to get the appreciation money going without delay the moment she finished her first number. And if Bessie ordered it, her followers would put the finger on you and run you right off the stage and out of sight, maybe forever.
>
> Bessie was in a pretty good position to dictate to the managers. She had me put on my act for her and said I was a long goody. But she told the men who ran No. 91 that she didn't want anyone else on the bill to sing the blues. I agreed to this. And when I went on I sang "I Want to Be Somebody's Baby Doll So I Can Get My Lovin' All the Time." But before I could finish this number the people out front started howling, "Blues! Blues! Come on, Stringbean, we want your blues!"
>
> Before the second show the manager went to Bessie's dressing room and told her he was going to revoke the order forbidding me to sing any blues. He said he couldn't have another such rumpus. There was quite a stormy discussion about this, and you could hear Bessie yelling things about "these northern bitches." But she agreed that after I took two or three bows for my first song, I should, if the crowd still insisted, sing "St. Louis Blues."
>
> I sensed this was the beginning of the uncrowning of her, the great and original Bessie Smith. I've never enjoyed seeing a champ go down, and Bessie was all champ. When I closed my engagement in that theater, Miss Bessie called me to her. "Come here, long goody," she said. "You ain't so bad. It's only that I never dreamed that anyone would be able to do this to me in my own territory and with my own people. And you know damn well that you can't sing worth a———!"

Ma Rainey in 1923. The pianist is the Reverend Thomas A. Dorsey, the gospel composer, in his earlier incarnation as blues pianist Georgia Tom.

Ethel Waters was born in Chester, Pennsylvania, in 1896. The chronology of her autobiography is labyrinthine, but the date indicated for this encounter is 1918. If Bessie Smith had been born even in 1894, she would have been twenty-four, only two years older than Ethel, and thus hardly likely to have occupied the exalted position and commanded the veneration Miss Waters associates with her at that time. It may be significant that Miss Waters brackets Bessie with Ma Rainey, who was born in 1886.

The story is valuable, too, as one of the very few documented glimpses of Bessie Smith in the earlier stages of her career. Tradition has it that she was heard, as a child, singing, either in the streets or in a theater, by Ma Rainey, when the latter was playing Chattanooga with her husband's company of F. S. Wolcott's Rabbit Foot Minstrels, and was taken into the troupe. With Ma Rainey, so the story goes, she served an instructive and fruitful apprenticeship. This is essentially the account given by Paul Oliver in his *Bessie Smith* (1959). Carman Moore, in his *Somebody's Angel Child* (1970), has Bessie kidnapped by Ma Rainey, and says she stayed with the "Foots" for three years.

More recent research, notably Chris Albertson's, has established all this as fanciful mythology. He dates her first professional experience to 1912, when she was recruited by her brother Clarence, a dancer and comedian, for a traveling show playing Chattanooga storefronts. Ma Rainey was in the company, but she and her husband would not have their own show until after 1916. Bessie, thereafter, traveled with a number of tent and carnival shows, working her way up from the chorus to star billing.

Beyond that simple fact, Albertson has been hardly more successful than others in rooting out details. "Information regarding that period of her life," he writes, "is still so scant and vague that we may never know the whole truth." He picks up her trail at the Douglas Gilmore Theater in Baltimore in 1918, and catches glimpses of her in the black press as far west as Muskogee, Oklahoma, and as far south as Atlanta. By 1921 she had worked her way north to Philadephia, where she played the New Standard Theater on South Street. During the summer of 1922 she is known to have worked at the Paradise Gardens in Atlantic City.

There is some confusion, too, about Bessie's earliest essays at recording. She may have made some records for the Emerson Record Company as early as 1921, but if so, they were not released, nor has their existence ever been confirmed. It is the same with the Columbia records referred to in a 1921 advertisement of Bessie's appearance at the New Standard Theater. Also in 1921, according to Paul Oliver, she had an abortive test with Harry Pace, an early black entrepreneur, who was W. C. Handy's partner in the music-publishing business and president of the Pace Phonograph Company, which issued race records on the Black Swan label. Pace's star at the time was Ethel Waters. Bessie, so the story goes, disgusted Pace when she held up a take, hollering, "Hold on, let me spit!"—and spat.

Both Clarence Williams, who would be the piano accompanist on her first authenticated records for Columbia, and Sidney Bechet, who was with her during her brief stay in Philadelphia with a musical comedy, *How Come?* remembered an unsuccessful audition for the

Okeh label in what must have been January 1923. All that is certain is that she was engaged by Frank Walker when he took over race records for Columbia at about that time. Warned by Clarence Williams, then Judge of Race Records for Columbia, that other companies had found Bessie's voice too rough, Walker, as the most plausible of many versions has it, said, "You just get her here."

Her first side for Columbia was " 'Tain't Nobody's Bizzness If I Do." The second was "Down Hearted Blues," a twelve-bar blues by Alberta Hunter and Lovie Austin, which, as sung by Miss Hunter, had already been a best seller in the Paramount race series. Bessie's record sold 780,000 copies in less than six months. She signed a one-year contract, effective April 20, 1923, requiring her to record twelve sides at $125 a usable side and guaranteeing her $1,500 with a one-year renewal option for twelve sides at $150.

Blessed with such professional and financial prospects, she married, on June 7, 1923, Jack Gee, a Philadelphia policeman (Chris Albertson says he was only a night watchman, but Carman Moore's book includes a photograph of him in the uniform of a Philadelphia patrolman), and set up housekeeping at 1226 Webster Street in South Philadelphia.

"Down Hearted Blues" included the line "Got the world in a jug, the stopper in my hand," and that was about how it was. In the next six years Bessie's records would sell somewhere between five and ten million copies. She would tour the country as one of the highest-paid stars of the black entertainment world, earning, it is said, as much as $2,500 a week. There was just one flaw in the picture: the world in her jug was liquid. As George Avakian wryly put it in his liner notes to Volume I of the 1951 CBS *The Bessie Smith Story*, "she drank to excess in her youth and increased her capacity as she rose to fame." Standing five feet nine inches and weighing in at 210 pounds, she was a formidable drunk.

Sidney Bechet said of her, "Bessie was a hell of a fine woman. She could be plenty tough; she could really hold her own. She always drank plenty, and she could hold it. But sometimes, after she'd been drinking a while, she'd get like there was no pleasing her. There were times you had to know just how to handle her right. She had this trouble in her, this thing that wouldn't let her rest sometimes, a meanness that came and took her over."

Oliver echoes Sidney: "When she was sober she was agreeable

enough, but when she had been drinking she became irascible, temperamental; and her drinking sprees became ever more frequent." Carman Moore, drawing upon Jack Gee's recollections of life with Bessie, says, "When Bessie was drinking she could be evil. She could punch people, throw things, and fire people who worked for her, sending a hail of cursing after them as they fled."

Any doubts that anyone may ever have entertained about Bessie's conduct when drinking are dispelled by Chris Albertson. He heard it all from Ruby Walker Smith, Bessie's niece by marriage and her companion on most of her tours. In *Bessie*, he passes on a distressing catalogue of brawls, binges, obscene curses, promiscuities, strandings, etcetera, including an outrageous performance at a reception given by Mr. and Mrs. Carl Van Vechten when Bessie got drunk and flattened Mrs. Van Vechten in full view of the other guests.

Just about everyone who knew Bessie Smith has spoken of a curious dualism in her character. One side of her, certainly, was rough and tough and coarse and crude. Another was warm, tender, affectionate and generous to the point of heedless extravagance. A widely circulated story tells how she interrupted a profitable tour when one of Frank Walker's children was ill to take over the housekeeping chores from Mrs. Walker until the child was out of danger. The two sides of her nature seem to have been in perpetual conflict, except when she was drinking. Then the rougher side took over.

One is tempted to think of her not as childish, but as childlike— until one has heard her account of a Mississippi flood in "Backwater Blues." Nothing childlike about that! It's a woman embracing the women and the families she had known. A *Time* writer said (April 13, 1970) that the blues, for Bessie Smith, was "a womanly wail that somehow remained proud of its woe." But in private life she remained a tough customer. One remembers the comment of May Wright Johnson, wife of James P. Johnson, Bessie's pianist on many of her finest records, "She would come over to the house, but, mind you, she wasn't my friend. She was very rough!"

She was a formidable competitor, too. Among her early records were many songs and blues recorded previously by other singers. Not only had "Down Hearted Blues" been recorded by Alberta Hunter and others; " 'Tain't Nobody's Bizzness" had been recorded by Sara Martin. At her second session Bessie sang "Aggravatin' Papa" and

"Beale Street Mama," which had recently provided hits for Lucille Hegamin, and Sara Martin's "Keeps On a-Rainin'."

Recording songs originated by, or associated with, other singers is known nowadays as "covering." In Bessie's time "carving" would have been closer to the meaning. It is a reasonable assumption that Bessie was out to demonstrate who was boss. A comparison of her records with those of others who were recording at the same time leaves no doubt as to her success. She was a superior performer and even more imposing as a personality. Thanks, probably, to Frank Walker, her records were technically superior to those made by other artists under other labels, particularly the records made prior to electrical recording.

Despite the abundance of her records, and the financial rewards they yielded, Bessie remained essentially a public performer. Between recording sessions she would be off on the road, back to "her own people" in the South, and to the top theaters on the black circuits in the North. Possibly because of her repertoire, possibly because of a style that was thought to be crude and primitive by the more sophisticated in the black communities, possibly because of disinclination, she never played what black entertainers in those days called "the white time," thus failing to achieve the relative national and even international celebrity enjoyed in the 1920s by such artists as Josephine Baker, Florence Mills and Ethel Waters. Many whites, however, went to black theaters and cabarets to hear her, especially the young jazz musicians and jazz enthusiasts, and their memoirs give us a vivid picture of the kind of performer she was.

Clarinetist Mezz Mezzrow, along with other such early jazzmen as Bix Beiderbecke, Eddie Condon, Jimmy and Tommy Dorsey, Frank Teschemacher and Dave Tough, heard her in Chicago in the mid-1920s, at the height of her career. This is how he remembered her in his *Really the Blues:*

> Bessie was a real woman, all woman, all the femaleness the world ever saw in one sweet package. She was tall and brown-skinned, with great big dimples creasing her cheeks, dripping good looks—just this side of voluptuous, buxom and massive, but stately, too, shapely as an hourglass, with a high-voltage magnet for a personality. When she was in a room her vitality flowed out like a cloud and stuffed the air till the walls bulged.

She didn't have any mannerisms, she never needed any twirls and twitches to send those golden notes of hers on their sunshiny way. She just stood there and sang, letting the love and the laughter run out of her, and the heaving sadness, too; she felt everything, and swayed just a little with the glory of being alive and feeling, and once in a while, with a grace that made you want to laugh and cry all at once, she made an eloquent little gesture with her hands. . . .

Her style was so individual that nobody else ever grasped it. The way she let her rich music tumble out was a perfect example of improvisation—the melody meant nothing to her, she made up her own melody to fit the poetry of her story, phrasing all around the original tune if it wasn't just right, making the vowels come out just the right length, dropping consonants that might trip up her story, putting just enough emphasis on each syllable to make you really know what she was getting at. She *lived* every story she sang; she was just telling you how it happened to her.

Bessie working a room was one thing; Bessie working from a theater stage was another. Carl Van Vechten heard her at the Orpheum Theater in Newark, New Jersey, on Thanksgiving Day, 1925, and contributed this ecstatic account to *Jazz Record*:

She was very large, and she wore a crimson robe sweeping up from her trim ankles and embroidered in multicolored sequins in designs. Her face was beautiful with the rich ripe beauty of southern darkness, a deep bronze brown, matching the bronze of her bare arms. Walking slowly to the footlights . . . she began her strange, rhythmic rites in a voice full of shouting and moaning and praying and suffering, a wild rough Ethiopian voice, harsh and volcanic, but seductive and sensuous, too, released between rouged lips and the whites of teeth, the singer swaying lightly to the beat, as is the Negro custom.

Now inspired partly by the expressive words, partly by the stumbling strain of the accompaniment, partly by the powerfully magnetic personality of this elemental conjure woman with her plangent African voice, quivering with passion and pain, sounding as if it had been developed at the sources of the Nile, the black and blue-black crowd, notable for the absence of mulattoes, burst into hysterical, semi-religious shrieks of sorrow and lamentation. Amens rent the air.

It is clear from the reports of all who experienced the art of Bessie Smith at first hand that she had a kind of innate majesty. In terms of sophistication she fell between the elemental, fundamental primitive demeanor and address of the tent shows and gin mills where she had begun and the polished showmanship of the next generation's stars.

Those who heard Bessie Smith in person in her prime have their memories. For the rest of us there are only the records (all 160 of them now reissued by Columbia). They constitute a treasurable legacy. They tell us little about a live performance before a live audience, but a great deal about what she sang and how. They tell us a lot, too, about the singers who came after her. They also raise some pertinent questions.

Most fundamental of these is how to reconcile what we hear on the recordings with the description of Bessie by Ethel Waters and others as a shouter. There is little on any record she ever made that sounds like shouting in the common sense of the term. Indeed, she would seem, by the recorded evidence, to have been incapable of making a strident or otherwise unseemly sound. Her contemporaries made many. Bessie's tone, except on some of her last records, is always rich, full, round and warm. The placement is wonderfully forward, the production natural, easy and fluent.

A quotation from the Savannah *Tribune*, a black newspaper, in *Billboard*, June 10, 1922, provides a clue. Miss Waters had just finished an engagement there, and the *Tribune* commented: "Her departure from the shouting, bellowing sort of blues singers we have been accustomed to hearing was a source of much pleasure to local music lovers. . . . Her interpretation of blues singing was, indeed, refreshing." No reference here to Bessie Smith specifically, but by the criteria thus implied, she would certainly have been numbered among the sinners. "Shouting," as Bessie's black contemporaries used the word, was associated with a category of performer. In their eyes it was a low category, however admirable the performance. One thinks of the classical musician who admires a great jazz musician without questioning a categorical distinction in the classical musician's favor, or even of the modern jazz musician who thinks of Sidney Bechet and Louis Armstrong as admirable primitives.

In assessing the art of Bessie Smith today it is helpful to note that while what we hear may not sound like shouting, it rarely sounds much like singing, either, in any conventional or traditional sense of the term. It is pertinent to add that the closer to conventional singing it comes, the less characteristic it is of Bessie Smith. Bessie was a talker. Her utterance, at its best, was like a passionate kind of oratory, intoned and sustained, and pretty loud, forceful and forthright, too, as would be required of one accustomed to addressing large congregations prior to the days of amplification. Bessie, like most of the "classic" blues singers, scorned even the megaphone.

Her breath was heavy on the vocal cords. The refinements of her vocal art—and there were many—were not dynamic. They were melodic. Within a limited range from top to bottom they called upon a limitless variety of pitch and color. Melody, for her, had little to do with do re me, or with tune, which is why she excelled in self-made or custom-made material. When she sang popular songs she altered tune and time to suit herself. The result was commonly a hybrid. It was not, as a rule, admirable. Other singers sang tunes better than she, although they may not have achieved so striking a performance.

Compared with the great black singers of a later time, she had an astonishingly short vocal compass. She rarely ventured outside the single octave C–C, and she had little to show for her exertion when she did. Above the upper C the voice became thin and uncharacteristic. Beneath the lower C it trailed off in barely audible cadences on barely identifiable pitches. Only the exceptional song, on records, covers the full octave, barring the occasional higher or lower pitch touched in a trail-off or *appoggiatura*. Mostly she remained within the span of a fifth or sixth.

Nor was she harmonically sophisticated or adventurous. She had a pronounced affinity for a tonal center, working around it with much imagination, but rarely straying far from it, and then always in a melodic rather than a chordal context. This predilection was shrewdly noted by Roberta Flack, a "soul" singer of our own time, in a Leonard Feather Blindfold Test in *Down Beat* (March 1972). Feather had played Bessie's 1933 recording of "Gimme a Pigfoot," and Roberta said:

I'm pretty sure that was Bessie Smith. . . . The thing that impresses me is the transition or the development of the blues vocal line. As we listen to it on that cut, it's very simple; she sticks right around the tonic even when they [the backing group] go from the tonic—sounded like it was E flat. When they went from E flat to the C seventh chord, she is still leaning somewhere around the E flat. Then they go to F seventh, then to B flat, and she's still somewhere around that E flat.

Bessie's art lay not in the seamless movement from one pitch to another in the diatonic major and minor modes, but in her discovery and exploitation of the uncharted microtonal areas between the pitches. That is why her shortness of range, in singing the blues, was no handicap. In terms of what she was saying, and how, she had all the range she needed. She probably had more, potentially. The quality of the voice suggests a true contralto with an easy two-octave range from F to F. But she never learned how to discipline her vocal apparatus to extend a characteristic sound beyond what came naturally. It is unlikely that she tried.

What has been said of her dealing with pitch applies similarly to her handling of rhythm. She accepted the 2/4 or 4/4 of European music, just as she and other black artists accepted the basic pitches of the European scales, but she refused to be bound by them. Like most jazz musicians of the 1920s, she sang pretty much on the beat, but it was largely a beat of her own making. In only one of her sessions for Columbia did she use drums, and in the theater she insisted on the drummer's restricting himself to brushes. She did not, apparently, wish to be dominated rhythmically by any drummer. She was a mistress of *rubato*, too. A spectacular example is afforded by her "Cold in Hand Blues," recorded with Louis Armstrong in 1925.

Her approach to diction, or enunciation, was all of a piece with her approach to melody and rhythm. She took pains to make herself understood. The vocabulary may be strange, even incomprehensible, at times, to the uninitiated, but the enunciation is usually distinct. It is, at the same time, free. She had no reservations about changing vowels to suit the melodic context. She added syllables and left syllables out, added or repeated a word here and there, and so on, in the manner made more familiar to the white public many years later in the gospel singing of Mahalia Jackson and others.

In view of all that has been said of the greatness, the uniqueness, of her art, one wonders, inevitably, how to explain her decline as the decade came to a close. My own proposition would be that it was not so much a decline as a disorientation. The depression was a factor, as were the inroads of radio and talking pictures upon the record market and vaudeville circuits. Her drinking was no help, nor was her decision to forsake the guidance and counsel of Frank Walker as her manager. But along with all that, and probably more fundamental for her career as a public performer, American black society was changing.

Bessie was a primitive, both as person and as performer. She had come North in the wake of a migration that brought hundreds of thousands of "her own people" to the big industrial and cultural centers. To them she was a voice from back home, and a great voice. But to a younger generation not rooted in the rural South, or only too anxious to forget its roots, she must have begun to seem old-fashioned, even embarrassing. One remembers Carl Van Vechten's observation of a conspicuous absence of mulattoes in her Newark audience in 1925, and Ethel Waters' statement: "I sensed this was the beginning of the uncrowning of her, the great and original Bessie Smith." A premature, even patronizing speculation in 1918, but there was something to it.

By 1930 it was no longer speculation. Bessie knew it. When she recorded "Need a Little Sugar in My Bowl" and "Safety Mama" in 1931, the initial order to the pressing plant called for only eight hundred copies. Of a previous coupling of "Long Old Road" and "Shipwreck Blues," released subsequently, only four hundred were pressed. Her recording career was at an end—and so was her marriage. When John Hammond brought her back from near oblivion two years later to do four sides for Columbia's European market, all she could command was $50 a side. Sales did not cover expenses.

Nor would she record the kind of blues that had made her famous. It was a jazz age, she said, and people didn't want to be depressed by the blues. Frank Walker said she had lost heart: "You might say she didn't have a hitching post to tie her horse to. She began to lose interest in life. She had no heart left, and she was singing differently. There was bitterness in her, and, you know, the blues aren't bitter."

Without the blues she was also without a proper repertoire. The kind of popular song she had been able to get away with in the early

1920s was out of date, as was her way with a popular song. So, doubtless with an ear to her grass-roots public, she veered toward the coarsely pornographic, the kind of tawdry stuff she had been reduced to in a declining career as a public performer. She also made a pass at pop-gospel. But her heart was not in it. Again, she was unfortunate in her choice of material, or in the material that was offered her.

The finest of her late records is "Long Old Road." Here we can hear the Bessie of old singing: "You can't trust nobody. You might as well be alone." She was alone, professionally, at least she who in 1925 had sung so exuberantly: "I ain't gonna play no second fiddle 'cause I'm used to playing lead!"

Prior to the publication of Albertson's *Bessie* in 1972, almost as little was known of her life subsequent to the end of her recording career as of her life before she began to record. One obvious reason was that she was not doing much. Four weeks at the Apollo in Harlem, for instance, was all that she had to show for 1935. But thanks to her parting from Jack Gee and a new relationship with Richard Morgan, a well-to-do Chicago bootlegger, her personal life was less tumultuous, and she was never, as legend has it, down and out. That, at least, is Albertson's conclusion.

Beginning with engagements at Connie's Inn at Broadway and Seventh Avenue in New York in 1936 (filling in for Billie Holiday!) and a sensational appearance at a Sunday-afternoon jam session at the Famous Door on 52nd Street, things began to look up. She had long runs in Philadelphia. Further recordings were in prospect, and she was touring the South with Winsted's *Broadway Rastus* show when she was fatally injured in a car crash on Route 61 between Memphis, Tennessee, and Clarksdale, Mississippi, in the early morning of September 26, 1937. Even in death she remained a figure of legend. Mezz Mezzrow, in *Really the Blues*, offered the traditional account:

> You ever hear what happened to that fine, full-of-life female woman? One day in 1937 she was in an automobile accident down in Mississippi, the Murder State, and her arm was almost tore out of its socket. They brought her to the hospital, but it seemed like there wasn't any room for her just then—the people around there didn't care for the color of her skin. The car turned around and drove away, with Bessie's blood dripping on the floor mat. She was finally admitted to another hospital where the

officials must have been colorblind, but by that time she had lost so much blood that they couldn't operate on her, and a little later she died. *See that lonesome road, Lawd, it got to end,* she used to sing. That was how the lonesome road ended up for the greatest folk singer this country ever had—with Jim Crow directing traffic.

Well, that's the ugly story—or at least one of many variants of the same story—as it has been passed down through the years. Edward Albee wrote a play about it, *The Death of Bessie Smith,* produced off Broadway in 1961. He would have done better to consult Paul Oliver's biography of Bessie, published in 1959:

> Of a dozen versions perhaps the most likely is the report that a prominent—but unnamed—Memphis surgeon was passing the scene of the accident and stopped to render aid. Whilst trying to lift the 200-pound body of the singer into his car, his own vehicle was struck by oncoming traffic and destroyed. An ambulance, summoned by another unknown person, arrived a few minutes later, and the mortally wounded Bessie was taken to the Negro ward of the G. T. Thomas Hospital at Clarksdale, Miss. One of the best surgeons is said to have amputated her arm, but the severe injuries that she suffered to her face, head and internal organs caused her death at quarter-past noon on the same day.

According to Sally Grimes, in an article, "The True Death of Bessie Smith," in the June 1969 issue of *Esquire,* the Memphis surgeon, now identified as Dr. Hugh Smith, a past president of the American Academy of Orthopedic Surgeons, when shown Oliver's version, said, "I think this man is accurate about this—that she was taken to this colored hospital and a damn good man took care of her, but . . . she'd just had too much. And of the dozen versions, the other eleven you'd better forget."

Dr. Smith gave detailed accounts of the incident to both Sally Grimes and Chris Albertson. It is his opinion that even with today's improved facilities, Bessie, given the critical condition in which he found her, would have had little chance of survival.

Her passing was hardly noted by the white press, but the following account, datelined Philadelphia, October 8, appeared in the Chicago *Defender* of October 9:

> Bessie Smith, "Queen" of the blues and the grandest trouper of them all, answered her final curtain call. Brought to an untimely death through an automobile accident in Clarksdale, Miss., the "Queen" took her last bow before the footlights and received the last respects of an admiring public and the homage of her theatrical colleagues in a simple but very impressive funeral service at the C. V. Catto Elks Home, 16th and Fitzwater Sts.
>
> Bessie Smith was dressed in a gorgeous flesh lace gown with pink slippers. She rested in an expensive open silver metallic casket trimmed in gold and draped in a two-toned lining. Being the first of the Race to have professional pallbearers in Philadelphia, the body was borne on the shoulders of the men out of the hall and a block down 16th St. between tightly packed rows of people, preceded by the choir softly intoning "Rest In Peace." . . .

Her grave remained unmarked until the summer of 1970.

> For some years [said Sally Grimes in her 1969 *Esquire* article] it was considered a scandal in the jazz world that no marker was placed upon her grave, although there had been numerous benefits to raise money for a fitting tombstone for the Queen of the Blues. Somehow the money never reached the right hands, and Bessie's unmarked grave is the final elusive fact of her death. But what Bessie Smith had was alive. And whatever the facts of her death, that Albee and others have recognized her more as a victim of racism than as a great American artist is, perhaps, the most telling injustice of all.

I'm not so sure. I was talking, just a few years ago, with the young, personable and gifted leader of a black gospel choir. We were speaking of the great gospel composer Thomas A. Dorsey, and I remarked that he had played fifty years or more ago for Ma Rainey and Bessie Smith.

"Who," she asked me, "was Bessie Smith?"

3

Ethel Waters

I don't know how Ethel Waters introduces herself today, or how she is introduced, as she tours the world, a black lady in her seventies, with Billy Graham. But I can think of no more appropriate way of introducing her here than the way she used to introduce herself in vaudeville fifty years ago. It was a device she worked out with her partner, Ethel Williams, for her entrance in a black variety road show called *Oh! Joy!* Here is her own account, as given in her autobiography, *His Eye Is on the Sparrow:*

> When I planned my routines for *Oh! Joy!* I wanted to make a different kind of entrance than other well-known record singers were using. They were going in for flash and class, one of their favorite entrances being coming on the stage through the door of an ornate phonograph. Just before my entrance in *Oh! Joy!* Ethel Williams would go out on the stage.
>
> "Where's that partner of mine?" she'd ask the orchestra leader. "Where's that Ethel Waters? What can be keeping her?" And she'd look all over the stage for me, behind the curtain, in the wings and, for a laugh, under the rug. She'd mutter, "How can I start our act without that gal?"
>
> After that build-up, I'd come out—in a funny hat and a gingham apron that was a gem. I was slim, and when Ethel

81

would ask, "Are you Ethel Waters?" I'd answer, "Well, I ain't
Bessie Smith!"

These two lines would wow the audience. Then I'd sing the
plaintive and heartbreaking song, "Georgia Blues." The number
told the story of a Southern gal who felt lost and homesick up
North. Georgia was home to her, no matter what else it was, and
the piece had universal appeal. It was like the cry from the heart
of all wanderers everywhere. And on the stage I was the bewil-
dered little colored girl who couldn't feel at peace and at ease so
far off from the scenes of her childhood.

Ethel Waters was not from Georgia, nor from anywhere else in
the South. Nor had she any reason to be homesick for the scenes of
her childhood. This had been spent in the sordid side streets of black
neighborhoods in Chester, Pennsylvania (where she was born illegitimately to a twelve-year-old girl on October 31, 1896), and in Philadelphia, where she grew up—fast.

In all other respects this was an informative introduction, both
for her audiences at the time and for ourselves now. It couples her
immediately, if only by way of striking and significant contrast, with
Bessie Smith. It reveals her as one of the first black recording artists.
And it shows her, thus early in her career, establishing the person, the
setting, the situation and the mood for a song of character and
characterization.

It is fitting, too, that we should meet her on stage. Far more
than Bessie Smith, far more, indeed, than any other black singer of
the century, Ethel Waters was a woman of the theater. In her teens,
as a substitute chambermaid at the Harrod Apartments in Philadelphia, she would hurry through her work in a room, then lock the
door, stand in front of the full-length mirror and transform herself
into Ethel Waters, the great actress, "playing all sorts of roles, and
also the audience, mugging and acting like mad."

Small wonder, then, that she should have achieved two of her
greatest successes in straight dramatic parts on Broadway—as Hagar
in Mamba's Daughters (1939) and as Berenice Sadie Brown, the
black cook, in The Member of the Wedding (1950). It is also too bad,
in a way, because the celebrity she earned as an actress has tended to
overshadow or obscure both the luster and the importance of her
accomplishments as a singer.

Ethel Waters in *The Member of the Wedding* ▶

Above, Lena Horne; *below*, Pearl Bailey

Along with Bessie Smith and Louis Armstrong, she was a fountainhead of all that is finest and most distinctive in American popular singing. Of the three, she may well have been the most widely and the most perceptibly influential. Louis Armstrong's vocalism, if not his phrasing, has defied imitation. Bessie Smith's singing was too little touched by white example. Bessie's influence has come down to us through gospel song and the blues. In Ethel Waters one hears almost everybody. In just about every popular singer who came after her one hears a bit of Ethel Waters.

She was, as a singer, a transitional figure and a towering one, summing up all that had been accumulated stylistically from minstrel show, ragtime and coon song, and anticipating the artful, jazz-touched Afro-American inflections of the swing era. She was one of the first and, after Bessie Smith, probably the best of the many excellent singers who made race records and sang to black audiences in nightclubs and theaters across the country throughout the 1920s. There are echoes, on her early records, of her black contemporaries, but one hears suggestions, too, of Nora Bayes, Fanny Brice, Marion Harris, Al Jolson, Blossom Seeley and Sophie Tucker. Mixed in with these echoes are foretastes not only of Pearl Bailey, Ella Fitzgerald, Billie Holiday, Lena Horne and Sarah Vaughan, but also of Mildred Bailey, Connee Boswell, Ethel Merman, Lee Morse, Kate Smith and Lee Wiley.

Yet there is never a sense of stylistic or idiomatic inconsistency or impropriety. Such was her genius in the comprehension and projection of a song, and such was the strength of her personality, that everything she did seemed to be uniquely hers and ultimately right. As much could probably be said of other singers, including some of her contemporaries, in a limited repertoire. But her talent and her nature defied categorical circumscription. Her repertoire ranged from quasi-blues and coon songs of the kind turned out in the 1920s by Lovie Austin, Shelton Brooks, Eubie Blake, Perry Bradford, W. C. Handy and Clarence Williams to the smart lyrics, sophisticated rhythms and infectious melodies of Harold Arlen, Irving Berlin, Vernon Duke and Arthur Schwartz.

Her awareness and subsequent cultivation of a talent richer and more widely ranging than that of other blues singers of her time she owed to the perception and persistence of Earl Dancer, a black vaudevillian and sometime entrepreneur, who heard her at Edmond's Cellar on Fifth Avenue and 132nd Street in Harlem, where she worked on and off for several years just after World War I, and to Lou Henley, her pianist at Edmond's. It was Henley who encouraged her to add popular tunes to her blues routine, and it was Dancer who talked her into having a go at "the white time."

She was already, at twenty-six or twenty-seven, a veteran trouper of the black time. We have met her, indeed, a few years earlier, as Sweet Mama Stringbean, an apprentice shaker and singer, exploding Bessie Smith's formidable wrath by singing "St. Louis Blues" to a Bessie Smith audience in Atlanta. Back home in Philadelphia, she had worked in Barney Gordon's Saloon at the corner of 13th and Kater Streets. As the first star of Harry H. Pace's Black Swan Records, she had toured the country on promotional jaunts with Fletcher Henderson's Black Swan Jazz Masters.

All of this was in the lowest bracket of show business, and Edmond's Cellar was far from being a glamor spot, even of Harlem. Miss Waters describes it as the last stop on the way down in show business. "After you had worked there," she remembers, "there was no place to go except into domestic service." She had already been in domestic service. She was still young, she was on her way up, and Earl Dancer knew it.

"Ethel," he told her, "believe me when I say you don't belong on the colored time. In those theaters you're playing now, your public will get fed up with you in two or three years. But if you would only let the white people hear you sing, they'd love you for the rest of your life. You don't have to sing as you do for colored people, verse after verse after verse of the blues. You can break it up; sing some blues, then talk the story in the song, and end up with more blues. They'll love it. You're a genius, Ethel."

In her own eyes at that time she was just a Fifth Avenue (Harlem) honky-tonk performer, and she was a fearful and reluctant convert. She was confident enough of her ability to get over with her own people, but she was equally certain that both her talent and her material would be lost on a white audience. She agreed at last to a break-in date with Earl at the Kedzie Theater in Chicago, "just to get rid of Earl's big talk and dreams," convinced that their act would be a flop and put an end to it. Instead, she was an instant success, and

Ethel Waters with Eubie Blake in *Lew Leslie's Blackbirds of 1929*

Josephine Baker

she toured the Keith-Orpheum circuit for a couple of years with Earl as her partner.

She was destined for even bigger things: for the Plantation Club at Broadway and 50th Street; for the Cotton Club in Harlem; for the Broadway theater, where she was first featured in *Africana* (1927) and *As Thousands Cheer* (1933) and then starred in *At Home Abroad* (1935) and *Cabin in the Sky* (1940); for Hollywood, and for the role of Beulah on television. It is no exaggeration to say that she achieved a success and enjoyed a fame, both as singer and actress, unprecedented for a black artist.

White critics were quick to detect her talent—and to confirm Earl Dancer's judgment. In Chicago, on the basis of that first outing at the Kedzie Theater, she was hailed by one critic as "the ebony Nora Bayes," by another as "the Yvette Guilbert of her race." A Cleveland critic wrote that if she had been born white she would have been a Raquel Meller or an Eleanora Duse. The comparison with Nora Bayes pleased her most. Miss Bayes, she tells us, "had elegance, dignity, class; she was the one who never gave out with any unladylike shouts and growls, but sang all her songs with refinement."

This tells us rather more about Ethel Waters than about Nora Bayes. Ethel's childhood, or what passed for childhood—she was first married at thirteen—left her tough, self-reliant—and scarred. She admired refinement and probably envied it, too, if only because there had been so little of it in her early environment. But she was also proud of her survival and of the toughness it had nurtured, a toughness which had indeed made survival possible. Her upbringing and the adventures of road life on the black time had left her suspicious and wary. She could be a charming lady. But she tended to be touchy, quick to take offense. She was rough when aroused.

Billie Holiday, in *Lady Sings the Blues*, gives us a glimpse of Ethel that is closer to Bessie Smith than to Nora Bayes. Billie had been sent to Philadelphia early in her career to audition for a show at the Nixon Grand Theater featuring Duke Ellington, the Brown Sisters and Ethel Waters. As Billie tells it:

> I told the piano player to give me "Underneath the Harlem Moon," which was real popular then. I hadn't finished the first chorus when Ethel Waters bounced up in the darkened theater. "Nobody's going to sing on this goddam stage," she

boomed, "but Miss Ethel Waters and the Brown Sisters." That settled that. "Underneath the Harlem Moon" was Miss Waters' big number. But nobody told me. I didn't have the faintest idea. So the stage manager handed me two dollars and told me to get on the bus and go home. I threw the money at him and told him to kiss my ass and tell Miss Waters to do the same. . . . Later on Miss Waters was quoted as saying that I sang like "my shoes were too tight."

Billie passed the story on to Lena Horne when she heard that Lena had been cast with Ethel for the moving-picture version of *Cabin in the Sky*. Although Lena, still relatively a youngster, watched her Ps and Qs accordingly, luck was against her. Trouble began with a number, "Honey in the Honeycomb," first to be sung by Lena, her singing then to be parodied by Ethel. There has always been a lot of Ethel Waters in Lena Horne's singing, and now, according to Miss Horne's account, she rather emphasized it in order to set up the parody. But when Lena's pre-recording was played back for Ethel, she heard it otherwise. Miss Horne, she felt, had made parody impossible by parodying *her*. She could not, she insisted, parody a parody of herself. This was bad enough. Worse was to follow when Lena chipped a bone in her ankle just before the shooting of a scene they had to play together.

The accident, Miss Horne recalls, in *Lena*,

. . . caused a certain amount of the attention to be focused on me, which was just exactly what I did not want to happen when I was working with Miss Waters. The atmosphere was very tense, and it exploded when a prop man brought a pillow for me to put under my sore ankle. Miss Waters started to blow like a hurricane. It was an all-encompassing outburst, touching everyone and everything that got in its way. Though I (or my ankle) may have been the immediate cause of it all, it was actually directed at everything that had made her life miserable, the whole system that had held her back and exploited her.

We had to shut down the set for the rest of the day. During the evening, apparently, some of the people at the studio were able to talk to her and calm her down, because the next day we were able to go on with the picture. We finished it without speaking. The silence was not sullen. It was just that there was nothing to say after that, nothing that could make things right between us.

Miss Waters gives no details of this encounter in her own memoirs, but she is explicit about its having been an unhappy set.

There was conflict between the studio and me from the beginning. For one thing, I objected violently to the way religion was being treated in the screen play. Eddie (Rochester) Anderson, Lena Horne and many other performers were in the cast. But all through that picture there was so much snarling and scrapping that I don't know how in the world *Cabin in the Sky* ever stayed up there.

Vernon Duke, forewarned, had brought out the other side of her when they were working together on the original stage production of *Cabin in the Sky*. "Ethel Waters was known far and wide as an extremely difficult woman to work with," he remembered, in his *Passport to Paris*, "but I won her over by a time-honored device—I heartily recommend it to composers wishing to please their leading ladies. I kissed her hand in lieu of 'Good morning' and 'Be seeing you.' " Duke introduced her in his book as "that wonderful woman."

A certain old-worldliness in Duke (he was Russian, née Vladimir Dukelsky) may have rendered him more aware of, and more sympathetic to, the sense of personal dignity, even of rank, characteristic of the older black artists. He was, accordingly, spared the lesson learned by John Latouche, lyricist of *Cabin in the Sky*, when Ethel enjoyed a success she had not expected with "Taking a Chance on Love." He rushed back stage to her dressing room to congratulate her, crying "Ethel!" He was going to say, "We've made it!" or something to that effect. He never did. She just sat there, looked up at him and said, "Miss Waters."

Ethel herself thought that Carl Van Vechten had achieved the best summing up of her character when he said to her: "Ethel, you never ask anyone for anything—and you never thank anyone for anything."

References to shouting and growling—and to refinement—are frequent in Ethel Waters' memoirs, and they are important. Her mother, on whom she modeled the role of Hagar in *Mamba's Daughters*, "went in for the old backwoods, down-home religion, closely resembling that of Holy Rollers and hard-shell Baptists." But her grandmother, whom she thought of as the Berenice Sadie Brown of *The Member of the Wedding*, saw religion differently. "You don't have to holler so," she used to tell Ethel's mother. "God has very big ears. He can hear you even if you whisper." It was her grandmother, not her mother, whom Ethel thought of as Mom, and whose epic struggle for a decent existence amid the vicious squalor of Chester and South Philadelphia shaped her character and inspired her throughout a long stage career.

But there was a bit of her mother too in her approach to religion—and to music. She seems always to have been both interdenominational and intersectarian, if not ambivalent, in her churchgoing. She was strongly attracted to the Catholic church as a child, and has remained so. She also attended Protestant churches, favoring the Methodists, but partial too to the free-swinging, uninhibited Baptist preachers.

"I came," she remembers, "to love and value the inner fire of a brimstone and hell-fire preacher. I sensed that there was something splendid about this kind of religion that exploded in the pastor's heart, enabling him to reach you and make you believe." The various sides of her religious nature and predilections would seem to have found a satisfactory accommodation in the interdenominational evangelism of Billy Graham, whom she joined in 1957, at a time when both her health and her stage career were threatened by the fact that the former "Sweet Mama Stringbean" and "long goody" was tipping the scales at 350.

The combination, or amalgam, of moderation and refinement on the one hand and unrestrained backwoods fervor on the other characterized not only her religion but also her singing. She could put plenty of heat into a song, but it was always tempered, sooner or later—or in the next song—by an innate, as well as by a professional, sense of propriety. She was always in control, even when she let go.

She thought of Ma Rainey, Bessie Smith and other blues singers as shouters. In her eyes it was the absence of shouting and growling in her own treatment of the same or similar material that distinguished her from her singer sisters. She could, as she put it, "riff and jam and growl, but I never had that loud approach." The contrast was noted, and favorably, in the press, including the black press. Certainly it contributed to her success with white audiences. More importantly for her growth as an artist, her independence of the clichés of blues singing left her better equipped than most of her contemporaries to work in other, more widely popular styles.

It may have been, to a considerable degree, simply a matter of innate taste. She was always a tasteful performer. Endowment may have had something to do with it, too. It seems unlikely, on the evidence that has come down to us on her records, that she could have been much of a shouter even had she been so inclined. Her voice was distinguished for its tonal quality and its resources of nuance rather than for either size or range.

Although she sings, on the records, from a low E to a high F sharp, or just over two octaves, the voice is consistently weak at either extreme. Her effective range was from an A flat below to an E flat above. Even this was stretching it, for above a C she always eased off into a thin, often nasal head voice. Because like most of the popular singers of her time, both white and black, she never mastered the vocal "passage" by which opera singers move inconspicuously from a chest to a head resonance, or achieve a blend of the two, her upper voice had none of the eloquent, dark, viola-like richness of the middle. To compound the mischief, she frequently chose, or had to accept, keys that lay uncomfortably high. Early in her career these may well have been the only keys in which her accompanists could play.

She had, in other words, a sometimes lovely, always expressive, but otherwise unexceptional voice, and neither the training nor the guidance to make the most of what she had in terms of size and range. She sang improperly, she sang a lot, and she paid for it. Her records of 1929 betray the node (blister) on a vocal cord that had to be removed in a delicate operation in London early in the following year. She claims that the operation added a note or two to her upper range, and her records support the claim, particularly her "Memories of You," cut on September 29, 1930, on which she floats a spectacular head-voice high F sharp.

Given these limitations of endowment and technique, she made the most resourceful use of what she had. She worked, as all the great popular singers have worked, out of language. Her genius was for characterization, and characterization, in song, begins with language. Her diction was immaculate and flexible. She colored vowels, diphthongs and consonants to suit both the substance and the style of a song, which may be why she reminds the attentive listener, in one song or another, of so many other singers.

In the kind of song that Jolson sang, "Memories of You," for example, she sounds like Jolson, with *memories* emerging dismembered and mauled as *mem-o-rrrreeees*. It sounds like a put-on, and may have been one. In other cases, where she is sending up Josephine Baker or Rudy Vallee, there is no doubt about the caricature. But there is a reverse side to it. She had, if I hear her correctly, such a sense of what suited a song that other singers had no choice but to follow her example.

She milked both rhythm and melody for all they could yield. Her rhythm, particularly, was strong and earthy. Far more than with Bessie Smith, it was an essential element in her phrasing. In this, as well as in other respects, she was closer to jazz than to the blues. She needed the pulse, the lift and the boot of a jazz-flavored backing as props and foils for her own rhythmic devices and inspirations. How acutely she reacted to those who backed her is reflected in what she has had to say about musicians who worked with her, especially the pianists.

She favored those who came out of ragtime—Charlie and James P. Johnson, Luckey Roberts, Willie (the Lion) Smith and her own pianist and companion of many years, Pearl Wright. "They," she recalls, "could make you sing until your tonsils fell out. Because you *wanted* to sing. They stirred you into joy and wild ecstasy. They could make you cry. And you'd do anything and work until you dropped for such musicians."

It was otherwise with Fletcher Henderson, highly educated (chemistry and mathematics at Atlanta University) and, in music, classically oriented. On tour with the Black Swan Jazz Masters in 1921, as she tells it, "Fletcher wouldn't give me what I call the damn-it-to-hell bass, that chump-chump stuff that real jazz needs." So she made him listen to James P. Johnson's piano rolls. This superimposition of a blues experience upon a classical background subsequently helped Fletcher Henderson to become one of the first and best of the sophisticated band arrangers of the ensuing swing era.

Very late in his career, just before he was crippled by a stroke in 1950 (he died in 1952), Henderson toured again as Ethel Waters' pianist. His classical predilections, according to her, were still in evidence. "Even today, almost thirty years later," she wrote, "I practically have to insult Fletcher Henderson to get him to play my accompaniments the way I want. When Fletch is in fine form, he is fine for me. When he doesn't play good, I say: 'Fletch, stop playing that B.C. music of yours!' "

It is curious that she should use the term "accompaniment." That is probably precisely what Henderson was playing. Just as probably, that was what was wrong with it. A classical singer wants an accompaniment. A singer working out of blues or jazz wants a backing. Given a congenial backing, Ethel Waters, in terms of tracing a melodic line and projecting tune and text, could do just about anything she chose to do, and whatever she chose to do always seemed right.

She could slur and swoop with the best of them. She could even shout and growl and plunge and boom, although she did it rarely, and usually with an implication of gay parody. She was both singer and swinger. On many of her records we hear her in both roles. She takes an opening chorus straight, then, on the second time around, she swings it, departing from the written notes to improvise in the manner of the jazz instrumentalists, even scatting from time to time, or humming, or talking through the tune in the manner of Al Jolson and Sophie Tucker.

Her ornaments and embellishments, modest by the standards of later singers, were always appropriate, and judiciously applied. She used appoggiature, mordents and portamenti, but sparingly probably because she was concerned not with vocal device or display but with text and syllabic inflection. Even in a sequence of octave skips in "You Can't Stop Me from Loving You," with every note hit lightly right on the nose—a feat that would score as pure virtuosity for a classical singer—she is merely giving additional bounce to a bouncy tune and a bit of sass to a saucy text.

She did not think in such terms, of course. She didn't know them. She never learned to read music. "My music," she used to say, "is all queer little things that come into my head. I feel these little trills [mordents] and things deep inside of me, and I sing them that way. All queer little things that I hum." These "queer little things" represent a richness of imagination, a wealth of invention and a model of taste hardly matched by any other singer of her time.

Like most of the great American popular singers, Ethel Waters has been underrated as a singer, or at least insufficiently appreciated, simply because she sang too well. She made it all sound so natural and easy and inevitable that the listener was unaware of any physical or intellectual accomplishment, or of the mastering of any special difficulties.

Miss Waters has suffered, too, because of her versatility, including her notable accomplishments as an actress. Critics and critic-historians tend to be specialists and to concentrate on artists identified with their specialty. They also tend to look askance on those artists who stray from their specialty, particularly if they stray into popular or commercial pastures and achieve popular and commercial success.

This is tough on artists. They cannot reach a wider public without widening their repertoire; yet they cannot widen repertoire without hazarding their status with the critics. By the esthetic conventions of our time, a blues singer, or jazz singer, is a cultural ornament. But he must take care lest he please too many people. Not the goblins but the snobs will get him if he doesn't watch out.

Ethel Waters was not just a blues singer, although she could sing the blues. Nor was she just one of those "cake-walking babies" who, in the 1920s, sang in that idiom midway between the true blues and the popular song, although she was at home in it. She could swing in the jazz idiom of the 1930s, and made many records with Bunny Berigan, Jimmy and Tommy Dorsey, Benny Goodman, Manny Klein, Eddie Lang and many more. But she is not generally thought of as a jazz singer, whatever that may be.

Part of the problem, of course, is the failure of those most closely identified with the subject to achieve a commonly acceptable definition of jazz, or even of the blues. Singers of Ethel Waters' generation, including Miss Waters, thought of themselves as blues singers, and of what they sang as blues, whether it conformed to a twelve-bar or sixteen-bar format or not. Researchers and historians since then, almost all of them white, have been inclined to restrict the term to those songs, or types of song, least "contaminated" by white, or European, influence.

Jazz critics, similarly, disown any element or characteristic of jazz the minute it gets caught up in the mainstream of popular music, and ostracize artists identified with such elements or characteristics. This has made things difficult, in terms of status, for those who sang with the bands in the 1930s and 1940s when jazz, as it happened, was

America's most popular music. It confuses our view, to this day, of such singers as Ella Fitzgerald and Peggy Lee, of Tony Bennett and Frank Sinatra.

Just how ludicrous this inevitably subjective categorization can be, and how unjust to the artists so categorized, is illustrated nicely by the conflicting estimates of Ethel Waters by two veteran, widely respected, widely read and widely influential jazz critics: Hugues Panassié and Leonard Feather. Panassié, author of *Le Jazz Hot*, or *Hot Jazz* (1934), described her in a later volume, *The Real Jazz* (1942), not only as a jazz singer, but as, among all jazz singers, the greatest.

> Her voice [he wrote], although a miracle of smoothness, is nonetheless firm and penetrating, clear and supple, swinging, caressing, cynical, with myriads of little touches and inflections going from mockery to profundity with amazing mastery. . . . Since 1930 she has been influenced to some degree by Louis Armstrong. As a matter of fact, Ethel Waters' influence on female jazz singers is almost as great as that of Louis Armstrong.

Panassié's credentials as an authority on what constitutes a jazz singer are compromised by the fact that his chapter on "The Singers" fails to mention any white singers. He has little to say about white instrumentalists, either, and that little rarely favorable. He goes out of his way, in his Preface, to deny a categorical prejudice in favor of black musicians. But the book itself refutes the denial.

Feather's bias is of a different order, but fully as exasperating. Ethel Waters, he says, in the entry under her name in his *New Encyclopedia of Jazz*, was "principally a great show business personality and only incidentally and indirectly a jazz performer."

It is a measure of Ethel Waters' stature that both Panassié and Feather are right. Certainly she was a great jazz singer. But she wasn't *just* a jazz singer. She was more than that. A lot more. Which is why she was a *great* singer.

4

Louis Armstrong

The Bessie Smith legend dates from her fatal injury in an automobile accident, and has been nurtured by tendentious accounts of what happened between the time of the crash and her death in a Clarksdale, Mississippi, hospital a few hours later. Not until many years had passed would a retrospective assessment of her artistic stature grant her a more satisfactory immortality.

How different the destiny of Louis Armstrong! He had been, at the time of his death, on July 6, 1971, a living legend for half a century, not just to his own black people, nor to the American people as a whole, but to millions of people around the world. He had been, probably, the most famous musician of the century. When a Johannesburg, South Africa, newspaper, in the summer of 1970, polled fifty-six persons at random to find out how many could remember the names of the Apollo 11 astronauts, one girl identified not Neil Armstrong, but Louis Armstrong, as the first man to set foot on the moon.

An exceptional, if charming, notion! The very word *legend* seems to imply semifiction, or history distorted and inflated by fancy. But Louis Armstrong, lunar adventure aside, had been everything the legend held him to be: the greatest of early jazz cornet and trumpet players; a unique and improbable vocalist; an exuberant and extrovert

celebrity; a showman of genius; and an American ambassador more widely known and more warmly accepted than anyone who ever left the White House with a letter of accreditation in his pocket.

It was all true. It was all attractive. Yet, in the end, it was all wrong. Not factually wrong, but wrong because the legend was unjust to the man. Most legendary figures, being only human, fail to live up to the legend. The failure is condoned or denied because the legend, for sentimental or political reasons, is preferred to the truth. In Louis Armstrong's case it was the other way around. The truth surpassed the legend—and challenged credulity!

It must seem not merely improbable, but sheerly impossible that any one man could have exerted so original and so decisive an influence on the evolution of Western music, least of all an essentially unlettered black trumpet player from the slums of New Orleans. But he did. Almost everything we have heard in the past forty years in jazz, and in a great amount of popular music not usually associated with jazz, short of folk and rock, derives from Armstrong. As jazz encyclopedist and critic Leonard Feather has written:

> Americans, unknowingly, live part of every day in the house that Satch built. A riff played by a swinging band on television, a nuance in a Sinatra phrase, the Muzak in the elevator, all owe something to the guidelines that Louis set.

It was he who liberated the improvising virtuoso jazz musician, as soloist, from the tight collective improvisation of New Orleans jazz. It was he who, by his own example on trumpet, pushed back the technical boundaries of traditional musical instruments. It was he who broke the stereotyped rhythmic procedures of early jazz. It was he, more decisively than Bessie Smith, who established those characteristics of American popular singing that distinguish it from any kind of singing based on traditional European conventions and example.

That he should have exerted so decisive an influence on the art of the American popular singer must seem, at first glance, paradoxical. Louis, although certainly one of the most popular singers of the century, was always thought of primarily as an instrumentalist, as a trumpet player, as one who abused his vocal cords to spare his much abused chops. The common view of his singular vocalism is that it proceeded from his playing, that he sang as he played insofar as limitations of vocal compass would permit. One is tempted to suggest that it may have been the other way around, that his playing was an extension of his singing.

His instrumental virtuosity was, I believe, deceptive. The high notes, those devastating excursions above high C, unique and unprecedented in their time, diverted attention from the pervasive oratorical character and eloquence of his playing. Among those whose attention was diverted, and disastrously, were the jazz players of the next generation, and not only the trumpet players. They equaled and even surpassed him in range and dexterity, but they overlooked or ignored or disdained his roots in song.

An important contribution to the vocal or rhetorical aspects of Louis' musicality may be identified, I would suggest, in his association with the "classic" blues singers in the 1920s. The records he made with Bessie Smith are the most familiar example. But he also recorded with many others, among them Chippie Hill, Ma Rainey and Clara Smith.

More was involved in this than Louis' influence upon them or theirs upon him. Jazz and blues converged in the 1920s, much as swing and rhythm-and-blues would converge briefly in Kansas City a decade later. Not only Louis Armstrong, but also Red Allen, Sidney Bechet, Jimmy Harrison, Coleman Hawkins, Fletcher Henderson, James P. Johnson, Tommy Ladnier and Don Redman, among others, worked behind the female blues singers of the time. This collaboration required a kind of playing markedly different from the polyphonic procedures of New Orleans jazz. The instrumentalist both complemented and commented upon the singer's vocal utterance, perpetuating the call and response patterns of some African and early American black idioms, and evolving a concept of instrumental attack, phrase and cadence that would become one of the most distinctive and also one of the most attractive characteristics of jazz.

That Louis Armstrong never forsook or slighted the musician's oratorical responsibility is attributable also to the sensible and restraining influence of Joe "King" Oliver, whose band he joined in Chicago in 1922. He emphasized his debt to Oliver in countless interviews.

Louis rejoiced, of course, in a prodigious facility. As a young man fresh from New Orleans, determined to make his mark in the big city, he was tempted to show off. What Oliver told him runs like a central theme through everything that Louis ever said about his development as a musician and about his musical philosophy.

"Joe would listen to my horn," he told Steve Allen in a radio interview late in his career, "and I was fly, making all kinds of variations like they're tryin' to call bebop. I instigated all that, 'cause I was so fast with my fingering. But Joe Oliver said: 'No, play lead, play more lead on that horn so the people can know what you're doing.' "

Similarly, he told Geoffrey Haydon, in a television interview for BBC filmed to coincide with his seventieth birthday on July 4, 1970: "I was just like a clarinet player, like the guys run up and down the horn nowadays, boppin' and things. I was doin' all that, fast fingers and everything, so he used to tell me: 'Play some lead on that horn, boy.' You know?" And in the same vein: "Ain't no sense playing a hundred notes if one will do. Joe Oliver always used to say, 'Think about that lead!' "

What Joe Oliver was talking about was melody line, or tune. Louis never became a tuneful performer, either on trumpet or as a singer, in the sense of faithfully adhering to the prescribed notes of a song. He made a stab at it in the early 1930s when his prodigious accomplishments on cornet and trumpet, and the unprecedented vocalism of his 1929 recording of Fats Waller's "Ain't Misbehavin'," swept him from the black entertainment world tributary into the white American popular music mainstream. The records he made then reveal a young man stylistically ill at ease, seeking to adapt his own musicality to the sweet, vapid, sentimental white popular songs and styles of the time.

Fortunately he failed. Whether as trumpeter or as singer, his musical individuality was too strong, his manner too vigorous, his inventive impulse too sheerly irrepressible. He came close enough to achieving adaptation to make some bad records. He never made a record that was not unmistakably Armstrong, although there are echoes here and there of Al Jolson, Bing Crosby and some of the black female singers who were working more closely to white styles than Bessie Smith and Ma Rainey had worked. Nor did he ever make a record on which he was not conspicuously superior to both the song and the arrangement. But he made many that were marred by creative inhibition and stylistic insecurity.

He solved the problem, eventually, by ignoring white conven-

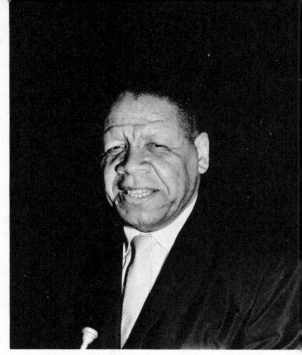

Red Allen
Fats Waller

DON SCHLITTEN/STEREO REVIEW

tions and recasting white music in his own personal and musical image. His heeding of King Oliver's counsel saved him from disaster. It is likely that he never in his entire career sang or played a familiar tune note for note, bar for bar, from beginning to end. But neither did he ever spurn the tune and its chord structure as a frame of melodic and harmonic reference. The modern jazz musician rejects both tune and chords as a frustration of his individual creative freedom, as a violation, so to speak, of a musician's right of free speech. Louis Armstrong had no fear of traditional discipline. It was a challenge both to his invention and his ingenuity. He could accept it with relish and zest. In so doing he set precedents that would become the conventions of American popular singing and give to the singer creative opportunities—and creative responsibilities, too—that he had not enjoyed in Western music since the latter part of the eighteenth century.

Adjectives trotted out to describe the sound of Louis Armstrong's voice have included "hoarse," "rasping" and "gravelly," the last of these being probably the most apt. Humphrey Lyttelton, in a BBC tribute on Louis' seventieth birthday, came up with "astrakhan." I should not have thought of "astrakhan" as a descriptive adjective, but it impressed me at the time as singularly felicitous. The image that has occurred to me most frequently in listening to his later records is that of someone singing through a gargle.

However one chooses to describe his voice, there is no mistaking it. An axiom in the study of singers has it that the great, as opposed to the merely very good, are immediately recognizable. A Caruso, a McCormack, a Tauber—one knows them within eight measures, just as one knows Nat Cole, Bing Crosby, Billie Holiday, Peggy Lee, Frank Sinatra and Bessie Smith. None was more distinctive, more readily identifiable, than Louis Armstrong.

This probably explains why he had no imitators. He was imitated, of course, but always with a parodistic purpose. The listener knew what the imitator was up to—that it was impersonation rather than emulation. Bing Crosby and Frank Sinatra each inspired a generation of emulators, some of them admirable. Red Allen, Jack Teagarden and Jabbo Smith worked close to Louis in style, but they didn't sound like him, although Jabbo Smith may have tried.

What made the sound of his voice so utterly unique was, I venture to suggest, the cumulative effect of night after night, month after month, year after year, of bad singing; bad, that is, in traditional terms of vocal production. His voice had not always been so hoarse, so rasping, so gravelly. He had, at the outset, a reasonably agreeable quality and a reasonably extensive range, roughly two octaves from A flat to A flat. This would represent, in European music, a low tenor or a high baritone.

Louis comes through, on his early records, more tenor than baritone, and that was, I suspect, the beginning of his vocal infirmities. Every once in a while, a fine, free baritone escaped him in the middle of his range, revealing what I hear as the natural color and pitch of the voice. Had he elected to sing conventional ballads in a conventional way, he would have chosen keys at least a third below those in which he actually sang them.

He might have got away with those higher keys, for a time, at least, if he had known how to move from one register to another, to negotiate the "passage," to disguise register breaks and to cover the tone as he moved up the scale. But he knew nothing of such matters. Preferring to work in the upper fifth of his range, he was continually under vocal strain. He did not seem to mind. He may even have liked it. Many black singers, particularly those least susceptible to European musical conventions, have shown a predilection for the sense and sound of exaltation, exhortation and incantation that require a vocal production somewhere between singing and shouting, and achievable only by raising both voice and pitch. Louis Armstrong was one of these.

His procedures as a trumpet player provide the clue. He played higher than anybody had ever played a cornet or a trumpet before him. It was not just the odd, climactic, high E flat, E or F. He played consistently high. The performance was not without its purely exhibitionistic side. He obviously reveled in his ability to astonish. He wasn't, as a young man, above carving the competition. Sam Price, a pianist who worked with most of the great jazzmen of the 1920s and 1930s, remembers an encounter between Louis and Jabbo Smith in Chicago: "Louis played about 110 high Cs, and sheet, that was it; and Jabbo could play."

But the stunting was, I suspect, a by-product. Louis, early in his career, probably didn't know how high he was playing, or that what he was playing was assumed to be impossible. Playing high and recklessly was simply a satisfactory outlet for a musically exuberant and ebullient nature. One of his favorite words was "wailing"—and he used it in special contexts, notably and memorably when he told the Pope, who had asked if he and his wife, Lucille, had any children: "No, but we're still right in there wailin', Daddy!"

He was a wailer as a vocalist, too, and no singer can wail in the middle register. So, singing in a manner which came naturally to him, he sang unnaturally high. Wailing on the trumpet takes its toll on the lips, or, as Louis would have said, the chops. This could be countered by salves. The toll on the vocal cords and the muscles and cartileges of the throat was beyond remedy. The upper A flats, Gs and F sharps of the early records did not last long. To an opera singer the loss would have been a disaster. To Louis it mattered very little. If one note was no longer available, he had others to put in its place.

An example of his resourcefulness, of his inexhaustible fund of musical invention, is afforded by a comparison of two recordings of "Ain't Misbehavin'," the one made in 1929, the second in 1955. On the first there are many high Gs. On the second there are none. But the two performances sound very much alike, and both are in the same key—E flat. Louis knew what he wanted to do with that song, and what he wanted did not essentially change in twenty-six years. If he could not get it one way, he could get it another. The casual listener, hearing the two records one after another, will not be aware that anything is missing, that anything was changed.

The earlier recording of "Ain't Misbehavin' " is instructive, too, as an example of how, with the great singers, the essential elements of their greatness are evident in their earliest work. It is true of early Crosby, of early Sinatra, of early Fitzgerald, of early Presley and of early Ray Charles. They may waver a bit as they hit midstream. They may give inferior performances, make inferior records and flounder stylistically as they seek to widen repertoire, to accommodate their native musicality to the requirements of commercial fashion, and to escape being typed as singers of one particular kind of song. Everything that made Louis Armstrong great is present in this earlier recording of "Ain't Misbehavin'." He subsequently made many inferior records with less congenial material before finally learning to discipline not himself, but the song.

He also learned a lot about his own singing. He never learned to sing. He would have been finished as a singer if he had. But he reacted instinctively to what was best in his singing. His phrasing was always as exemplary as it was original, including the trumpet-derived scatting. His improvisatory flights were almost always just right. But his diction, initially, was negligent and slovenly. He was thinking instrumentally, granting that his trumpet playing was rooted in vocalism. As he grew older he learned about the music of language. His diction improved. He mastered the art of milking text. He must have sensed, again probably instinctively, the musicality of his own speech. As his technical prowess and physical resources waned, both vocally and instrumentally, he became more of a talker and less of a wailer.

In the end, as seems to happen with all great singers, he also became the creature of his own distinctive characteristics. He fell into mannerism. His enunciation became meticulous and overarticulated. His swoops, slurs and growls became the clichés of predictable artifice rather than the unpredictable expressions of irrepressible artistic impulse. But so profound was his musicality that his procedures, even as mannerisms, still worked. There had always been too much music in his speech to suffer constraint by a mere tune. He had never been, as I have noted, a tuneful musician. As he became even less tuneful with the years, he became somehow more musical.

This was his legacy to those who came after him. All, with the exception of Billie Holiday, were more tuneful than he. They had better, more agreeable, more extensive voices. But from him they learned to escape the strictures of the printed notes and the pre-scribed rhythms, to distort meter in favor of a more flexibly musical prosody, to work out of syllables rather than words, to take the melodic and rhythmic structure of a song apart and put it together again so that the singer talked as he sang and sang as he talked.

They were untroubled by what remained throughout Louis Armstrong's career his principal shortcoming as an artist and espe-cially as a singer—his lack of emotional identification or involvement with whatever he was singing about. I was often moved by him both in personal performance and on record, but my response was one of sheer delight with his genius, his taste, his invention and his own obvious pleasure in making music. He was always a joyous, jubilant musician. The toothy smile, the waving white handkerchief, the invitation to the audience to sit back and enjoy some of the "old goodies," the gay palaver with his sidemen—all this was genuine. All this was fun.

It would be unjust, probably inaccurate, to suggest that he was ever anything but serious in his approach to a song. But it may be permissible to suggest that he rarely, if ever, took a song seriously. His identification with the music was intimate, his relationship with the textual content casual and detached, often conveying an undertone of benevolent raillery. But the devices of his musicianship have proved both valid and invaluable to those who have taken their songs more seriously than he—or made you believe they did—notably Frank Sinatra.

Louis Armstrong's importance to musical history is difficult to overestimate, and responsible critics and historians have not shied away from hyperbole. André Hodeir, for example, in his *Jazz, Its Evolution and Essence*, has said of the records Louis made with the Hot Five and the Hot Seven between 1925 and 1928: "I wouldn't go so far as to state that Louis Armstrong was the man who 'invented' jazz, but listening to these records might make me think so."

One of those records was "West End Blues," of which Gunther Schuller, in his *Early Jazz*, has said:

> The clarion call of "West End Blues" served notice that jazz had the potential capacity to compete with the highest order of previously known musical expression. Although nurtured by the crass entertainment and nightclub world of the Prohibition era, Armstrong's music transcended this context and its implications. This was music for music's sake, not for the first time in jazz, to be sure, but never before in such brilliant and unequivocal form. The beauties of this music were those of any great, compelling musical experience: expressive fervor, intense artistic commitment, and an intuitive sense for structural logic.

Armstrong's reaction to this kind of commentary was characteristic. When Geoffrey Haydon, in the BBC-TV birthday program mentioned previously, asked him if he had been aware when making these records with the Hot Five and the Hot Seven that he was doing something very important, he replied, "No, we was just glad to play. We weren't paid no money, just was glad to play." Music, as Schuller noted, for music's sake.

The lay music lover or jazz fan, accustomed to think of Louis Armstrong as an amiable and irrepressible entertainer, even as a venerable and lovable clown, would be astonished to learn of the extent of scholarly literature devoted to his music. No one could have been more astonished than Louis himself, or could have found it more bewildering, more incomprehensible. He was not an intellect. But his improvisatory explosions have been copied down note for note and bar for bar in countless books and periodicals, and have been subjected to the most painstaking melodic, harmonic and rhythmic analysis.

The significance of his innovations is implicit in the fact that none of this analysis really works. Notation is inseparable from the European conventions it was evolved to record and represent. It cannot reflect the myriad shadings of attack, color, vibrato, release and so on that distinguish Louis Armstrong's playing and singing. It cannot document the slight deviations from pitch, and their harmonic and melodic connotations. Nor can it reproduce, visually, rhythmic subtleties so foreign to the fractional subdivisions of units of time in the rhythmic organization of European music.

Armstrong's own career after 1930 helped to frustrate any just evaluation of his achievement outside an inner circle of sympathetic and perceptive scholars. By the end of the 1920s he was already a celebrity. Indeed, as early as 1925, when he was twenty-five, he was being billed, probably accurately, as "the world's greatest trumpet player." The role of celebrity suited both his talent and his disposition. He drifted, or was drawn, into the mainstream of popular music, playing anything and everything that came his way. He appeared in moving pictures—usually as Louis Armstrong. He played and sang with popular musicians and popular singers, and not always with the best. He clowned and mugged and rejoiced in such monikers as "Satchmo" and "Pops."

Whatever he played or sang, he did in his own way, and there is no denying that the "way" commonly transcended the "what." He even survived an "Uncle Tom" label that would have been fatal to any other black musician after the mid-1950s. "Sure, Pops toms," said Billie Holiday, "but he toms with class!" As Benny Green, the English jazz critic, pointed out in a seventieth-birthday profile for the London *Observer:*

> The complaints have all come either from purist critics or political rebels. There is not a single musician of any consequence who takes exception to the personality Armstrong projects on

the stage, and for a very good reason. It takes a performer to know a performer.

If he played and sang to the grandstand, and too often accepted the grandstand's image not only of Louis Armstrong but of jazz itself, he knew exactly what he was doing. "I belong to the old school, you know," he told the French journalist Philippe Adler in 1968, "to the guys who think only of pleasing the public. I gave up the idea of playing for the critics or for musicians long ago." To Geoffrey Haydon he said: "A musician has no business being bored as long as he's pleasing the public." To Max Jones, as recounted in Jones's *Salute to Satchmo,* he said: "You understand, I'm doing my day's work, pleasing the public and enjoying my horn."

The jazz world, whose snobbery is, if anything, even more distasteful than the complacent snobbery of classical music, never quite forgave him. Sometimes, granting an exception for a seventieth birthday, it seemed almost to have forgotten him—or abandoned him to popular music, although jazz musicians of the generation immediately after his were usually eager to honor their debt. The best of the popular singers, too, acknowledged what their phrasing owed to his example.

Twenty years before Louis' seventieth birthday, Bing Crosby told Ken Murray, in a *Down Beat* interview: "Yes, Ken, I'm proud to acknowledge my debt to the Rev. Satchelmouth. He is the beginning and the end of music in America." Similarly, Billy Eckstine, speaking to Max Jones in the winter of 1970: "Everybody singing got something from him because he puts it down basically, gives you that feeling. It's right there. You don't have to look for it."

But to younger artists, further removed from the source in time and example, he seemed an anachronism, both as man and musician. Or he appeared, to put a better face upon it, as a legend. In one sense it was a mark of his stature. Where other musicians of his generation had either to adapt their style to changing fashion or perish, he could adhere to his own style and not only survive, but prosper. But there was tragedy in it, too. He lived to see what was unique and wondrous in his early work become the clichés of the mainstream. He saw the inspired distortions that were the secret of his genius distorted beyond recognition in the work of some of his successors. He did not enjoy the experience.

He made only one bitter record, a parody of the "Whiffenpoof Song," in which he had some wry fun at the expense of the be-boppers, and on that one subject there was no mellowing with the passage of time. He sang the "Boppinpoof Song" on a Flip Wilson television program in the spring of 1971, just a few months before his death. "What's scattin' but notes—but the *right* notes?" he asked Geoffrey Haydon. "Just to be scattin' and makin' a whole lotta noise and faces, slobbin' all over yourself? No. Let them notes come out right, you know?"

In the span of Louis Armstrong's life and career this bitterness was only a passing shadow.

My whole life [he said in a letter to Max Jones] has been happiness. Through all the misfortunes, etc., I did not plan anything. Life was there for me, and I accepted it. And life, whatever came out, has been beautiful to me, and I love everybody.

Even in the jails, in the old days in New Orleans, I had loads of fans. One morning on my way to court, the prisoners raked pans on their cell bars and applauded thunderously, saying "Louie . . . Louie Armstrong," until the guy who was taking me to court said: "Who are you, anyway?" I said to him, "Oh, just one of the cats."

And that's how it has always been.

5

Jimmie Rodgers

When the Country Music Association established the Country Music Hall of Fame and Museum in Nashville, Tennessee, in 1961, it was a foregone conclusion that the first singers to be enshrined would be Jimmie Rodgers (the "Singing Brakeman") and Hank Williams. The citation supporting Jimmie's election described him as "the man who started it all."

It all refers, of course, to the American musical idiom now known as "country," centered in Nashville, and represented today by such stars as Glen Campbell, Johnny Cash, Ernie Ford, Merle Haggard, Buck Owens, Hank Snow and Hank Williams, Jr. In Jimmie Rodgers' time, in the late 1920s and early 1930s, the idiom was called "hillbilly," a pejorative designation which gave way to an intermediate "country-and-western" after World War II, as the music became nationally and even internationally, rather than merely regionally, familiar and popular.

Rodgers, also known as the "Blue Yodeler," was not the first country singer to seek and find fame and fortune. Nor was he the first to make records. Vernon Dalhart ("The Prisoner's Song"), Wendell Hall ("It Ain't Gonna Rain No Mo' "), Carson Robison and many others were ahead of him by five years or more. Nor was he even the first to yodel on records. Riley Puckett had been yodeling on records as early as 1924. But Jimmie was at once the most successful, the most original, the most versatile and the most influential.

> In assessing Jimmie Rodgers' influence on American folk music and on a later generation of commercial performers [wrote Bill C. Malone in his definitive *Country Music, U.S.A.*] one can safely use the adjective "phenomenal." Indeed, one would be hard pressed to find a performer in the whole broad field of "pop" music—whether it be Al Jolson, Bing Crosby or Frank Sinatra—who has exerted a more profound and recognizable influence on later generations of entertainers. No one as yet has made a full-scale attempt to determine how many of his songs have been accepted by the folk or gone into oral tradition, and there is no way to measure the number of people, amateur and professional, who have been inspired by him to take up the guitar or try their luck at singing.
>
> Rodgers single-handedly originated a new tradition in country music and stimulated legions of his followers—most of whom heard him only on record—to become country musicians. The new group of performers arising in the late twenties and early thirties would have repertoires of a less traditional character and would perform them in styles that were often direct imitations of Jimmie Rodgers.

Ernest Tubb, who was one of the first to follow in his footsteps, has estimated that perhaps 75 percent of the leading country singers of today and yesterday were influenced, directly or indirectly, by Jimmie Rodgers. Paul Ackerman, of *Billboard* Magazine, has thus summed up his place in the history of country music:

> Some regard him as America's "truly native" balladeer. Others consider him the father of the country music field. And many more, thinking of Rodgers' big pop hits, which cut across all musical categories, place him in that select group whose compelling talent established the phonograph as an important medium of home entertainment. . . . Someone at that early date had to fuse and synthesize these musical elements (pop, folk, country, blues and jazz) to prepare the way for the Elvis Presleys and Johnny Cashes of today. It was Rodgers who did this.

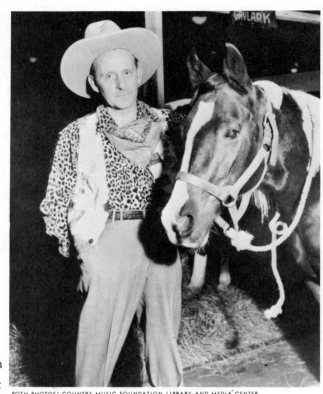

Carson Robison
Vernon Dalhart

Quite by accident, but with fortunate propriety, my own awareness of country music as an idiom worthy of sympathetic study began
with Jimmie Rodgers, which is not to say that his records were my
introduction to country music. That introduction occurred in 1955,
when, on an automobile trip through the South, Southwest and
Middle West, my car radio taught me, a Philadelphian long resident
in Europe, that country, rather than jazz, was rapidly becoming, or
had already become, the music of a great part of middle America.
The big hit at the time was Webb Pierce's "In the Jailhouse Now." I
must have heard it fifty times or more as I drove through Virginia,
North Carolina, Tennessee, Alabama, Mississippi, Louisiana, Texas,
Oklahoma and Missouri. I thought it pretty awful.

I regarded country music then—and I probably called it "hillbilly"—as beyond the pale. Like most musicians classically educated
and European-oriented, I noted only that the voices were unschooled,
sometimes thin and reedy, and often nasal; that the melodies were
one very like another; that the lyrics were homespun, sentimental,
even maudlin, and that the harmonic scheme rarely ventured beyond
the chords of the tonic, subdominant and dominant.

So I thought no more about it until one day, about five years
later, at the PX in Bad Godesberg, near Bonn, where I was stationed
at the time, my eye fell on a record album, the jacket heralding *Never
No Mo' Blues*. The title was in large yellow letters above a blown-up
pencil sketch of a friendly, cheerful, sympathetic countenance
crowned by a soft visored cap and underlined by a neat black bow tie.
Below the face I read: "Jimmie Rodgers Memorial Album." On the
reverse side was the photograph from which the jacket design sketch
had been drawn, showing the singer in railroad brakeman's garb, a
guitar on his lap, an amiable smile on his face, and his fists facing the
camera, thumbs up!

I think I was drawn by the face and the slender figure even
before I noted the song titles. These were intriguing: "Blue Yodel
No. 4 (California Blues)," "Pistol Packin' Papa" and "Old Pal of My
Heart," among others. There was something boyish, almost childlike,
about that face, but something, too, possibly the thumbs-up pose, as
well as the cheery smile, that suggested optimism in the face of
adversity. Then there was the variety of style and subject matter
reflected in the song titles. I read the liner notes—and bought the
album.

I took it home, put it on the turntable and—as one says nowadays—flipped! "Blue Yodel No. 6"—here was a white country boy singing a classical twelve-bar blues. But where a black bluesman would have been interposing a blues riff on the guitar between verses, Jimmie Rodgers was yodeling! And how he yodeled! I had heard plenty of yodeling during tours of duty with the Army and the Foreign Service in Switzerland, Bavaria and Austria, but never anything quite like this. It was sweeter than any yodeling I had ever heard, more melodious, wider in range—a true falsetto extending upward to the E flat above high C—more accurate in pitch, more imaginative in its figuration, and somehow compellingly and uniquely plaintive.

I'm not sure that "plaintive" is the right word. "Wistful" may be better. As I write, I am reminded of how many other great singers have expressed that same sense of loneliness and vulnerability: Judy Garland, Billie Holiday, Edith Piaf, Frank Sinatra, Hank Williams. . . . In their singing one has heard the cry of those for whom the world has seemed too much. Among those I have named—and there have been others—only Sinatra survived the hurt that exploded into song, and even Sinatra did not emerge unscathed.

Many singers have been able to simulate it, which is a function of art. Some, for whom the hurt may have been real enough, have simply whimpered or bawled. The greatest artists have not asked for sympathy—for themselves. They tend to be a proud lot. They have told us, rather, of other people's problems—and ours—with insight and appreciation born of their own troubles, awakening a feeling of fellowship, of companionship, in the hearts of millions. It has made them famous and rich without—it goes almost without saying—making them much the happier.

This last may not be quite true of Jimmie Rodgers. His frailties were physical—tuberculosis—rather than mental or personal. He seems always to have been a happy, cheerful fellow, or to have made a good show of being one, even in the face of professional disappointment and, in the last years of his short life—he died in 1933 at the age of thirty-five—the certainty of early death. "My time ain't long," he is supposed to have said when he journeyed to New York in 1933 to make his last records.

One's awareness of this indomitability in the face of hardship (including poverty) and doom excites sympathy and admiration in us who listen to his records today, and who know the story of his life.

But this hardly explains the affection he aroused in those who heard him in the flesh and on records forty and more years ago, and who bought enough of his 111 records (an estimated twenty million copies) to place him among the biggest sellers of early recording history. Few of those listeners would have had any inkling of the impending tragedy, nor would they have known much of Rodgers' story beyond the fact that he had begun life as a railroader. Something in the quality of his voice and in his way with a song told them that *he was one of them.*

The first thing about Jimmie Rodgers' voice that impresses an uninitiated listener hearing it on records for the first time is its insignificance. It was small, nondescript, and given to nasality on such words as *now, want, mine, I'm, on, way, say,* etcetera. The range was short, hardly more than an octave and a third, discounting the considerable upward extension in falsetto. It has commonly been described as a tenor, probably because the sound was higher than the actual pitch. The C–E range, however, identifies it as a baritone, although a light one. Rodgers sang up to F and even F sharp from time to time, but he had to back off into head voice to do it. Even then, he sometimes barely made it.

Well, great voices do not great singers make. Great singers are made by what musically creative men and women do with the voices God gave them. I am reminded of this as I review the notes I made at a first hearing of another of RCA's Jimmie Rodgers reissue albums, *Train Whistle Blues.* By the time I got to track 7, "High-Powered Mama," I was writing: "The voice grows on you—a lovely voice!" What grew on me was not so much the voice as what was being done with it—the phrasing, the coloring, the gentle slurring, the lightest and briefest of grace notes, mordents and *appoggiature,* and, above all, the enunciation!

Time and again I find in my notes: "Lovely enunciation!" This was no accident. Jimmie had a thing about words, as revealed in many passages in Carrie Rodgers' book, *My Husband Jimmie Rodgers.* He disliked intensely, she wrote, "listening to a singer, highbrow or lowbrow, if he couldn't make out every word, every syllable." She recalled his comments on listening to records: "That guy ought to tone down that banjo. Got a pretty good voice, but shucks, what's the use havin' a good voice if it's all the time drowned out?" Or "Doggone! That guy's a humdinger on that mandolin, but his singin' is a pain in the neck. Too loud and whangy. 'Sides that, what's he singin' about, anyway? Can't make out a word he's sayin'."

There was more to it than simply distinct enunciation. Of another singer Jimmie observed: "You can make out what he's singing about, too. Only thing is, no way of tellin' if he's feeling bad about it—or good about it." Jimmie wanted the listener to get not only the words and the story they told, but also the *feel* of the story. In this context it should be noted that most of the songs he sang and recorded were his own, or his own extensive adaptations or rearrangements of other people's songs. Mrs. Rodgers summed it up in one perceptive paragraph:

> He scorned alike context, subject, sequence and all the tenses; sometimes even the genders! And plurals and singulars got themselves gaily tangled up continuously. No matter. Did it sound right? That was all that mattered to Jimmie Rodgers, minstrel. He wanted to be sure that voice and strings expressed his moods perfectly; told the stories he had to tell, whether carefree or rowdy, or heart-breakingly tender.

Voice and strings—yes, strings were a part of it. Jimmie rarely left his message to the voice alone. He played both banjo and guitar. He was no virtuoso on either, but the guitar, particularly, which he came to favor during his recording career, was an integral part of almost every song he ever sang. Rhythmic patterns were carefully tailored to tune and text. When he took a guitar chorus it was all of a piece with the vocal chorus that had gone before.

A lovely example is "Treasures Untold." My notes on a first hearing—and on a second, too—include: "Plays guitar with *precisely* the same phrasings, colorings, slurs, as his singing. Makes guitar talk." His yodels, similarly, were varied to suit the material. Then there were the train whistles—his only whistling accomplishment, according to Carrie Rodgers—which gave to all his many railroad songs, most memorably "Hobo Bill's Last Ride" and "Ben Dewberry's Final Run," a unique sense of authenticity. That sound could not have been achieved by anyone who had not grown up with railroading in his blood and environment.

Which was true, of course, of Jimmie Rodgers. He was born in Meridian, Mississippi, on September 8, 1897. His father was foreman of an extra gang on the Mobile and Ohio Railroad. Jimmie, when he went to work as his father's assistant at the age of fourteen, had already served an apprenticeship carrying water for the workers in the Meridian railroad yards. Until tuberculosis forced his retirement from railroading fourteen years later, he rode the rails throughout the South and Southwest as flagman, brakeman and, no doubt, in many other capacities. Mrs. Rodgers included call boy and baggage man among his railroad occupations.

Music, during this time, was for him avocation and recreation. It was, surprisingly, mostly instrumental, although there had been a hint of things to come when, at the age of twelve, he won an amateur contest at a Meridian theater, singing "Bill Bailey" and "Steamboat Bill." As a boy, he had picked up both banjo and guitar. He played for friends and companions, for social gatherings, for dances, and so on. He played for, and with, the black workers in the railroad yards. It is generally assumed that from them he learned the blues conventions, both vocal and instrumental, of his subsequent "blue yodels" and of many others of his songs not specifically categorized as blues. In playing for dances and social gatherings he learned the popular white musical lore of the time and the region, thus laying the groundwork for what would later be a repertoire astonishingly wide-ranging both in style and in idiom.

Retirement from railroading forced him to make a profession of avocation, first as a blackface entertainer with a medicine (or "physic") show touring Kentucky and Tennessee, then as leader of his own Jimmie Rodgers Entertainers (which he called his "hillbilly ork") in Asheville, North Carolina, whither he and his wife had moved in search of a climate congenial to his tubercular condition. It was while working out of Asheville that he had his first fleeting taste of real public success. "Mother," he told his wife after a one-nighter, "I don't know if they were kidding me or not, but kind of sounded like they ovationed me!"

He broadcast for a time from Station WWNC (Wonderful Western North Carolina), and he moonlighted (or was it the other way around?) as private detective, janitor and furnaceman. Eventually, he and his group took to the road, and it was while they were on tour that he heard of Ralph Peer, the former Okeh Records executive and talent scout (he had cut the first blues records with Mamie Smith), who was holding field auditions in Bristol, on the Virginia-Tennessee border, for the Victor Talking Machine Company.

Jimmie and his group auditioned separately. There are conflicting stories as to why. Mrs. Rodgers' account suggests that the group walked out on him, and she quotes Jimmie as saying, "The boys have made arrangements with Mr. Peer to make a test record—without me!" According to another and, I think, likelier version, Peer realized that group and singer were mismatched, and advised them to audition separately. There may have been a misunderstanding. In any event, the separate audition probably made Jimmie's fortune. It took place on August 4, 1927. Jimmie cut two sides. One was a traditional Southern lullaby, "Sleep, Baby, Sleep." The other was his own adaptation of an old song, "Soldier's Sweetheart," the adaptation inspired by the tragedy of a friend of his, killed in action in World War I.

The choice of songs came as a surprise to Carrie Rodgers. She had expected him to sing a song of his own called "T for Texas" (Blue Yodel No. 1), with which he had enjoyed some success in Asheville. His reasons for choosing as he did are recounted in her book in his words as she remembered them. Both the reasons and the manner of their telling reveal much of the singer and the man:

> When Victor's deciding board listens to my record, I want 'em to get the music! See what mean? Want 'em to be able to judge the quality of my voice and my playin'; I mean the way I try to make the guitar strings a part of my voice, make 'em say what I do and feel what I do. And when they're listening, I want 'em to be able to make out what I'm saying'—without havin' to think about it. I don't want the words themselves to get all the attention.
>
> If I'd given 'em Thelma [in "T for Texas"] some of 'em would be surprised, some shocked and some tickled; but there wouldn't any of 'em, maybe, stop to figure out whether I really had a voice or not, and maybe they wouldn't even know if I'd played a guitar. They'd all be thinkin'—well, about my shootin' poor Thelma. Those fellas up there, they're bound to be more critical than the radio listeners. . . . Maybe they'd like Thelma —maybe they wouldn't; but I'll make a guess they'd think maybe the public wouldn't.
>
> If those fellas up there at the factory are smart like I think they are, they know that's the kind of stuff the public's ripe for right now. Folks are about fed up on smart-Aleck jazz and jungle stuff. Well—if they do happen to like me—my voice and my

playin'—and these pretty old-fashioned numbers, why they'll have sense enough to know I can put over all those old hillbilly things, sentimental or rowdy.

What impresses one even more than this evidence of Jimmie Rodgers' good sense is the language in which the reasoning is couched. As Carrie Rodgers expressed it elsewhere in her book, "His singin' speech was exactly the same as his loafin' on the corner speech." Affinity of language and native musicality has been characteristic of all country singers. It is, to a considerable degree, what country music is all about. Jimmie Rodgers was probably the first to make this affinity manifest to a large public. Subsequent singers either followed his example or were encouraged by his success to put aside any inhibitions they may have had about singing in public, on radio and on phonograph records the way they spoke at home among themselves.

Country music and, of course, the blues demonstrate more vividly than any other Afro-American musical styles except gospel the relationship between music and language, or, to put it more dogmatically, music's origin in speech. In the art of Jimmie Rodgers one hears song not only as an extension of speech, but, more significantly, as a sublimation of speech. I remember thinking, when I first played his records: "This is not just a man speaking or singing. It's a whole countryside, an entire people, the American South—exclusive, of course, of the plantation and mercantile elite." The innocent rhetoric of Jimmie Rodgers and of all the fine country singers who came after him can be appreciated only in this context.

Who were these people? W. J. Cash (unrelated to Johnny) answers the question in his *The Mind of the South* (1941):

> . . . obviously and simply, in the large, and outside the oldest regions, the residue of the generally homogeneous population of the old backwoods of the eighteenth century, from which the main body of the ruling class had been selected out. The relatively and absolutely unsuccessful, the less industrious and thrifty, the less ambitious and pushing, the less cunning and lucky—the majority here as everywhere.
>
> The plantation system had driven these people back to the less desirable lands. . . . It had, to a very great extent, walled them up and locked them in there—had blocked them off from escape or any considerable and social advance as a body. . . .

They were the people to whom the term "cracker" properly applied—the "white trash" and "po' buckra" of the house niggers, within the narrowest meaning of those epithets.

They were the people who, almost anywhere in the South in the early 1930s, would enter a general store and say, "Let me have a pound of butter, a dozen eggs and the latest Jimmie Rodgers record." Jimmie was not a country boy in the sense that he worked the land, but he was of the stock that Cash was writing about. First as a railroader, later as an entertainer, he moved among them from Florida to Arizona. He spoke their language as one of them. He sang their songs, and he made up songs of his own, fashioned in their image. Being a railroader may have rendered him just a bit of an outsider—an outsider, that is, in any given neighborhood. It saved him, in any case, from the insularity of a lifetime spent in one community.

It undoubtedly accounted for the wide range of style represented not only in what he recorded, but also in what he wrote: railroad songs, hillbilly heart and roisterer songs, coon songs, blues, western songs, even a bit of jazz. In my notes on his recording of "Blue Yodel No. 5" I find: "This very beautiful—he takes rhythmic liberties that are the very essence of jazz." On some of his blues records he is backed by jazz musicians, including, allegedly, on "Blue Yodel No. 9," Louis Armstrong and Earl "Fatha" Hines.

Although his repertoire encompassed this considerable variety of style, it never strayed beyond what his listeners could recognize and comprehend. The presentation conformed to the homespun flavor of the words and music. Bill C. Malone gives this picture of Jimmie at work before a live audience:

For his stage appearances he generally dressed in a white or tan light-weight suit, and sported a jauntily cocked straw sailor hat. (He often posed for publicity pictures in a cowboy uniform or railroad brakeman's attire, but seldom dressed this way during a performance.) He looked and acted the part of a young man-about-town out for an evening of pleasure. He would put his foot on a chair, cradle his guitar across his knee, and captivate his audience with a selection of both rakish and sentimental tunes that generally consumed no more than twenty minutes. In a voice unmistakably southern, he kidded his audiences in a whimsical fashion and beguiled them with songs that seemed to catalogue the varied memories, yearnings and experiences of small-town and rural Americans: nostalgia for the departed mother, or "the old southern town" of childhood; pathos for the homeless hobo dying in a boxcar or trying to bum a south-bound freight; unrequited memories of the sweetheart who proved unfaithful; laughter for the rakes and rogues who "loved and left them" in every town; and a variety of other experiences with which most people could identify.

The total effect of his performances was an air of effortless informality, marked by a very personal approach which insinuated its way into the hearts of listeners, making them feel that the song was meant just for them. His voice . . . was capable of adjusting itself to almost every kind of song. . . . He sang them all with sincerity and in the particular spirit in which they were written. When his audiences of railroad workers, truck drivers, laborers, farmers and small-town people heard his songs, they recognized him as one of their own, and the deadening, bleak years of the depression were thereby made more endurable.

In all except the heart songs, in which his style was as white—or poor white—as white could be, Jimmie Rodgers' art revealed more of the interrelationship of black and white than that of any country singer who came after him. He certainly owed his affinity for the black man's music, and his mastery of its conventions, to his early associations with black workers on the road gangs and in the railroad yards of the Mississippi delta. But the stylistic breadth of his repertoire suggests an extraordinarily assimilative nature. The accuracy and authenticity of his blues singing stand as an instructive early memorial—on records—to the interaction of white and black that has so profoundly enriched Western music in the cities and the heartlands of America.

Still, he never sounds truly black on these blues records. White soul singers of our own time have tried to duplicate the black vocal sound, the black vocal production, often so successfully that black singers, on blindfold tests, have been fooled. Jimmie Rodgers was too much his own man for that. He simply picked up what he heard, and did it in his own way. What is remarkable is that he did it so acutely, so expertly, including especially the upward slurs and the octave leaps into falsetto from the terminal note of a descending phrase, characteristic of the early black blues singers of the delta.

The inspiration for his yodeling and guitar playing is less easy to identify precisely. Many singers were yodeling in those days, emulating Swiss entertainers who were then a familiar and popular attraction on the American vaudeville circuits. Carrie Rodgers wrote that Jimmie first yodeled during an automobile trip to Arizona in the mid-1920s, from which it has been inferred that he picked up yodeling from cowboys. But they, in turn, may have learned it from the Swiss.

Similarly with his guitar playing, which often sounded more Hawaiian than black. Certainly he knew all about Hawaiian guitar playing, having at one time briefly led a Hawaiian group touring with a carnival. But the black blues singers, working with guitar, used the same slurring devices, probably profiting from Hawaiian example, in which they found an escape from what they felt to be the melodic and rhetorical inhibitions of strict adherence to diatonic pitches. Jimmie would seem to have been the first, in any case, to introduce yodeling, if not slurred guitar inflections, into the blues.

His reasons for doing so were characteristically pragmatic. "That's a new way," he told his wife, "to spell the blues. You yodel 'em." What he meant, presumably, was that it provided a means of "spelling" the monotony of a sequence of repetitive vocal refrains. Even though voiced, the falsetto sound was a change. The melody was left behind, and there were no words. He used guitar choruses similarly, following the melody more closely than was usual with black blues singers.

Jimmie Rodgers' blues, although probably preferred by sophisticated listeners studying his vocal and narrative art today, were not his most popular offerings in his own time. The heart songs were. In choosing heart songs for his test records in Bristol he was guided by his knowledge of his own people. It speaks for his native intelligence that he addressed himself on that occasion to a potential record audience rather than to the presumed tastes and predilections of the executives up North.

He would seem to have assumed—correctly, as it turned out—that the latter would be more interested in what Southern buyers might like than in what they, the executives, fancied. Peer, for one, approved of what he heard. He paid Jimmie twenty dollars in cash as an option. Jimmie and his wife promptly moved into the best hotel in Bristol. "I want," he told her, "to feel like somebody."

Fame and fortune did not follow immediately, but the interval was not long. He and his wife spent the winter of 1927–28 in Washington, D.C., Jimmie taking singing jobs where he could find them, she working as a waitress in a Happiness Tea Room. But then came the call from Camden. His test records were selling, and Victor wanted more. He was ready and prepared to oblige.

Just a year and a half later Jimmie could build a $50,000 mansion in Kerrville, in the Texas hill country, the location determined by its proximity to a tuberculosis sanitarium. He called it "Blue Yodeler's Paradise," inspired, no doubt, by the example of Gene Austin, who had befriended and sponsored him during that winter in Washington, and who had taken him and his wife cruising on the Potomac aboard Gene's yacht, "Blue Heaven," named after his greatest hit.

From that time on, Jimmie's life was touring—always in the South—and recording. But his health deteriorated predictably. There were periods of hospitalization. Medical expenses mounted. He had to sell "Blue Yodeler's Paradise" and move to San Antonio. When he traveled to New York in May 1933 to make what he almost certainly knew would be his final records, it was because he needed the money. He was already so weak that he had to lie down on a cot between numbers. Only a stiff shot of whiskey would subdue the cough long enough to get him through a song. The voice, too, was weak, as may be heard on those records.

He made the last of them on May 24—although more had been scheduled—and died two days later in the Manger Hotel (now the Taft). His body was taken to his native Meridian for interment. The train arrived late at night, and the engineer blew a long, mournful blast on the whistle as it pulled in, well aware that the "Singing Brakeman" who had sung so hauntingly of Hobo Bill and Ben Dewberry had just taken his own last ride.

6

Bing Crosby

Of the great American popular singers, Bing Crosby has been among the most profoundly and decisively influential. It might be more accurate to say that he has been among the most *immediately* influential. The impact of earlier innovators, notably Al Jolson, Bessie Smith and Ethel Waters, was indirect, filtered to a considerable extent through Bing—and the microphone. The two elements contributing to a new, distinctive vocal idiom—an Afro-American approach to phrasing, and radio, bringing with it the microphone—met in him. They were synthesized in his singing, and passed on to all who came after him.

Certainly the art of no other singer has been so deceptive, if only because Bing's singing, at its best, has always seemed so easy, so free of artistic pretension, so devoid of any suggestion of accomplishment. No other singer, it seems to me, has been so inadequately assessed.

Not that he has been underrated, or that his achievements, either as singer or movie actor, have gone unacknowledged or unrewarded. Nor that recognition has been a matter of fame and fortune alone. Long past is the "groaner." Almost everyone today acknowledges the mellow richness of the voice, the elegance of the phrasing, the easy, buoyant rhythm, the fastidiousness of the diction, the "way with a song."

127

Like Louis Armstrong, he has been a legend in his own lifetime. But, as with Louis, the legend, attractive and flattering as it may be, does the man less than justice. Like Louis, he is probably unaware, possibly even incapable of understanding, the wider implications of his influence upon the art of the singer. But there the parallel ends. Louis was a fully formed, intuitive and inspired original right from the start. Once having absorbed all that King Oliver could give him, he was his own man, unique in the world of music at twenty-five, influencing all who ventured within range of his horn or his voice, and virtually immune, it would seem, to any outside influence.

One might be tempted, at first glance, to say the same of Bing. He would appear, on the evidence of the finest records from the best years of his career, to be as original in his way as Louis. The extent of his influence is documented in the work of a hundred other and lesser singers. But there is an important difference. Louis' most distinctive records were made before he was thirty. Bing's were made in middle age and later.

Although the artist is evident in Bing's earliest records, what one hears on them is stylistically embryonic, tentative, inconsistent, with none of the assertive assurance and idiomatic self-confidence of the young Armstrong. Bing's career suggests rather an assimilative, adaptive disposition. As man and musician he was a creature of his time. He was influential not so much because he was original, but because he reflected or embodied, both in his singing and his person, his own social and musical environment.

Louis Armstrong was a heroic figure, the exuberant, uncomplicated, uninhibited conqueror. Bing Crosby has been the antihero, or nonhero, the ordinary middle-class, middle-city (Tacoma and Spokane) American male, whose only outstanding attribute, initially, was his ears. "A camera pointed at you," Jim Ryan, casting director at Fox's Western Avenue Studio, told him after a test in 1930, "would make you look like a taxi with both doors open." Long before he reached middle age, his hair was thinning on top. He tended, as do most men of his stocky build, to put on weight. He dressed casually and comfortably. He smoked a pipe. His hobbies and enthusiasms were unexceptional—and unexceptionable: golf, baseball, hunting, fishing, the race track, the family. He was, in the language of his own generation, Joe Average. This was a basis of his appeal to millions of Americans—and non-Americans, too—as both movie actor and singer.

Although he rose to fame in the 1930s, he was a product of the 1920s, of a generation challenging the conventions and restraints of a pre-World War I social order. Outward symbols of the challenge were raccoon coats, loud clothes, hip flasks, a slangy vocabulary, cheek-to-cheek dancing, rumble-seat cuddling, flivvers, jalopies—and jazz! For the girls there were bobbed hair, short skirts, drinking and smoking. When Bing Crosby filmed *College Humor*, shortly after his arrival in Hollywood, he knew the scene. He had been a part of it. His later Joe Average was simply an older Joe College who had stayed with the music of his youth.

It may have been a rebellious generation, but it was lighthearted in its rebellion and quick to become conventional in the acceptance of the fruits of victory. The young dissenters of the Korean and Vietnam war generations have been a solemn, defiant, even sullen and despairing lot, resentful of an older generation on whom, in their view, the imperfections and injustices of society sit too lightly. Bing's generation found its elders too serious, too concerned with propriety and with outward appearances. Its defiance was jaunty, debonair, irreverent and fashionably irresponsible. It would be unfair to Bing to suggest that he has been either irreverent or irresponsible, once his wild oats were sown. But jaunty and debonair he was, and has remained. The manner in which he has sustained, for his generation, the image of its youth may well account for the extraordinary longevity of his hold upon the affections of an enormous public.

He has sustained it not only as a movie actor and radio and television personality, but also as a singer. His vocalism has, if anything, grown more relaxed, casual, effortless and "average" with the years. It has been essential to the image that it be, or seem to be, as natural, as uncontrived, as inevitable and as unexceptional as it sounds. No one has understood this better than Bing himself. Seeking to explain, in his autobiographical *Call Me Lucky*, why his singing has always been attractive to men as well as to women, he wrote:

> I think—and I'm confident that my assumption is correct—that every man who sees one of my movies, or who listens to my records, or who hears me on the radio, believes firmly that he sings as well as I do, especially when he's in the bathroom shower. It's no trick for him to believe this, because I have none of the mannerisms of a trained singer, and I have very little

voice. If I've achieved any success as a warbler, it's because I've managed to keep the kind of naturalness in my style, my phrasing and my mannerisms which any Joe Doakes possesses. . . . It's my hunch that most men feel that if they had gotten the opportunities I've had, they could have done just as well. I don't doubt that there's a lot of truth in that.

With all due respect, I doubt it very much. There is a curious ambiguity in what Bing at one time or another has had to say about his singing. In one breath he presents himself as just an ordinary Joe with an ordinary bathroom baritone who made it big by not trying to be anything more than that. In the next, he will be making observations that betray, beneath the nonchalance, a thoughtful and perceptive student and critic of his own work. Popular singers are not, as a rule, fruitful sources of information about how and why they sing as they do. Bing is, up to a point, an exception. Take, for example, this candid self-appraisal, again from *Call Me Lucky*:

> When I'm asked to describe what I do, I say, "I'm not a singer; I'm a phraser." That means that I don't think of a song in terms of notes; I try to think of what it purports to say lyrically. That way it sounds more natural, and anything natural is more listenable. Time was when I let the lyrics roll out of me without thinking how they sounded. Playing some of the records I made in the 1930s, I notice that in many of them I was tired; my voice was bad, and had a lot of frogs in it. The notes were generally in key, but sometimes I barely made them, and they sounded strained. But I paid no attention to whether they were bad or good when I made them. And they sold. They were popular. When I play back some of the records I've made in the past year or two [*Call Me Lucky* was published in 1953] they're too vocal. They're over-sung. I'm listening too much to what I sing when I sing it, and it makes me self-conscious.

The records Bing has made since then offer persuasive documentation of a lesson learned and taken to heart. But it wasn't, in fact, so simple as all that. His apparent unawareness of the many idiomatic and technical influences evident in his records over a span of forty years may well resolve the contradiction implicit in the man who tells us on the one hand that he does no more than what comes naturally to him and to most men, and on the other, talks so

The young Bing

thoughtfully and so knowledgeably about what has been good and what has been bad in his singing.

The clue may lie in the fact that he has been, as I have suggested earlier, an unconsciously assimilative rather than a consciously innovative artist, a reflector rather than an analyst of idiomatic, stylistic and technical phenomena. This would help explain, too, why his talent and artistry matured so slowly, so erratically, so almost imperceptibly. He was always musical, but his musical education was haphazard, picked up along the way, so to speak, and acquired from the exigencies of the moment.

At Gonzaga High School, in Spokane, he had played drums in a Dixieland group called the Juicy Seven. As a freshman at Gonzaga University, in 1921, when he was seventeen, he graduated to a more sophisticated outfit called the Musicaladers, and became its vocalist. Out of this association grew the partnership with Al Rinker (Mildred Bailey's brother), which was to lead to Paul Whiteman and the Rhythm Boys (Crosby and Rinker plus Harry Barris).

Success came early, and Bing was a long time learning to live with it—or to sing with it. He played around too much. He drank too much. He sang too much. He sang uncritically. A young man of twenty-five doesn't question a formula that works. What Bing has to say about his records of the 1930s is true enough. He sang badly, and the records sold. But it was not, I think, just the casual, relaxed phrasing that sold them. Bing's phrasing, while always individual and engaging, was not so distinctive then as it became later on. The records sold because of the sound of the voice in the best part of its range.

The octave B flat to B flat in Bing's voice at that time is, to my ears, one of the loveliest I have heard in forty-five years of listening to baritones, both classical and popular. It dropped conspicuously in later years. Since the mid-1950s, Bing has been more comfortable in a bass range while maintaining a baritone quality, with the best octave being G to G, or even F to F. In a recording he made of "Dardanella" with Louis Armstrong in 1960, he attacks lightly and easily on a low E flat. This is lower than most opera basses care to venture, and they tend to sound as if they were in the cellar when they get there.

Bing is right when he says that he has very little voice. He is wrong in assuming that what voice he has is ordinary. The error is not surprising to those acquainted with his early records. They show him to have been either slow in appreciating what was best in his voice or reluctant to acknowledge that what was best was all there was. For years he persisted in carrying a lot of voice up to E flat, E, F and even an occasional F sharp. It was always a precarious endeavor, not just because, as he says, he often barely made it, but, more importantly, because his voice then lost its characteristic timbre. Above the B flat it took on a tenor quality. The sound, even when the notes were securely landed, was unexceptional.

He found a way around the difficulty quite early on, but seems to have regarded it as an alternative rather than a solution. By moving into head voice, or a mixed chest and head resonance, at a lower area of the scale than previous baritones had done, he was able to sustain a characteristic sound into the upper areas of his range. He had to sacrifice volume, forcefulness and intensity to do it, and he had to ease off in the middle in order to preserve an even scale. This was a sacrifice baritones of his generation were reluctant to make. It implied a loss of virility, a shying away from the challenges of the big climaxes, an easy way out.

This may seem irrelevant to generations conditioned by the singing of popular baritones who came after Bing and profited by his example. But it must be remembered that in the early days of Bing's career the distinction between popular singers and classical singers was not so clearly drawn as it is today. John McCormack, at that time, was a popular singer. Some of the songs Bing was singing in the 1930s were also sung by Lawrence Tibbett, John Charles Thomas, Nelson Eddy and other opera baritones, all of whom rejoiced in ringing high Fs, F sharps and Gs. Bing did not have them.

What he may not have understood at the time, although he seems to have reacted to it instinctively, was that, with radio, phonograph and soundtrack supplementing and even supplanting public performance, and with amplification available when public performance was required, a singer no longer needed them. Opera singers needed them, to be sure. They still do, because they sing the same old opera repertoire, unamplified, in the same old amphitheatrical opera houses. For any other singer, unencumbered by a stagnant and aging repertoire, or by nineteenth-century concepts of vocalism conditioned by the requirements of that repertoire, the arrival of radio and the public-address system had opened the way to, had indeed demanded, a less forceful, more intimate, more natural kind of vocal production and vocal communication.

Marguerite Haymes, mother of baritone Dick Haymes, and an extraordinarily perceptive vocal coach, described this manner of production and communication in a book, *The Haymes Way* (1945), as "that 'in the room' intimacy, the sort of intimacy that is typical of Crosby—you talk on sound, singing the melody very softly. . . . It means that you sing as though you were speaking." Roland Dick, a radio announcer of that time, used to say that Bing "sounds as if he were leaning over the piano in your own parlor singing to you." Similarly, Charles Henderson, in *How to Sing for Money*, wrote of Bing that "you get the feeling that he's letting you in on something very important to you, something he wants to tell you about, now that you and he are alone together." Henderson coined the term "phonogenic" to describe Bing's voice. He might have coined "microgenic," too.

Rudy Vallee, when Bing Crosby was still a Rhythm Boy, had used a megaphone to carry over into the dance hall or large auditorium the "crooning" techniques of radio singing, techniques which Vallee, in his *Vagabond Dreams Come True* (1930), says he picked up from the blues singing of Al Bernard and Marion Harris. It was Vallee, according to his own account, who, in 1930, introduced electronic amplification of music into the public auditorium. "It sounds like a real Goldberg contraption," he told Paul Whiteman, "but it works. I borrowed an old carbon mike from NBC, hooked up a homemade amplifier with some radios, and I've got a sort of electronic megaphone. I had the legs sawed off the radios so they don't look so strange."

By thus bringing the radio into the public auditorium, Vallee had done more than just saw off the legs of radio sets. He had, in fact, knocked the last props from under the traditional concepts of vocal objective and vocal production. Radio had removed size of voice as a competitive factor. When the turn of a knob could make any voice sound as big as any other voice, a singer, in order to excel, had to look for other areas of excellence. Rudy Vallee had already sensed where that area lay when he first took a megaphone from the bell of his sax and put it to his mouth:

Rudy Vallee

Russ Columbo

My use of the megaphone came through absolute necessity as, although my voice is very loud when I speak or shout, yet when I use it musically it is not penetrating or strong, and the megaphone simply *projects the sound in the direction* in which I am singing. What I did was simply to risk the censure of public opinion by using it *on every song*, and singing many songs through it, because I believe that one of the biggest defects in most people who sing songs is that they get the *melody* out but not the words.

Not just the melody, then, nor just the voice giving out the melody, but the text must be the thing. It was not only that the words should be heard and understood. They must be heard and understood in a musical and colloquial context. The singer must work henceforth not just from the music of a tune, but also from the music of language. Along with Vallee's megaphone and Goldbergian public-address system, electronic amplification had, in less than a decade, taken singing back about 300 years to the objectives and practices of the early seventeenth-century reformers, Caccini, Monteverdi and Cavalli. These men had freed vocal music, with opera, at least, from the artificial melodizing of renaissance polyphony and wedded it to the music of Italian speech. The language of the new epoch, in the twentieth century, would be American English.

There were others, in the late 1920s, who "crooned"—Russ Columbo, Bennie Fields, Little Jack Little and Will Osborne—but it was Bing Crosby, more than any other, whose voice and approach to song and text lent themselves to amplification. Bing knew, whether from instinct or from calculation, how to make the microphone work for him. Of his early records, Martin Williams, in a review of *The Bing Crosby Story* (Epic E2E 202 and E2E 201) in the June 29, 1968, issue of *Saturday Review*, observed perceptively:

One thing that Crosby helped accomplish, a thing his natural talents prepared him for, was the carrying of popular music into the electronic age. Crosby does not sound like a singer *using* a microphone for some of his most telling effects. He was, in effect, overheard by the microphone. To say that he is effortless, natural, intimate, as is often said, is to say that he uses the mike to reach the members of his audience more directly. He could be as emotionally effective as the next singer without raising his general volume level—or perhaps more effective simply because he did not raise it. But personal statements like "Paradise," and person-to-person gossip like "Sweet Georgia Brown" therefore work far better for him than pseudo-grandiloquence like "Without a Song" or "Lord, You Made the Night Too Long."

Williams may have been influenced, to some extent, by his familiarity with recordings made later in Bing's career. Bing's mike technique on these earlier records is not always so good. What Williams says is true. Bing did, indeed, carry popular music into the electronic age, but he also carried into it initially, some of the habits and concepts of the previous acoustic age into which he had been born. The longevity of his career, and his ultimate mastery of the microphone, make it easy to forget that he was essentially a transitional figure.

He broke into show business not with radio, but as a performer in public places, and he made his mark in public places without the assistance of amplification or, for that matter, of a megaphone. For those who persist in thinking that the microphone makes a singer, I offer this last quotation from Rudy Vallee. Rudy had gone to Baltimore in 1927 with a pickup band from the Ben Bernie organization to play for a debutante ball. Whiteman was there with the Rhythm Boys, and:

> It was a crowded place, and the trio [the Rhythm Boys], working with only a piano, was back against the wall of the gym, and nobody paid much attention to their performance. Suddenly, however, one of them walked to the center of the floor and delivered a popular song of the day, "Montmartre Rose." There were no amplifying systems in those days, and I could scarcely hear his rendition. When he had finished, there was a deafening roar of applause which would have called for at least one or two encores. Instead, he walked off the floor past where we sat, his classic features expressionless, his patrician nose just a bit up in the air. You might have thought him deaf, so unaware he seemed of the sensation he had created. But then, this insouciance has always characterized Bing Crosby.

Just a year earlier, Hugo Friedhofer, subsequently to become one of Hollywood's finest film composers and arrangers, had heard Bing and Al Rinker at the Granada Theater in San Francisco. Friedhofer was then cellist and arranger for the theater orchestra, and as he tells the story:

> The team worked *sans* orchestra—in fact, we didn't even know what the duo was going to do until the first show. After the M.C.'s announcement, we played the boys on with a short intro, during which they emerged from the wings pushing a small upright piano which had a small sock cymbal at one end. What followed was (for 1926) some of the farthest-out jazz we had ever heard. Even at that time our Mr. Crosby had that wonderfully loose-jointed, totally relaxed vocal style which later made him a world figure. At that time, most of the audience didn't know what the hell was going on, but we in the band were completely gassed. Oh, yes—Bing, without ever being a belter, somehow managed to project without benefit of microphone in a theater seating 1,750, which ain't bad at all.

Bing sang on records and radio, in the early 1930s, at least, much as he sang in public. Granted, his way of singing in public lent itself readily to amplification. Working with a trio had taught him to sing lightly and with the forward production essential to distinct enunciation, particularly in up-tempo numbers. He was one of the first of many fine popular singers to benefit from the disciplines of ensemble singing, especially the requirement of singing in time and in tune, of modulating the voice to suit the group, the song, and the exigencies of time and place.

Had he listened to his records then as he might listen to them now with the perception gained from forty years of subsequent experience and growth, he could easily have detected precisely what areas of his voice and what characteristics of his phrasing offered the most fruitful targets of isolation, concentration, development and exploitation. As it was, the practices of nearly a decade of preamplification show biz were ingrained. It was only over another decade devoted more and more exclusively to soundtrack, radio and records that he began slowly to sort out what worked on the microphone and to eliminate what was superfluous or incompatible.

Even then, it was not entirely an intellectual or technical accomplishment. Bing has been lucky even in his vices.

The Rhythm Boys with, left to right, Bing Crosby, Harry Barris and Al ▶ Rinker

One of my Boswells [he recounts in *Call Me Lucky*, discussing his long stand with the Rhythm Boys at the Coconut Grove in Los Angeles in 1930] has since made the statement that I "wooed my listeners with a husky whisper." That could be true. Some nights, after singing four or five hours, including two on the radio, a husky whisper was all I had left.

With the coming of fame, we became regular callers at Agua Caliente. Since we had Sunday and Monday off, we'd go there occasionally for a weekend. What with driving about 150 miles each way and playing roulette, golf and the races and belting a little tequila around, come Tuesday, when I stood or swayed in front of the microphone, my pipes were shot.

His growth as a stylist, too, was as gradual and haphazard as his technical accommodation to the opportunities afforded by the microphone. Ralph J. Gleason, the jazz critic, in a review of *Call Me Lucky*, said of Bing that "he is the personification of the whole jazz movement—the relaxed, casual, natural and uninhibited approach to art." In the same review he observed of both Bing and Frank Sinatra that "they have the rhythmic feeling for jazz and the gift of free melodic articulation that is the essence of jazz." In Bing's case, this was truer of his earlier and later singing than of the period in the 1930s when he was accommodating himself to life as a soloist and coming to terms with the microphone.

As a kid Dixieland drummer he had grown up with jazz. The great jazz musicians of the time were his idols. He heard them all—Louis Armstrong, Mildred Bailey, Cab Calloway, Ethel Waters and many more—and as a member of the Whiteman orchestra he was greatly impressed by Bix Beiderbecke (with whom he roomed for a while), Eddie Lang, Jack Teagarden, Frankie Trumbauer and Joe Venuti. But the impact of this association is reflected more vividly in his records as one of the Rhythm Boys, which reveal him as a natural and precocious "scatter," than in those he made immediately after he left Whiteman and, subsequently, the Rhythm Boys to go out on his own. Deprived suddenly of the jazz format, the arrangements, and the company of Al Rinker and Harry Barris, he moved closer to the popular music mainstream of the time, compelled to do so, probably, by a ballad rather than a "novelty" repertoire, and fell back to a considerable extent upon his very first singer model, Al Jolson.

Bing, as a schoolboy and as "assistant or flunky in the prop department of Spokane's Auditorium Theater," had heard Jolson in *Sinbad* and *Bombo*. For a while, he tells us, he tried to sing like Jolson and studied Jolson's records. One is tempted to observe that in later years he often sang like Jolson without trying. But that would be to overstate the case. He never "sang like Jolson," but in the records he made early in his career, after the break-up of the Rhythm Boys, there was a lot of Jolson in his singing. There are traces of Jolson in his singing to this day.

The Jolson influence has been overlooked in most assessments of Bing's early vocal style, probably because critics, and particularly the jazz critics, do not listen to Jolson records if they can help it, and they expel the experience from their memory as quickly as possible when they do. One who has listened attentively to Jolson, however, will recognize the stylistic source of Bing's slurring, his whistling, his occasional ventures into song-speech. They will also recognize, probably not without distaste, the Jolsonesque nasality of the diphthongs in such words as *way, may, mine, divine,* etcetera. Bing, on his early records, sounds most like Jolson, and least like Bing, when he carries a full voice into the upper part of his range.

The Jolson example was no help to him in belting out the high ones, and it marred many of his recordings. But for the rest, Bing simply took what Jolson had done and did it more tastefully. Or he transformed it in his own image, not always so tastefully. His slurring, for example, is more appropriate, more expressive, more varied and more musical than Jolson's, reflecting a jazz as well as a Jolsonesque stylistic origin. He overdid it from time to time and has had to live with the "groaner" label as a consequence. But it was an important factor in his getting away from the lyrical inhibitions of precise intonation on prescribed pitches.

To the slurs he added (although he could probably not have identified or defined) the mordent, which became an early hallmark of his singing. A mordent is simply the introduction of an unscheduled short note adjacent to the note of destination. The additional note may be the note above or the note below. Bing's mordents were light and fast, and they produced that effect of a slight catch, or choke, or sob which was to remain one of the most attractive of his vocal devices. Initially he used only the upper mordent. In later years he added the lower, articulating it more slowly and very effectively.

Compared with singers who came after him, notably Sinatra,

Ella Fitzgerald and Sarah Vaughan, Bing's embellishments, and his melodic and rhythmic deviations, are modest. They were, initially, tentative. One hears in the early records four measures here, four measures there, which forecast the master phraser of the future. In the next measures of the same song he can sound pretty square. He was clearly, if probably unwittingly, working toward that articulation of text and tune, independent of prescribed pitches, note values and bar lines, that now distinguishes the best of American popular singing from any previous vocal conventions in Western music.

He was also working toward a similarly innovative concept of vocal production. He sought melodic and rhythmic liberation in order to sing more intimately, more conversationally. In this he was guided, as Jolson had been guided before him, by the Afro-American— and Jewish—oral, or oratorical, concept of song. Bing's most original contribution was the lowering of the voice, not so much in pitch as in intensity, to a conversational level.

It is only paraphrasing Bing himself to say that he grew as a singer the less he tried to sing. It was in this accomplishment that he discovered and demonstrated the implications of the microphone for the present and the future of the vocal art. As Peter Reilly put it in a perceptive review of Bing's recent *Bing 'n Basie* album for *Stereo Review:* "After the advent of Crosby, pop singers stopped singing *at* you, like Jolson, and began singing *to* you, like Bing."

It is a mark of Bing's stature as artist and man that he will be remembered by all but students and historians not as an innovator, but simply as a singer of songs. As with all the great singers, the elements of his greatness can be detected in his very earliest work. Again, as with other great singers, you recognize him immediately. In less than half a measure of "Where the Blue of the Night," or any other song he ever sang, you welcome the voice and salute the master.

But there is more to it than that, more indeed than can be said of many great singers. As with John McCormack or Richard Tauber or Louis Armstrong, when we hear Bing Crosby we recognize the voice of an old and treasured friend.

7

Mildred Bailey

Mildred Bailey, more than any other of the great American popular singers, was a jazz musician's singer, a jazz musician's delight. This was the secret of her unique success. But it also had a lot to do with the commercial limitations of that success.

> Jazz singing, until the late 1920s [wrote Leonard Feather in *The Book of Jazz*] was largely confined to the Negro artists, and, despite occasional exceptions, such as Armstrong and Waters, was limited in substance to the form of the blues. The break on both levels may have been completed with the advent of Mildred Bailey. Where earlier white singers with pretensions to a jazz identification had captured only the surface qualities of the Negro styles, Mildred contrived to invest her thin, high-pitched voice with a vibrato, an easy sense of jazz phrasing that might almost have been Bessie Smith's overtones.

She sang popular music. Indeed, she sang every kind of popular music, from blues and pseudo-blues, gospel and pseudo-gospel, through Tin Pan Alley and show tunes to Charles Wakefield Cadman's "From the Land of the Sky-Blue Water." And she sang it all idiomatically—with the possible exception of the Cadman piece, which had once figured in the programs of Lillian Nordica. Her career in radio, her numerous records, her association with the Paul Whiteman, Red Norvo and Benny Goodman bands and her work as a single in prestigious nightclubs earned her a considerable portion of fame and money. Yet she never quite made it, as show-biz terminology has it, really big.

Mildred blamed it on her personal appearance. She was fat. For a variety of reasons, probably representing a fatal combination of biological and psychological factors, she was never able to keep her weight down. She loved to eat. She ate too much. She ate compulsively. Even in the later stages of the diabetes that killed her—on December 12, 1951, at the age of forty-four—she used to say: "Now, I've ate the diet, so bring on the food."

Obesity may have had something to do with it. She was no beauty. Dainty feet and trim ankles could not divert the onlooker's eye from the hulk they supported. She had, moreover, plenty of prettier contemporaries, some of whom made it bigger than she without being in her class as a singer or musician. But there were, I suspect, other, more musical reasons.

She was, to begin with, ahead of her time. As a featured vocalist with Paul Whiteman, beginning in 1929, she became the first girl singer to front a jazz band, or, in the jargon of the period, a jazz orchestra. More significantly, she and Connee Boswell were the first white singers, male or female, to absorb and master the blues, or rather the early jazz idiom of the black singers of the 1920s. Mildred Bailey was singing bluesy jazz, and swinging, when the rest of white America had hardly got beyond the Charleston.

Her place in American musical history is with those white musicians who as youngsters in the 1920s were listening to Sidney Bechet and Louis Armstrong, to Bessie Smith and Ethel Waters, at a time when middle-class America's idea of jazz was Ben Bernie, Vincent Lopez, Fred Waring and Paul Whiteman—or Gene Austin, Al Jolson, Harry Richman, Sophie Tucker and Rudy Vallee.

Many of those youngsters went on to great careers—Jimmy and Tommy Dorsey, Benny Goodman, Woody Herman, Harry James and Glenn Miller. Others—Bix Beiderbecke, Bunny Berigan and Dave Tough, for example—achieved only posthumous recognition. For all of them, however, the transition years from the Jazz Age to the Swing Era were difficult and precarious. The musicians knew what they had heard in the black nightclubs and theaters of Chicago

and New York, and on race records. They had learned to play it. But the general public was not ready for it, or for anything very much like it.

What these young musicians heard, and what they wanted to play, was, in ethno-musical terms, something closer to a black original than was being offered by the white theater and dance bands of the 1920s. Benny Goodman made the breakthrough in 1935–36. Swing, if not yet the blues, was in. The musicians had been swinging, privately and on records, for years. One of the most exciting, and also one of the most instructive, ways of hearing what they were up to, individually and collectively, is to listen to them playing behind Mildred in more or less ad hoc groups on the records she made in 1933–34–35.

The personnel on these dates reads like a Who's Who of early swing: Bunny Berigan, Chu Berry, Jimmy and Tommy Dorsey, Benny Goodman, Coleman Hawkins, Johnny Hodges, Gene Krupa, Red Norvo, Teddy Wilson and many more. The presence of black musicians is significant. This was before Benny Goodman and Artie Shaw had broken the color line in public performance, Benny with Wilson and Lionel Hampton, Artie with Billie Holiday. But behind the scenes, and in the recording studios, jazz was one world. Benny Goodman's famous trio was hatched, it is pertinent to recall, when he met Teddy Wilson at Mildred Bailey's home on Long Island.

Mildred, on these records, appears with bands variously designated. There are the Dorsey Brothers' Orchestra, Benny Goodman and His Orchestra, and Red Norvo and His Orchestra, all subsequently famous. There are more ephemeral titles: Mildred Bailey and Her Orchestra, Mildred Bailey and Her Alley Cats, and Mildred Bailey and Her Oxford Greys, the personnel sprinkled with names now hallowed. Listening to those records, and noting how Mildred always emerges not just as a singer fronting a band but as the lead voice in any band she worked with, one is tempted to forget the names of the bands and think of them simply as Mildred Bailey and Her Friends.

They were her friends. Red Norvo was her second husband. This was her music. So it had been since she was a young girl. Bing Crosby remembers her singing in Charlie Dale's Cabaret in Spokane (she was born in Tekoa, Washington, in 1907) during his college days, when he and Mildred's brother, Al Rinker, had a six-piece band called the Musicaladers. Mildred, he recalled in a prose portrait for

CBS's *Her Greatest Performances* album, "used to get some great records from the east from time to time, and Alton and I and our band would copy them. Believe me, with such a library in those days in Spokane, we were pretty *avant*. This was in 1925."

Mildred married and went on to Los Angeles. Bing and Al Rinker, then on their way to becoming the Rhythm Boys, found her there a year later, working in a club called The Swede's.

> I'll never forget my first visit there [Bing recalls] how my eyes bugged when I saw Gene Pallette, eminent actor of the period, lay a *Benjy* [a hundred-dollar bill, so called because it bears a portrait of Benjamin Franklin] on her for two choruses of "Oh, Daddy!" "Ace in the Hole" was good for a brace of *Benjies*. And "Sweet Mama, Where Did You Stay Last Night" might get pretty near anything.
>
> There it was that she introduced us to Marco, at that time a very big theatrical producer, and we were on our way—with a lot of her material, I might add. Ah! She was *mucha mujer*. A genuine artist, with a heart as big as the Yankee Stadium, and a gal who really loved to laugh it up. She had a beautiful sense of humor, and a way of talking that was unique. Even then, I can recall her describing a town that was nowhere as "Tiredsville."

Obviously, Mildred was closer to jazz than were other white singers of the time. She was listening to race records, and not only singing, but also talking, in the jazz idiom, as she would continue to do for the rest of her life. "Oh, Daddy!" had been Ethel Waters' first record hit. Another of Mildred's favorites was "Down Hearted Blues," recorded by Ethel Waters in 1921 and by Bessie Smith at her first session for Columbia in 1923. Mildred's own recording of it, in 1935, is one of her finest. When Bessie Smith made her last public appearance in New York, impromptu, in a jam session at the Famous Door on 52nd Street, Mildred was so moved that she declined to follow.

Red Norvo, reminiscing with Whitney Balliett for a *New Yorker* Profile, told how life was at their home on Pilgrim Circle in Forest Hills:

> Bessie Smith and her husband came to the house, too. Bessie was crazy about Mildred. She and Mildred used to laugh

Connee Boswell

Lee Wiley

at each other and do this routine. They were both big women, and when they saw each other one of them would say: "Look, I've got this brand-new dress, but it's too *big* for me, so why don't you take it?" Fats Waller came out. And Jess Stacy and Hugues Panassié and Spike Hughes and Lee Wiley and Bunny Berigan and Alec Wilder. Red Nichols lived right across the street. . . .

It may have been this sense of total identification with jazz, especially with jazz as it was emerging in the early 1930s, and with the young musicians, black and white, who were playing it, that inhibited Mildred's communication with a wider public. Where musicians are so obviously having a ball, so obviously playing for each other, admiring each other and liking each other, the lay public, excluding the "hot jazz" buffs of the time, may have felt excluded. The musicians were playing their own music and on their own terms.

Another problem for Mildred, probably, was the way in which her singing tended to suggest another instrument, or, as jazz musicians would put it, another horn. There was a paradox in this, for no other singer has rejoiced in a lovelier voice. But it was not the voice that suggested a horn. It was what she did with it. Her way with a phrase or a tune, particularly in the early days, tended to be an instrumentalist's way.

This has always been a way calculated to win the approval of jazz musicians, jazz critics and jazz fans. Their highest praise is to say of a singer that he uses his voice, or phrases, like a horn. It is essentially what they are talking about when they speak of a singer as being a "jazz singer." The praise has seduced and inhibited many a fine singer. It is nonsense.

Not in the sense that it can't be done, of course; but in the sense that it *should* be done. To encourage the singer to emulate the instrumentalist is to stand music on its head. It is to forget that the instrument is a vocal substitute, that the best instrumentalists are those who are the best singers on their instruments. What has confused and distorted our view of the singer-instrumentalist relationship in jazz has been the fact that the greatest jazz instrumentalists— Louis Armstrong and Sidney Bechet, for example—have "sung" so well on their instruments.

They learned from the singers. One notes the backing personnel on countless recordings of the 1920s by Bessie Smith, Ethel Waters, and their contemporaries. There they all are: Red Allen, Louis Armstrong, Buster Bailey, Sidney Bechet, Bunny Berigan, Henry Brashear, Jimmy and Tommy Dorsey, Benny Goodman, Charlie Green, Jimmy Harrison, Coleman Hawkins, Fletcher Henderson, James P. Johnson, Eddie Lang, Joe Smith, Jack Teagarden and so on. It is easy to miss the point when a Frank Sinatra says he learned all he knows about phrasing from listening to Tommy Dorsey play the trombone. He probably did. But Dorsey learned what he knew about phrasing from Henry Brashear, Charlie Green, Jimmy Harrison and Jack Teagarden. And they, in turn, learned from the black singers.

In Mildred Bailey's time, particularly in the early 1930s, an instrumental approach to singing was neither so hazardous nor so distinctive as it became later on, when jazz departed disastrously from its roots in song. The best instrumentalists were admirable models for a singer simply because they had modeled their own phrasing on such excellent singers, and "sang" so well. But for a singer of Mildred's extraordinary musicality, their virtuosity and invention were also a temptation. She could do with her voice what they did with their horns. Sometimes she would deliberately imitate an instrument—a trumpet, a trombone or a sax. She could do it marvelously. She enjoyed doing it.

It was not so much that she sang in an instrumental manner as that she thought instrumentally. Her enunciation was a model of clarity. The sound was vocal and feminine. But the effect was often as if a lead instrument had somehow acquired the capacity of articulating words. What one heard was admirable and delightful. The sheer virtuosity, however, sometimes overshadowed the articulation of a lyric and the probing of textual substance.

Any first-class jazz musician of the time could have taken a Mildred Bailey chorus and reproduced it on his instrument note for note, deviation for deviation, slur for slur, rubato for rubato, without the slightest suggestion of incongruity. She worked with a tune as the instrumentalists did, improvising from and around it, but never losing touch with it. This ability, and this predilection, help to explain why, on these early records, she comes through so strikingly as a member of the band.

The dangers, for a singer, of an instrumental style were compounded in Mildred Bailey's case and time, if she wished to reach a white audience, by the fact that the style itself was so blues-flavored.

All the white instrumentalists with whom she worked were also phrasing in the manner of their black contemporaries. For Mildred, as a singer, phrase was inseparable from language. So she adopted not only the black musician's way with a phrase, but also his way with a word and his vocal sound, including the pronounced nasal resonance—not nasality—which has characterized the great black female singers from Bessie Smith to Aretha Franklin.

For one born and raised in the state of Washington in the American Northwest, two or three thousand miles from the deep South and from Southern speech, Mildred's enunciation in any song requiring or even suggesting a blues inflection is astonishing. I have often played Mildred Bailey records of this type of song for unsuspecting visitors, both black and white, and asked them to describe the singer. The response, without exception, has been: "Well, to begin with, she's black." In more European material she doesn't sound black at all. I reckon it a sign of an acutely sensitive musicality that she reacted instinctively and profoundly to the indivisibility of music and language.

For all her concern with language, rendered the more conspicuous by the unfailing distinctness of her enunciation, the melody of language would seem to have been more important to her than its meaning. This has always been a problem for singers in whom musicality is combined with a beautiful voice. It has something to do with the fact that the greatest dramatic artists among the great singers in any category have rarely been those with the loveliest and most tractable voices. With the superbly endowed, the endowment takes precedence. Their singing tends to be more delightful than exciting. The fault may lie, to be sure, with the listener, so beguiled by the sound that he misses the substance.

Records Mildred made at the close of her career reveal a voice as fresh as that of records made fifteen years earlier. There is not a trace of blemish, no evidence of wear and tear, no falling of pitch. The explanation is apparent in the records themselves; there was never any wear or tear in her singing. One is tempted to put it all down to exemplary vocal production, as one can do, in good conscience, in accounting for Ella Fitzgerald's vocal longevity. What one hears in Mildred's singing is indeed exemplary. But it is only what Mildred would let you hear. It speaks more of artful resource, of taste and discretion, than, as with Ella, of technical mastery.

She would seem to have been a bit lazy as a singer, and possibly not just as a singer. It may be more than idle coincidence that the song most intimately associated with her is Hoagy Carmichael's "Rockin' Chair," and that she was known in her prime as "the rockin' chair lady." The best photograph ever taken of her shows her idly swatting a fly on her arm as she reposes in that rocking chair.

Not that her singing was ever slovenly. She was too fine a musician for that, too conscientious an artist, and sufficiently inventive to evade difficulties without betraying the evasion. A telling example is a recording of "Can't Help Lovin' Dat Man," where she repeatedly passes up a low E on "lovin'," reshaping the melody so artfully that only the purposefully attentive will note the discrepancy.

Those funked low Es are not the only remarkable or revealing feature of that performance. It is even more remarkable that the low Es are there to funk. She sings the Kern song in A flat, a fifth below the original E flat, in which she could easily have sung it without having to pass up any notes at all. This curious choice of key tells a lot about Mildred Bailey. It tells a lot, too, about the art and the vocalism of other admirable singers working in the Afro-American idiom.

A term encountered over and over again in descriptions of Mildred's voice by those who knew her well and heard her often is "high-pitched." It was no such thing. She is frequently referred to as a soprano. She was not. The sound could seem high, even soprano-like, but the actual pitch was low. Her effective range was from a G below to an E above, or an octave and a sixth. She probably had more below. She certainly had more above, as may be heard on her 1939 recording of "St. Louis Blues," where she suddenly and easily comes up with a high G.

She had, then, a mezzo-soprano's normal two octaves from G to G. But she preferred to work in a narrower range. When a song, or the chosen key of a song, took her out of that range, she simply altered the notes to suit herself, as in "Can't Help Lovin' Dat Man." Even within her favored octave and a sixth, she took things comfortably, passing into head voice very early in the ascending scale.

This passing into head voice has been noted as a characteristic of both Bessie Smith and Ethel Waters. They had not the vocal technique to carry the full sound of the middle voice any farther. With both of them, the register break is conspicuous and sometimes disquieting. With Mildred it is not.

She, too, probably lacked the technical know-how. But she would seem to have been more aware of the break and its esthetic consequences than either Bessie or Ethel were, and she got around it, as Bing Crosby was doing at about the same time, by easing into head voice well before it became the only alternative to vocal disaster. Instead of seeking, as opera singers do, to extend the quality of the middle voice upward, she extended the character of the light head voice downward, thus achieving a delightfully homogeneous quality throughout her range, if not without some sacrifice of fullness, power and amplitude in precisely those areas of the vocal compass where such attributes repose naturally.

She ascribed this evenness of scale to her experience as a child and young girl singing Indian music. Her mother was part Indian and, according to Barry Ulanov in his *A History of Jazz in America*, used to run through Indian songs with her. When the family moved to Spokane, her mother often took her over to the nearby Coeur d'Alene reservation. Ulanov quotes Mildred on what she learned there:

> I don't know whether this music compares with jazz or the classics, but I do know that it offers a young singer a remarkable background and training. It takes a squeaky soprano and straightens out the clinkers that make it squeak; it removes the bass boom from the contralto voice, this Indian music does, because you have to sing a lot of notes to get by, and you've got to cover an awful range.

A matching of registers by easing off in the middle instead of stretching at the top has been common to many popular singers, who never learned it from the Indians, but may have learned it from Mildred Bailey. It has much to do with the failure or reluctance of European-oriented vocal connoisseurs to appreciate them as vocalists and artists. The connoisseurs note the absence of the big sound while overlooking the subtleties made possible by its avoidance.

Mildred Bailey could have sung "Can't Help Lovin' Dat Man" in any one of several keys between E flat and A flat. She chose the lowest because it best served her communicative purpose. That the

Mildred Bailey with Red Norvo

choice involved a melodic alteration betraying shortness of range at the bottom of the scale would not have troubled her for an instant, nor, probably, would it have troubled Jerome Kern.

It may have troubled less discerning listeners, not because they would have been aware of the distant transposition, but because they would have missed the vocal tension they were accustomed to in performances by other singers in higher keys. The opera singer Eleanor Steber, for example, transposed the same song upward to F and threw in a superfluous but vocally exciting high B flat, and a far too arty cadenza.

Mildred, as Red Norvo remembers her, "made you feel that she was not singing a song because she wanted you to hear how she could sing, but to make you hear and value that song." She may well have been to some extent a victim of her own good musical taste. She would have liked to be a commercial success. She made records with the strings and choir backings she thought would appeal to a wider public and thus offended her jazz-oriented admirers. As Bucklin Moon puts it, in his contribution to the CBS album:

> She chose to be neither the one thing nor the other, but a combination of all that was good in both. She was too deeply rooted in jazz to have a large popular following, and too commercial to be accepted by a jazz cult which, until recently, was unwilling even to admit that a musician who could read music could play jazz. . . . Songs that she introduced, records that she made, had an alarming habit of turning up as somebody else's hits. . . . She never lacked for a tight little following who loved and admired her, but somehow, just about the time you figured she had made it finally, it all started to come undone again.

The result was a sense of frustration and resentment ill-housed in an ever volatile temperament. She was not always the laughing lady of Bing Crosby's portrait. Moon says that she was "salty as a fishwife," and he describes her rages as "monumental." John Hammond, producer of many of her CBS records, calls them "towering." Norvo, who knew her better than anyone else, passed on to Whitney Balliett an affectionate reminiscence of Mildred with her dander up. Norvo and Benny Goodman had gone fishing on Long Island. What with moving from one fishing hole to the next, they were gone two days instead of one.

When I got home, I could tell that Mildred was hacked. Things were cool, but I didn't say anything, and a night or two after, when we were sitting in front of the fire—I was on a love seat on one side and she was on one on the other side—Mildred suddenly got up and took this brand-new hat she had bought me at Cavanaugh's and threw it in the fire. So I got up and threw a white fox stole of hers in the fire, and she got a Burberry I'd got in Canada and threw *that* in. By this time she was screaming at me and I was yelling at her, so finally I picked up a cushion from one of the love seats, and in it went. The fire was really burning. In fact, it was licking right out the front and up the mantel, and that was the end of the fight because we had to call the Fire Department to come and put it out.

Mildred's tragedy was not her weight, nor her diabetes nor her rages. These were problems, and they brought with them vicissitudes and bitterness. Her tragedy was that people could not hear her, during her short life, in the perspective we bring to her singing today. It is an old story. Ned Rorem, in his *Music and People*, has summed it up in a way which at once illuminates the inevitable frailty of contemporary evaluation and does tardy justice to Mildred Bailey:

> The open question of what will come is vain but tantalizing. Tantalizing, because it is the primal question of human nature. Vain, because historic events, even history itself, switch focus every year as we funnel faster toward novel philosophies. Certainly we listen now to Mozart in a mannner inconceivable to him: he was ignorant of Mascagni and Mildred Bailey, who came between to recondition us. . . .

Similarly, we hear Mildred today with ears conditioned by our experience of Ella Fitzgerald, Billie Holiday and Frank Sinatra. Thanks to them, the vocal art that was uniquely hers in her youth is now widely appreciated. She was a great and lonely artist, born just a few years too soon. That was her tragedy, mitigated, one hopes, by the fact that she lived just long enough to see her genius and her insights perpetuated in the art of the great singers whom she inspired.

8

Billie Holiday

Certain leads or opening sentences to articles or books stick in one's mind. I have always remembered and cherished, for example, the opening sentence of Rafael Sabatini's *Scaramouche:* "He was born with the gift of laughter and a sense that the world was mad." It was my favorite until I opened Billie Holiday's *Lady Sings the Blues* and read: "Ma and Pop were just a couple of kids when they got married. He was eighteen, she was sixteen, and I was three."

This was more than just a flip gambit. It established immediately the setting and background for one of the most troubled careers in the annals of American music. The book traces, with significant candor, not only the professional life of a great singer, but also a sordid history of adolescent prostitution and subsequent drug addiction, the scene switching back and forth between more or less prestigious nightclubs, supper clubs, theaters and auditoriums to police courts, reformatories, sanatoriums and jails.

Billie Holiday made a lot of news, most of it bad. She made and spent a lot of money. Her two-hundred-odd records constitute a legacy of much that was finest in her era of jazz, a precious documentation of her own unique art as a singer and of the art of the splendid musicians, both white and black, who worked with her. But it was her losing struggle with adversity, bad luck, and personal weak-

nesses and inadequacies, rather than her hoarsely eloquent voice and her way with a phrase or a song, that made her a legend in her own time.

She is to be numbered among the self-destructive waifs of modern musical history, along with Mildred Bailey, Bix Beiderbecke, Judy Garland, Charlie Parker, Edith Piaf, Bessie Smith and Hank Williams. They were all gifted beyond the lot even of those destined to become the most accomplished professionals. But they were denied the compensatory attributes of self-knowledge and self-discipline, prerequisites for survival in the merciless world of show biz. Toward the end of Billie Holiday's career, a magazine asked her for the "real lowdown inside story of her life." She summed it up in a single sentence. "I wish," she wrote, in *Lady Sings the Blues*, "I knew it myself."

She didn't know it. But both her book, written with William Dufty, and her work on records offer clues. From the book, for example:

> It's a wonder my mother didn't end up in the workhouse and me as a foundling. But Sadie Fagan loved me from the time I was just a swift kick in the ribs while she scrubbed floors. She went to the hospital and made a deal with the head woman there. She told them she'd scrub floors and wait on the other bitches laying up there to have their kids so she could pay her way and mine. And she did. Mom was thirteen that Wednesday, April 7, 1915, in Baltimore, when I was born.

It is an eloquent paragraph, not just because it tells a story of desperate nobility so simply and so affectionately, but also because it projects succinctly and ingeniously the juxtaposition of feigned or ingrained toughness and vulgarity on the one hand, and on the other, the real pride and tenderness that characterized and complicated Billie Holiday's public and private performance throughout the forty-four years of her life.

Her vocabulary was as unoriginal and unimaginative as it was coarse. Women were bitches, girls were chicks, lesbians were dikes, musicians were cats, money was loot, whores were whores and policemen were fuzz. To be arrested was to be busted. This from the singer who was known throughout most of her professional life as Lady Day, or Lady, for short.

Her Christian name was Eleanora, but her father, Clarence Holiday, a jazz musician, called her Bill because she was such a tomboy. She changed it to Billie after Billie Dove, her idol on the silent-movie screens of her childhood. "Lady" was conferred upon her early in her public career by the other girls at Jerry Preston's Log Cabin in Harlem when she refused to pick up tips from customers' tables without using her hands. Lester Young, then playing tenor in Fletcher Henderson's band, and who later played some of his most beautiful choruses behind her, combined it with the "day" of Holiday to make Lady Day. She returned the compliment by calling him "Prez," thus putting him on a pedestal alongside another of her idols, President Roosevelt.

Max Jones, veteran critic of *Melody Maker*, saw behind the mask when he met her, wrapped from head to foot in blue mink, at a London airport in 1954. "She was outspoken, bright, tough and transparently sincere most of the time," he wrote not long afterwards. "She was obviously an imposing woman, an inch or two taller than I had expected, with a strong, well-boned face and a lot of natural magnetism and dignity."

The operative word is *dignity*. She had it. She could not always sustain it, least of all when it was overlooked, ignored, offended or defied by others. Thanks in part, no doubt, to an Irish (Fagan) great-grandfather on her mother's side, she had a low boiling point. Exposed to real or imagined slights, she could respond in an undignified fashion, sometimes with her fists, sometimes with any hard movable object within reach.

Louis Armstrong characterized her for the benefit of the producer, director and stage crew on the set of *New Orleans* in Hollywood in 1946, when Lady Day, unhappy at being cast as a maid, but unable to escape her contract, broke into tears. "Better look out," said Pops. "I know Lady, and when she starts crying, the next thing she's going to do is start fighting."

Many elements in the Billie Holiday story recall the career of Ethel Waters. Both were children of the Northern slums. Both were born illegitimately to slum children, and both were grownups before they were even properly adolescent. Ethel was first married, it will be recalled, when she was thirteen. Billie was raped when she was ten. Both did menial work, Ethel as scullery- and chambermaid, Billie scrubbing the famous white steps of Baltimore's brick row houses.

Both served a rough, tough apprenticeship as singers in the swinging gin mills of prohibition Harlem.

More significantly, perhaps, both tasted Jim Crow under circumstances more galling, even, than those experienced by their less renowned black contemporaries. They had to endure the outrage of being admired, even loved, by whites as artists while being directed to the tradesmen's entrance and excluded from hotels, dining rooms and restaurants as persons. They earned well. They were accorded many privileges normally denied black Americans at that time. But their apparent good fortune only made the facts of black life seem blacker.

Billie Holiday had an especially grueling time of it as the first black vocalist to be featured with a white band. The year was 1938. The band was Artie Shaw's. As she remembered it nearly twenty years later:

> It wasn't long before the roughest days with the Basie band began to look like a breeze. It got to the point where I hardly ever ate, slept or went to the bathroom without having a major NAACP-type production.
>
> Most of the cats in the band were wonderful to me, but I got so tired of scenes in crummy roadside restaurants over getting served, I used to beg Georgie Auld, Tony Pastor and Chuck Peterson to just let me sit in the bus and rest—and let them bring out something in a sack. Some places they wouldn't even let me eat in the kitchen. Sometimes it was choice between me eating and the whole band starving. I got tired of having a federal case over breakfast, lunch and dinner.

Continual humiliation on this order left both Billie and Ethel, to use their own terminology, salty. Ethel was the stronger character of the two, certainly the more self-reliant. Billie fought, and fought hard, both against society and against the person that society had made of her. But there was something pathetic about the performance. The odds against her were too great.

Lena Horne came to know her well in New York in the early 1940s, when Billie was working at Kelly's Stable and Lena at Café Society Downtown, and as she remembered her in *Lena*:

> Her life was so tragic and so corrupted by other people—by white people and by her own people. There was no place for her to go, except, finally, into that little private world of dope. She

was just too sensitive to survive. And such a gentle person. We never talked much about singing. The thing I remember talking to her about most was her dogs; her animals were really her only trusted friends.

Small wonder that she was, as an admiring white singer once said of her to me, "a hard one to get through to."

Her career and Ethel Waters', after Harlem, differed considerably and significantly. Their respective ages had something to do with it. Ethel, twenty years older than Billie, was early enough on the scene to make a career in both black and white vaudeville, a preparation that revealed the talent and established the professional accomplishments for her subsequent triumphs as an actress in *Mamba's Daughters* and *The Member of the Wedding*.

Ethel was, in any case, far more a woman of the theater than Lady Day, not only in terms of experience, but also in terms of disposition and predilection, and it showed in her singing. In just about every song that Ethel Waters ever sang she projected a character. Hers was, indeed, an art of characterization, whether she was playing a part or singing a song. Billie Holiday never projected anybody but Billie. This was reflected even in her stage deportment. She had no routine. As Martin Williams remembered her in an article for *Jazz Journal*, "Billie Holiday—Actress Without an Act," "she came out, sang, bowed and left—no vaudeville showmanship."

The article is misleading only in the title. It might better have been called "An Act Without an Actress." But it wasn't even an act—discounting the white dress, the white gardenia and, as she ruefully appended to her own description of her stage appearance, the white junk. It was just Lady Day, who was Billie Holiday. Her way with a song was to take it apart and put it together again in her own image.

Even the image would change with the circumstances of the moment and according to her mood and passing fancy. "I hate straight singing," she used to say. "I have to change a tune to my way of doing it. That's all I know." Her way of doing it changed, too: "I can't stand to sing the same song the same way two nights in succession, let alone two years or ten years. If you can, then it ain't music; it's close-order drill, or exercise, or yodeling or something, not music."

There were other reasons why she changed the music. She had to fit a song not only to herself, to her state of mind and body, and to an extraordinarily acute sense of style, but also to a meager voice—small, hoarse at the bottom and thinly shrill at the top, with top and bottom never very far apart. She had hardly more than an octave and a third. She worked, as a rule, as Bessie Smith had worked, within an octave, tailoring the melody to fit the congenial span.

Given these physical limitations, what she achieved in terms of color, shadings, nuances and articulation, and in terms of the variety of sound and inflection she could summon from such slender resources, may be counted among the wonders of vocal history. She did it by moving, with somnambulistic security, along—or back and forth across—the thin, never precisely definable, line separating, or joining, speech and song.

This accomplishment, or ambiguity, has always been characteristic of the greatest blues singers. In this respect, Billie Holiday was a child of Bessie Smith, although she rarely sang a traditional blues. Her 1936 recording of "Billie's Blues" gives us a glimpse of what a blues singer she might have been had she chosen to be one.

Playing back to back the records made by Ethel Waters and Billie Holiday at about the same time in the early 1930s, one notes how much closer Ethel Waters was to Broadway. She was more versatile, more professional and, stylistically, whiter. Ethel was of a generation of black vaudeville and recording artists greatly influenced by the white headliners of the time—Nora Bayes, Ruth Etting, Al Jolson and Sophie Tucker. Played today, her records sound a bit dated. They are certainly easy to date.

In those years, Billie Holiday, then in her late teens and early twenties, seemed untouched by Broadway and show biz. She probably was. The only vocal models she ever acknowledged were Bessie Smith and Louis Armstrong. As a child in an East Baltimore slum, she had run errands for a whorehouse madam just to be allowed to sit in the front parlor and listen to Louis and Bessie on the Victrola. "Unless it was the records of Bessie Smith and Louis Armstrong I heard as a kid," she recalled later, "I don't know anybody who actually influenced my singing, then or now. I always wanted Bessie's big sound and Pops' feeling." Lady Day was probably entitled to say, as she did, that "before anybody could compare me with other singers, they were comparing other singers with me."

Bessie's big sound she never had, nor do her records suggest that she tried for it. She may have belted a bit in the very early days, working without a mike in Harlem clubs. But hers was not a voice that would have responded generously or amiably to the kind of treatment that Bessie's voice rewarded with that big sound. On records and on mike in clubs, Billie's breath was wonderfully light on the vocal cords, which is why a voice neither rich in texture nor ample in size could be so eloquently tender. This lightness of the breath on the cords also contributed to immaculate enunciation, as it has with subsequent singers, notably Nat Cole, Ella Fitzgerald, Peggy Lee and Frank Sinatra.

Louis' feeling she had, and then some, although one wonders what precisely she meant by "Pops' feeling." It can hardly have been feeling in an emotional sense, for Louis' involvement with any song was always more a matter of exuberant and affectionate virtuosity than of personal commitment. She may have meant his feeling for words and phrases, and his way of shaping, or reshaping, a song to suit his own musicality. In this she equaled and may even have surpassed the master.

Louis can be heard in just about every phrase Billie ever sang. His example is conspicuous in her way of wrapping a sound around a word or syllable, enveloping it, so to speak, in an *appoggiatura*, a slur, a mordent or a turn, in her habit of widening the vibrato during the life of a sustained tone. But what was musical fun and games to Louis Armstrong, who lived the better part of his seventy years at peace with the world, was life in the raw to Billie Holiday. What you had when she finished with a song was not just invention tempered by superb craftsmanship, although there was plenty of each, but untempered autobiography.

Lady Sings the Blues, when it appeared in 1956, three years before her death, was welcomed as a recital of the facts of her life—or at least some of the facts—but regretted for its failure to reveal much of the woman behind the facts. It did, indeed, fail in this respect. But the failure was inconsequential. Anyone who has heard Billie Holiday sing, in person or on record, "Strange Fruit," "God Bless the Child," "Come Rain or Come Shine," "Don't Explain" or "Prelude to a Kiss" does not need to look for her in a ghostwritten autobiography. "She, of all singers in jazz," wrote Max Jones, "laid herself most bare when she sang; and it was primarily this raw, human quality, communicated through her voice and her technique, which troubled the hearts and minds of her listeners."

What little voice Billie ever had deteriorated toward the end of her life. In her progress along the dividing line between speech and sustained melody she wandered more often, and ever farther, in the direction of speech. She also tended to wander farther and farther from pitch. She favored ever slower tempi. She was always a languorous singer except in out-and-out up-tempo songs, in which she could achieve and sustain astonishing speeds. Listening to the records she made in the mid-1950s, I am always reminded of George Bernard Shaw's description of Lady Hallé, in London, setting a tempo for the first movement of the Beethoven Septet "at about two-thirds of the lowest speed needed to sustain life." Lady Hallé's tempo may have been prompted by either conviction or discretion. Billie's tempi, on some occasions, at least, were probably dictated by vocal insecurity. But generally they would seem to have been determined by her life-long love affair with words.

She herself preferred her later records to the earlier ones, and not without reason. She had learned a lot, both about life and about her own singing. She was more resourceful. Her ornamentation was richer and more varied. The voice, formerly weak at the bottom, now had lovely dark tones down to the low G and F and even below.

"Anybody who knows anything about singing," she wrote at that time, "says I'm for sure singing better than I ever have in my life. If you don't think so, just listen to some of my old sides like 'Lover Come Back' and 'Yesterdays,' and then listen to the same tunes as I have recorded them in recent years. Listen, and trust your own ears."

She was probably right. But speaking for myself, and probably for others, I find that the earlier records have an imperishable charm, especially those she made with Teddy Wilson and a number of upcoming studio sidemen at the very beginning of her recording career. While she had not then the artistic accomplishment of a later time, the raw material was there, and the genius too, a spontaneous, original, fearless and irresistible way with voice and song.

There was something special about the backings, too, both in those early recordings and in those of a few years later, after she had established her association with the Count Basie band in 1937. Her work with the Basie men remained the happiest memory of her recording career, and her recollection of it offers a delightful and fascinating insight into how records were made in those days:

> Most of my experience with bands before then had been in hanging out with Benny Goodman. I used to listen to him rehearse with high-paid radio studio bands and his own groups. He always had big arrangements. He would spend a fortune on arrangements for a little dog-assed vocalist. But with Basie we had something no expensive arrangements could touch. The cats would come in, somebody would hum a tune. Then someone else would play it over on the piano once or twice. Then someone would set up a riff, a ba-deep, a ba-dop. Then Daddy Basie would two finger it a little. And then things would start to happen.
>
> Half the cats couldn't have read music if they'd had it. They didn't want to be bothered anyway. Maybe sometimes one cat would bring in a written arrangement, and the others would run over it. But by the time Jack Wadlin, Skeet Henderson, Buck Clayton, Freddie Green and Basie were through running over it, taking off, changing it, the arrangement wouldn't be recognizable anyway.
>
> I know that's the way we worked out "Love of My Life" and "Them There Eyes" for me. Everything that happened, happened by ear. For the two years I was with the band we had a book of a hundred songs, and everyone of us carried every last damn note of them in our heads.

Billie herself could not read music. Her art might have survived literacy. But it would have gained nothing from it. What she heard in her mind's ear and translated into vocal utterance had nothing to do with the notes on a printed page. Nor has it come down to us in any printed form. Even her records account for only a part of her musical estate. Hear it from one whose art has been an embodiment of her legacy:

> With few exceptions [wrote Frank Sinatra in an article for *Ebony*] every major pop singer in the United States during her generation has been touched in some way by her genius. It is Billie Holiday, whom I first heard in 52nd Street clubs in the

early 30s, who was, and still remains, the greatest single musical influence on me.

He had not changed his mind fifteen years later. An album released just after the announcement of his retirement in the spring of 1971, and recorded in October of 1970, includes a song called "Lady Day"—a tribute to Billie Holiday.

She would have been pleased.

9

Ella Fitzgerald

Gerald Moore, the English accompanist, tells about the time Dietrich Fischer-Dieskau, following a matinee recital Moore and the German Lieder singer had given together in Washington, D.C., rushed to the National Airport and took the first plane to New York in order to hear Duke Ellington and Ella Fitzgerald at Carnegie Hall.

"Ella and the Duke together!" Fischer-Dieskau exclaimed to Moore. "One just doesn't know when there might be a chance to hear that again!"

The story is illustrative of the unique position that both Ella Fitzgerald and Duke Ellington occupy in the musical history of our century. More than any other artists working in the Afro-American idiom, they have caught the attention and excited the admiration of that other world of European classical, or serious, music.

Ella's achievement, in purely musical terms, is the more remarkable of the two, if only because she has never ventured into the no-man's-land of semiclassical or third-stream music separating the two idioms. Duke Ellington is a familiar figure on the stage at symphony concerts, as both pianist and composer, in his jazz-flavored symphonic suites. Ella has ranged widely between the ill-defined areas known as "jazz" and "popular," but not into classical, although she has sung

the songs of the great American songwriters—Arlen, Gershwin, Porter, Rodgers, for example—with symphony orchestras. Many classical singers, however, like Fischer-Dieskau, are among her most appreciative admirers.

Unchallenged preeminence in her own field has had something to do with it, along with consistent performance throughout a career that has already extended over nearly forty years. Although she has never been, in her private life, a maker of headlines, her honors have been so many that word of them has filtered through to many who never saw a copy of *Billboard* or *Down Beat* and never will.

To enumerate those honors would be tedious. Suffice it to say, citing the entry under her name in Leonard Feather's *New Encyclopedia of Jazz*, that, between 1953 and 1960 alone, she was placed first in *Metronome*, *Down Beat* and *Playboy* polls in either the "jazz singer" or "popular singer" categories, or both, no fewer than twenty-four times. She had been a poll winner long before that—she won the *Esquire* Gold Award in 1946—and she is heading the polls in both categories to this day.

With Frank Sinatra and Peggy Lee, she shares the distinction of having achieved a nearly universal popularity and esteem without sacrificing those aspects of her vocal and musical art that so endear her to fellow professionals and to the most fastidious of critics and lay listeners. Not even Frank and Peggy are admired so unanimously. The refinements of their art often fall on unappreciative or hostile ears. But with Ella, the exclamation "She's the greatest!" runs like a refrain through everything one reads or hears about her. One is as likely to hear it from an opera singer as from Bing Crosby ("Man, woman and child, Ella Fitzgerald is the greatest!").

Of what does her greatness consist? What does she have that other excellent singers do not have? The virtues are both obvious and conspicuous, and there is general agreement about them. She has a lovely voice, one of the warmest and most radiant in its natural range that I have heard in a lifetime of listening to singers in every category. She has an impeccable and ultimately sophisticated rhythmic sense, and flawless intonation. Her harmonic sensibility is extraordinary. She is endlessly inventive. Her melodic deviations and embellishments are as varied as they are invariably appropriate. And she is versatile, moving easily from up-tempo scatting on such songs

◀ Ella with Frank Sinatra

as "Flying Home," "How High the Moon?" and "Lady Be Good" to the simplest ballad gently intoned over a cushion of strings.

One could attribute any one, or even several, of these talents and attainments to other singers. Ella has them all. She has them in greater degree. She knows better than any other singer how to use them. What distinguishes her most decisively from her singing contemporaries, however, is less tangible. It has to do with style and taste. Listening to her—and I have heard her in person more often than any other singer under discussion in these pages—I sometimes find myself thinking that it is not so much what she does, or even the way she does it, as what she does not do. What she does not do, putting it as simply as possible, is anything wrong. There is simply nothing in her performance to which one would want to take exception. What she sings has that suggestion of inevitability that is always a hallmark of great art. Everything seems to be just right. One would not want it any other way. Nor can one, for the moment, imagine it any other way.

For all the recognition and adulation that has come her way, however, Ella Fitzgerald remains, I think, an imperfectly understood singer, especially as concerns her vocalism. The general assumption seems to be that it is perfect. That she has sung in public for so many years—and still, when on tour, may do two sixty-minute sets six or seven nights a week—with so little evidence of vocal wear and tear would seem to support that assumption. Her vocalism is, in fact, as I hear it, less than perfect. "Ingenious" and "resourceful" would be more appropriate adjectives.

She has, as many great singers in every category have had, limitations of both endowment and technique. But, also like other great singers, she has devised ways of her own to disguise them, to get around them, or even to turn them into apparent assets. Ella's vocal problems have been concentrated in that area of the range already identified in the case of earlier singers as the "passage." She has never solved them. She has survived them and surmounted them.

She commands, in public performance and on record, an extraordinary range of two octaves and a sixth, from the low D or D flat to the high B flat and possibly higher. This is a greater range, especially at the bottom, than is required or expected of most opera singers. But there is a catch to it. Opera singers, as they approach the "passage," depress the larynx and open the throat—somewhat as in yawning—and, focusing the tone in the head, soar on upward. The best of them master the knack of preserving, as they enter the upper register, the natural color and timbre of the normal middle register, bringing to the upper notes a far greater weight of voice than Ella Fitzgerald does. Even the floated *pianissimo* head tones of, say, a Montserrat Caballé should not be confused with the tones that Ella produces at the upper extremes of her range.

Ella does not depress the larynx, or "cover," as she reaches the "passage." She either eases off, conceding in weight of breath and muscular control what a recalcitrant vocal apparatus will not accommodate, or she brazens through it, accepting the all too evident muscular strain. From this she is released as she emerges upward into a free-floating falsetto. She does not, in other words, so much pass from one register into another as from one voice into another. As Roberta Flack has noted perceptively: "Ella doesn't shift gears. She goes from lower to higher register, the same all the way through."

The strain audible when Ella is singing in the "passage" contributes to a sense of extraordinary altitude when she continues upward. In this she reminds me of some opera tenors who appear to be in trouble—and often are—in their "passage" (at about F, F sharp and G) and achieve the greater impression of physical conquest when they go on up to an easy, sovereign B flat. The listener experiences anxiety, tension, suspense, relief and amazement. It is not good singing by the canons of *bel canto*, which reckon any evidence of strain deplorable. But it is exciting, and in the performance of a dramatic or athletic aria, effective.

Both this sense of strain in that critical area of Ella's voice, and the striking contrast of the free sound above the "passage" may help to explain why so many accounts of her singing refer to notes "incredibly high." Sometimes they are. The high A flat, A and B flat, even in falsetto, must be regarded as exceptional in a singer who also descends to the low D. But more often than not they sound higher than they are. Time and again, while checking out Ella's range on records, I have heard what I took to be a high G or A flat, only to go to the piano and find that it was no higher than an E or an F. What is so deceptive about her voice above the "passage" is that the *sound* is high, with a thin, girlish quality conspicuously different from the rich, viola-like splendor of her middle range. It is not so much the contrast with the pitches that have gone before as the contrast with the sound that has gone before.

In purely vocal-technical terms, then, what distinguishes Ella from her operatic sisters is her use of falsetto; what distinguishes her from most of her popular-singer sisters is her mastery of it. One may hear examples of its undisciplined use in public performance and on records today in the singing of many women, especially in the folk-music field. With most of them the tone tends to become thin, tenuous, quavery and erratic in intonation as they venture beyond their natural range. They have not mastered falsetto. Ella has. So has Sarah Vaughan. So has Ella and Sarah's admirable virtuoso English counterpart, Cleo Laine.

The "girlish" sound of the female falsetto may offer a clue to its cultivation by Ella Fitzgerald, and to some fundamental character-istics of her vocal art. It is, for her, a compatible sound, happily attuned to her nature and to the circumstances of her career. She entered professional life while still a girl. Her first hit record, "A-Tisket A-Tasket," was the song of a little girl who had lost her yellow basket. The girl of the song must have been a congenial object of identification for a young singer, born in Newport News, Virginia, who spent her childhood first in an orphanage, later with an aunt in Yonkers, New York, who drifted as a young dancer into Harlem clubs, and who fell into a singing career in an amateur contest at the Harlem Opera House when she was too scared to dance.

"It was a dare from some girl friends," she recalls today. "They bet me I wouldn't go on. I got up there and got cold feet. I was going to dance. The man said since I was up there I had better do some-thing. So I tried to sing like Connee Boswell—'The Object of My Affection.' "

According to all the jazz lexicons, Ella was born on April 25, 1918, and entered that Harlem Opera House competition, which she won, in 1934, when she would have been sixteen. She became vocalist with the Chick Webb band the following year, was adopted by the Webb family and, following Chick's death in 1939, carried on as leader of the band until 1942. She would then have been all of twenty-four, with ten years of professional experience behind her.

According to Norman Granz, who has been her manager throughout the greater part of her career, she was younger than that.

Granz says that she was born in 1920 and had to represent herself as older, when she first turned up in Harlem, to evade the child-labor laws. She was adopted by the Webbs because a parental consent was a legal prerequisite for employment.

It should hardly be surprising, then, that her voice, when she began with the Chick Webb band, and as it can be heard now on her early records, was that of a little girl. She was only fourteen. She was a precocious little girl, to be sure, and probably matured early, as other black entertainers did—Ethel Waters and Billie Holiday, for example—who grew up in the tough clubs and dance halls of Harlem while other girls were still in secondary school. What mattered with Ella, however, and affected her subsequent career, was that the little girl could also sound like a young woman—and was irresistible.

The sound worked, and so did the little girl. Ella has never entirely discarded either the girl or the sound. She was, and has remained, a shy, retiring, rather insecure person. To this day when, as a woman of matronly appearance and generous proportions, she addresses an audience, it is always in a tone of voice, and with a manner of speech, suggesting the delighted surprise, and the humility, too, of a child performer whose efforts have been applauded beyond her reasonable expectations.

Nor has Ella ever forsaken her roots in jazz. George T. Simon, in *The Big Bands*, remembers watching her at the Savoy Ballroom in Harlem when she was with Chick Webb:

> When she wasn't singing, she would usually stand at the side of the band, and, as the various sections blew their ensemble phrases, she'd be up there singing along with all of them, often gesturing with her hands as though she were leading the band.

The fruits of such early enthusiasm and practice may be heard today in Ella's appearances with the bands of Count Basie and Duke Ellington, when one or more instrumental soloists step forward to join her in a round of "taking fours," with Ella's voice assuming the character and color of a variety of instruments as she plunges exuberantly into chorus after chorus of syllabic improvisation (scatting).

Ella owes at least some of her virtuosity in this type of display, or at least the opportunity to develop and exploit it, to Norman Granz and her many years' association with his Jazz at the Philharmonic tours. Benny Green, the English jazz critic, thus describes the importance of this association to the shaping of Ella Fitzgerald's art and career:

> When Ella first began appearing as a vocal guest on what were, after all, the primarily instrumental jazz recitals of Norman Granz, it might have seemed at the time like imaginative commercial programming and nothing more. In fact, as time was to prove, it turned out to be the most memorable manager-artist partnership of the post-war years, one which quite dramatically changed the shape and direction of Ella's career. Granz used Ella, not as a vocal cherry stuck on top of an iced cake of jazz, but as an artist integrated thoroughly into the jam session context of the performance. When given a jazz background, Ella was able to exhibit much more freely her gifts as an instrumental-type improvisor.

Elsewhere, reviewing an appearance by Ella with the Basie band in London in 1971, Green has described as vividly and succinctly as possible the phenomenon of Ella working in an instrumental jazz context:

> The effect on Ella is to galvanize her into activity so violent that the more subtle nuances of the song readings are swept away in a riot of vocal improvisation which, because it casts lyrics to the winds, is the diametric opposite of her other, lullaby, self. And while it is true that for a singer to mistake herself for a trumpet is a disastrous course of action, it has to be admitted that Ella's way with a chord sequence, her ability to coin her own melodic phrases, her sense of time, the speed with which her ear perceives harmonic changes, turn her Basie concerts into tightrope exhibitions of the most dazzling kind.

It was her activity with Jazz at the Philharmonic that exposed and exploited the singular duality of Ella Fitzgerald's musical personality. Between 1942, when her career as a band leader came to an end, and 1946, when she joined Granz, she had marked time, so to speak, as an admired but hardly sensational singer of popular songs. With Jazz at the Philharmonic, she was back with jazz.

The timing was right. Bop had arrived, and Ella was with it, incorporating into her vocal improvisations the adventurous harmonic deviations and melodic flights of Dizzy Gillespie and Charlie

Parker. Indeed, according to Barry Ulanov, in his *A History of Jazz in America*, the very term "bop," or "bebop," can be traced to Ella's interpolation of a syllabic invention, "rebop," at the close of her recording of " 'T'ain't What You Do, It's the Way That You Do It" in 1939.

She has cultivated and treasured this duality ever since, and wisely so. Singers who have adhered more or less exclusively to an instrumental style of singing, using the voice, as jazz terminology has it, "like a horn," have won the admiration and homage of jazz musicians and jazz critics, but they have failed to win the enduring and financially rewarding affections of a wider public. Others have stuck to ballads and won the public but failed to achieve the artistic prestige associated with recognition as a jazz singer. Ella, more than any other singer, has had it both ways.

Norman Granz, again, has had a lot to do with it. When Ella's recording contract with Decca expired in 1955, she signed with Granz's Verve label and inaugurated, in that same year, a series of Song Book albums, each devoted to a single songwriter, that took her over a span of twelve years through an enormous repertoire of fine songs, some of them unfamiliar, by Harold Arlen, Irving Berlin, Duke Ellington, George Gershwin, Johnny Mercer, Cole Porter and Richard Rodgers.

These were the first albums to give star billing to individual songwriters, and they served the double purpose of acknowledging and demonstrating the genius of American composers while providing Ella with popular material worthy of her vocal art. "I never knew how good our songs were," Ira Gershwin once said to George T. Simon, "until I heard Ella Fitzgerald sing them."

As a jazz singer Ella has been pretty much in a class by herself, and that in a period rejoicing in many excellent ones, notably Billie Holiday, Peggy Lee, Carmen McRae, Anita O'Day, Jo Stafford, Kay Starr and Sarah Vaughan, not to overlook, in England, Cleo Laine. I am using the term "jazz singer" here in the sense that jazz musicians use it, referring to a singer who works—or can work—in a jazz musician's instrumental style, improvising as a jazz musician improvises. Ella was, of course, building on the techniques first perfected, if not originated, by Louis Armstrong, tailoring and extending his devices according to the new conventions of bop.

There is a good deal of Armstrong in Ella's ballads, too, although none of his idiosyncrasies and eccentricities. What she shared with Louis in a popular ballad was a certain detachment—in her case a kind of classic serenity, or, as Benny Green puts it, a "lullaby" quality—that has rendered her, in the opinion of some of us, less moving than admirable and delightful. In terms of tone quality, variety and richness of vocal color, enunciation, phrasing, rhythm, melodic invention and embellishment, her singing has always been immaculate and impeccable, unequaled, let alone surpassed, by any other singer. But in exposing the heart of a lyric she must take second place, in my assessment, at least, to Frank Sinatra, Billie Holiday, Peggy Lee and Ethel Waters.

This may well be because she has never been one for exposing her own heart in public. She shares with an audience her pleasures, not her troubles. She has not been an autobiographical singer, as Billie and Frank were, nor a character-projecting actress, as Ethel Waters and Peggy Lee have been, which may be why her phrasing, despite exemplary enunciation, has always tended to be more instrumental than oral, less given to the *rubato* devices of singers more closely attuned to the lyrical characteristics of speech.

What she has offered her listeners has been her love of melody, her joy in singing, her delight in public performance and her accomplishments, the latter born of talent and ripened by experience, hard work and relentless self-discipline. Like Louis, she has always seemed to be having a ball. For the listener, when she has finished, the ball is over. It has been a joyous, exhilarating, memorable, but hardly an emotional, experience.

Also, like Louis, she has addressed herself primarily to a white rather than a black public, not because she has in any sense denied her own people, but rather because, in a country where blacks make up only between 10 and 20 percent of the population, white musical tastes and predilections are dominant. They must be accommodated by any black artist aspiring to national and international recognition and acceptance. In more recent years, younger whites have tended to favor a blacker music. A B. B. King has been able to achieve national celebrity where a Bessie Smith, fifty years earlier, could not. When Ella was a girl, what the white majority liked was white music enriched by the more elemental and more inventive musicality of black singers and black instrumentalists.

Ella's singing, aside from the characteristic rhythmic physical

Anita O'Day
Kay Starr

VERVE RECORDS   CAPITOL RECORDS

participation, the finger-popping and hip-swinging, and the obviously congenial scatting, has never been specifically or conspicuously black. It represents rather the happy blend of black and white which had been working its way into the conventions of American popular singing since the turn of the century, and which can be traced in the careers of Al Jolson, Sophie Tucker, Ethel Waters, Mildred Bailey and Bing Crosby.

When Ella was a girl, black singers—those in organized show business, at any rate—were modeling themselves on the white singing stars of the time, and many white singers were modeling themselves on the charmingly imperfect imitation. It is significant that Ella's first model was Connee Boswell. A comparison of the records they both made in the late 1930s shows again how perceptive an ear Ella had from the first. But it is just as significant that Connee Boswell belonged to a generation of jazz-oriented white singers—others were Mildred Bailey and Lee Wiley—who had been listening to Bessie Smith and, above all, to Ethel Waters.

Again like Louis Armstrong, Ella Fitzgerald has achieved that rarest of distinctions: the love and admiration of singers, instrumentalists, critics and the great lay public. But while she may be for the jazzman a musicians' musician, and for the lay public the First Lady of Song, she has always been more than anything else a singers' singer. Jon Hendricks, of Lambert, Hendricks and Ross fame, has put it well, responding to an Ella Fitzgerald record on a *Jazz Journal* blindfold test:

> Well, of course, she's my favorite—she's tops! I just love her. She's Mama! I try and sing my ballads like she does. I was working in a hotel in Chicago, and Johnny Mathis came in to hear me. I had just finished singing a new ballad I was doing at the time, and he came up to me and said, "Jon, you sure love your old Fitzgerald, don't you?"
> "Yes," I replied, "and don't you, too?"
> "We all do!" he said.
> And that's it. Everyone who sings just loves little old Fitzgerald!

10

Frank Sinatra

Frank Sinatra, as of this writing, has given voice to second thoughts about the retirement he announced in the spring of 1971. Not alone among the great singers of his or any other category, he may have found life without at least intermittent communion with an adoring public insupportable. But there can be little doubt that at the time of his announcement he meant it.

That decision, although unexpected, cannot have come as too great a shock to those who noted the kind of song he had favored since his fiftieth birthday, December 12, 1965. Certain titles speak for themselves: "September of My Years," "Cycles," "My Way," etc. They all have an autumnal flavor, especially "My Way," with that sobering line, "The end is near."

Others have sung "My Way," of course. But only with Sinatra does one have the feeling that Paul Anka's song must have been written for him. Anka says that it was. Certainly it strikes the listener—and it must have struck Sinatra, too—as pure autobiography. It's all there: the independent spirit, the high aspirations, the self-assisted disasters, the coups and goofs, the ups and downs, the defiance, the toughness, the arrogance and the breezy assumption that "my way" was somehow, and inevitably, an admirable way.

In Sinatra's case it is pretty hard not to admire that way,

although it has been strewn with words and deeds not always admirable. What remains in the public consciousness, when the marriages and divorces, the brawls, the adolescent antics and posturings of the Clan have been forgotten, is the voice, the rapport with song and audience, and the epic of a young champ who picked himself up off the deck and fought his way back to a nobler and more enduring supremacy than he had enjoyed as the pied piper of the bobby-soxers in the early and middle 1940s.

The face today, and the voice, too, on the late records, reflect the severity and the tensions of the struggle. This makes it difficult, without recourse to the old records and the old photographs and caricatures, to evoke in one's mind's eye, or hear in one's mind's ear, the hollow-cheeked, skinny kid "with jug-handle ears and golf-ball Adam's apple," who, with his light, appealing voice, inspired the term "Swoonatra" and induced in the adolescent female population of America—and not only America—what someone at the time called a "Sinatrance."

Those of us over forty-five remember the hysteria as one of the sociological phenomena of the century. Younger readers have seen it duplicated with the Beatles. Many psychological and sociological explanations were offered to account for it—he filled in for the sweetheart away in the service, he spoke for the adolescent against an uncomprehending adult world, and so on.

There was, I believe, something more fundamental, something that Sinatra and the Beatles had in common. That "something" was a suggestion of wistfulness, of tenderness, of innocence, of helplessness and, most telling in Sinatra's case, of vulnerability. Awaken the mother in young girls, and, given the right sound at the right time, you don't have to be pied to pipe up a few millions—and inspire the envy and hostility of less fortunate males.

The catch is that it does not last. With Frank Sinatra it lasted about five years, a long time for a fad, but not for a career. He started skidding toward the end of 1947. There were a number of contributing factors. His bobby-soxers were growing up. Taste in songs was changing, and new singers were coming along to sing the new songs: Tony Bennett, Perry Como, Vic Damone, Billy Eckstine, Eddie Fisher, Dick Haymes, Dean Martin, Johnnie Ray and Mel Tormé. The old master, Bing Crosby, was, of course, holding his own.

To make matters worse, Frank was having throat trouble. This

Mabel Mercer

was hardly surprising when one learns that in 1946 he had done as many as forty-five shows a week, averaging eighty to one hundred songs a day. At the Copacabana, in the spring of 1950, his voice failed him in the middle of a show and he had to cancel the engagement. As if that were not enough, he was involved with Ava Gardner, and his marriage to his boyhood sweetheart, Nancy Barbato, was on the rocks. By the end of 1952 he was without a movie contract, without a recording contract, and without a management.

The road back, as all the world knows, began with his nonsinging role as Private Maggio in *From Here to Eternity*, which revealed the former singing sailor of such tawdry ephemera as *Ship Ahoy!* and *Anchors Aweigh!* as a fine actor. At about the same time his move from Columbia to Capitol Records wrought the transformation of the swooner into a swinger, or at least a swinging balladeer. The frail, pleading, moonstruck boyfriend was reborn as the confident, easy-riding, hard-driving, irresistible and unchallenged Chairman of the Board, addressing himself to an audience of all ages and both sexes.

It has been said that Sinatra reversed the usual procedure by moving from pop to jazz. But it may be doubted that he changed so much. He had, after all, sung with Harry James from June 1939 until the end of that year, and with Tommy Dorsey from January 1940 until September 1942. His early models were jazz musicians, notably Tommy Dorsey, of whom he has often said: "He taught me everything I know about phrasing." He has also acknowledged the influence of Billie Holiday. According to Tony Bennett, both he and Frank, in the late 1940s and early 1950s, were listening carefully to Mabel Mercer, a statement corroborated, as far as Frank is concerned, by Ava Gardner, who once told her publicist, David Hanna, as she played a Mercer record, "I used to hear her every night when I was first married to Frank. He said that, more than anyone, she taught him to handle a lyric."

What changed was not so much the singer as the song and the backing. Toward the end of his contract with Columbia he had complained about the kind of song material he was getting. Some sides he cut at that time with backings by Sy Oliver and Phil Moore suggest that he sensed, even then, the need of livelier, more imaginative, gutsier arrangements than he had been receiving at Columbia from Axel Stordahl.

With the move to Capitol, Stordahl gave way to Nelson Riddle,

Frank Sinatra with Nelson Riddle

Billy May and Gordon Jenkins. Riddle, especially, according to Sinatra's biographer, Arnold Shaw, was "the major architect of the swinging Capitol Sinatra." The languishing strings were not banished, but they were made to fit into a breezier, more buoyant context. On up-tempo numbers the backing was big band. A vocalist who could manage both the melancholy "In the Wee Small Hours" and the exuberant "Anything Goes" was predestined for that moment in American musical history when swing left the dance floor and moved in behind the singers.

Also new was the fact that Sinatra was now listened to as a singer. During his earlier incarnation people were more concerned with what he was doing to the bobby-soxers than with what he was doing with his voice. As far as singing was concerned he was regarded as a no-voice freak. Even with the earlier crooning styles of Rudy Vallee, Russ Columbo and Bing Crosby fresh in their ears, most listeners found it impossible to take this gentle breathing and sighing, moaning and mooing (as it seemed to them) seriously as singing.

Actually, what was so admirable in Sinatra's singing in the last twenty years of his career can be heard today in his earliest records. Voice and style were not so mature, or so rich in the subtleties and refinements of phrase and enunciation, or in the variety of vocal coloration. The voice itself was lighter, lacking the later dark warmth of the middle and lower registers. The upper notes were sometimes ill-focused. But all the elements that subsequently combined to make him one of the great singers of the century—a seamless legato, an intuitive grasp of phrasing, a feeling for the meaning and music of words, and the warmth and intimacy of the voice itself, conveying a sense of sympathy and sincerity—were present then and can be heard on the records he made with Harry James and Tommy Dorsey.

The one man who, from the very beginning, sensed his true worth and potential was—Frank Sinatra. Harry James, back in 1939, years before anything happened, told a *Down Beat* staffer: "He considers himself the greatest vocalist in the business. Get that! No one ever heard of him. He's never had a hit record. He looks like a wet rag. But he says he's the greatest!"

E. J. Kahn, in a *New Yorker* Profile in 1946, noted:

He regards his voice as an instrument without equal, and although he tries scrupulously to be polite about the possessors of other renowned voices, he is apt—if the name of a competitor comes up abruptly in conversation—to remark: "I can sing that son of a bitch off the stage any day in the week!"

Harry Meyerson, the RCA A&R man who supervised the two sessions in 1942 when Frank recorded "Night and Day," "The Night We Called It a Day," "The Song Is You" and "The Lamplighter's Serenade" with the Dorsey band, recalls:

> Frank was not like a band vocalist at all. He came in self-assured, slugging. He knew exactly what he wanted. Most singers tend to begin with the humble bit. At first they're licking your hand. Then, the moment they catch a big one, you can't get them on the phone. Popularity didn't really change Sinatra. On that first date he stood his ground and displayed no humility, phoney or real.

Musicians were quicker than others to sense the musical genius behind the charisma. Jo Stafford, for instance, who was with Dorsey as lead singer of the Pied Pipers (little knowing that her new colleague would shortly be the greatest pied piper of them all), remembers his first appearance with the band: "As Frank came up to the mike, I just thought, Hmmm—kinda thin. But by the end of eight bars I was thinking, This is the greatest sound I've ever heard. But he had more. Call it talent. You knew he couldn't do a number badly."

John Garvey, now on the faculty of the University of Illinois, and director of the university's famous jazz band, was playing violin with the Jan Savitt orchestra in Pittsburgh in 1943 when Sinatra did some dates with them.

> The musicians were skeptical [he recalls] until one day, at rehearsal, Sinatra and the orchestra were handed a new song. Sinatra just stood there with the lead sheet in one hand, the other hand cupping his ear, following along silently while the orchestra read through the Stordahl chart. A second time through he sang in half voice. The third time through he took over. We all knew then that we had an extraordinary intuitive musician on our hands.

What stumped the less perceptive, and encouraged them to dismiss Sinatra as a singer, was, paradoxically, just those characteristics in his singing that brought him closer to the art of the classical singer than any other popular vocalist had ever come. What un-sophisticated listeners, brought up on Rudy Vallee and Bing Crosby, heard as "mooing" was, in fact, the long line, the seamless legato, of *bel canto*. Frank knew it.

> When I started singing in the mid-1930's [he wrote in an ar-ticle, "Me and My Music" for *Life* in 1965] everybody was trying to copy the Crosby style—the casual kind of raspy sound in the throat. Bing was on top, and a bunch of us—Dick Todd, Bob Eberly, Perry Como and Dean Martin—were trying to break in. It occurred to me that maybe the world didn't need *another* Crosby. I decided to experiment a little and come up with some-thing different. What I finally hit on was more the *bel canto* Italian school of singing, without making a point of it. That meant I had to stay in better shape because I had to sing more. It was more difficult than Crosby's style, much more difficult.

Frank was actually working closer to *bel canto* than he knew, or than has been generally acknowledged by others to this day. Consider the following:

> Let him take care that the higher the notes, the more neces-sary it is to touch them with softness, to avoid screaming.
> Let him learn the manner to glide with the vowels, and to drag the voice gently from the high to the lower notes.
> Let him take care that the words are uttered in such a manner that they be distinctly understood, and no one syllable lost.
> In repeating the air, he that does not vary it for the better is no great master.
> Whoever does not know how to steal the time in singing [tempo rubato] is destitute of the best taste and knowledge. The stealing of time in the pathetic is an honorable theft in one that sings better than others, provided he makes a restitution with ingenuity.
> Oh! How great a master is the heart!

If Frank Sinatra were ever to conduct master classes for aspiring vocalists, he might well address his students in just such a fashion. Not in those words, to be sure. The language is far from his. But the advice to singers, and the admonitions, recouched in his own North Jersey American, might stand as a tidy summation of the fundamental principles, the distinguishing characteristics, and even the specific devices of his own vocal art.

It is the more remarkable, therefore, and certainly the more significant, that the counsel set forth above, so pertinent to and so admirably exampled in the art of this utterly twentieth-century and utterly American man, should have been offered by Pier Francesco Tosi, of the Philharmonic Society of Bologna, in *Observations on the Florid Song*, first published in Bologna in 1723.

Nor does Tosi's counsel cover everything in Sinatra's singing that looked back to *bel canto*. Frank was a master of *appoggiatura*, knowing not only when and how to use it, but also when *not* to use it. He employed the slur and *portamento* (sometimes referred to as *glissando* in critical assessments of his singing) with exemplary propriety. His melodic deviations were rarely extravagant, but they were always tasteful. And he was extraordinarily inventive in devising codas (tails) for his songs—"One For My Baby" and "How About You?" for example.

Frank was not the first popular singer to be guided unwittingly by the objectives and criteria of *bel canto* as codified by Tosi. Others before him had worked intuitively toward a kind of singing closer to the rhetorical objectives of early Italian opera, and Frank could profit by their example. His accomplishment was to unite the rhetorical with the melodic, much as Italian singers of the seventeenth century had done as they progressed from the *recitativo*, *parlando* and *arioso* procedures of Caccini and Monteverdi to the more sustained, mellifluous manner of singing represented by the term *bel canto*.

Sinatra, in other words, was neither pioneer nor radical. He was simply a musical genius who arrived at a moment predestined for that genius. The ground had been prepared for him as a singer by Al Jolson, Bessie Smith, Ethel Waters, Louis Armstrong, Billie Holiday and—Bing Crosby. In reviewing his own work, Sinatra has always singled out Tommy Dorsey and Billie Holiday as his principal influences. They were, undoubtedly, his principal *immediate* influences. But any appreciation of his style must take into account the earlier singers—and instrumentalists—who influenced *them*. Billie Holiday went back to Bessie Smith and Louis Armstrong. Tommy Dorsey looked back to Jack Teagarden, Jimmy Harrison and Charlie Green.

Perry Como   Eddie Fisher   Mel Tormé

Frank may have overlooked, or, as is more likely, he may have been unaware of, how much he owed to Bing Crosby, although he has acknowledged that Bing was his boyhood idol and that Bing's picture was hung in his room at home. He has been perceptive in identifying what distinguished his own vocal art from Crosby's. He *sang* more. He sustained more. He achieved a wider dynamic range, and within that range he found a greater variety of shading, color and nuance. But he and Bing had much in common—the intimate way with song and listener and the mastery and exploitation of the microphone as a means of establishing and maintaining that intimacy. It may well be, of course, that by the time Sinatra came along, what Crosby—and Rudy Vallee and Russ Columbo—had minted was common currency. In 1940 a young singer could easily be forgiven for taking it all for granted. This was the singer's world he had grown up in. He had never known any other.

Bing says of himself, "I'm not a singer; I'm a phraser." Sinatra has certainly been a phraser, too. He inherited, or shared, Bing's affection for words, and he mastered more completely than Bing the art of projecting a text in four- or eight-measure arches, grouping words or syllables without being bound precisely by the time values of the individual notes to which they are attached, or, as he once put it, "talking words expressively to a background of music."

But he also had an Italian's delight in voice and in vocal line. It was this Italian predilection, probably, that drew him to Tommy Dorsey and, curiously, to Jascha Heifetz. Sinatra's own account, in his article for *Life*, of what he learned from Dorsey and Heifetz, and how, tells a great deal about his approach to singing. It should be required reading for all who think, as most classical musicians and critics do, that the good popular singer is just a guy or gal who stands up there in front of the microphone and makes with the pipes.

The thing that influenced me most [he wrote] was the way Tommy played his trombone. He would take a musical phrase and play it all the way through without breathing, for eight, ten, maybe sixteen bars. How in the hell did he do it? Why couldn't a singer do that, too? Fascinated, I began listening to other soloists. I bought every Jascha Heifetz record I could find, and listened to him play the violin hour after hour. His constant bowing, where you never heard a break, carried the melody line straight on through, just like Dorsey's trombone. It was my idea to make my voice work in the same way as a trombone or violin—not sounding like them, but "playing" the voice like those instruments. . . .

The first thing I needed was extraordinary breath control, which I didn't have. I began swimming every chance I got in public pools—taking laps under water and thinking song lyrics to myself as I swam, holding my breath. I worked out on the track at the Stevens Institute in Hoboken, running one lap, trotting the next. Pretty soon I had good breath control, but that still wasn't the whole answer. I still had to learn to sneak a breath without being too obvious.

Instead of singing only two bars or four bars of music at a time—like most of the others guys around—I was able to sing six bars and, in some songs, eight bars without taking a visible or audible breath. This gave the melody a flowing, unbroken quality, and that—if anything—was what made me sound different. It wasn't the voice alone; in fact, my voice was always a little too high, I thought, and not as good in natural quality as some of the competition.

Although Sinatra has never, to my knowledge, expressed himself on the subject, it has often occurred to me in listening to him that he may have picked up from Dorsey, and possibly from Heifetz, too, more than just the long, flowing, seamless phrase. Both trombone and violin are instruments of unfixed pitch. The trombone, particularly, invites or at least permits an ambiguity of intonation that has often been characteristic of Sinatra's phrasing. This ambiguity or flexibility or variability had been attractive to black musicians in the earliest days of New Orleans jazz, probably as a means of escape from the fixed pitches of the European major and minor modes. It made it possible for them to phrase in a manner closer to speech.

As used by Dorsey, and before him by Jack Teagarden, it could also be used to create suspense. While a note might not be, strictly speaking, out of tune, it could be just far enough off center for the listener to feel its resolution to be imperative, and to experience a sense of relief and satisfaction when it was resolved. It is a familiar device of gypsy fiddle players, who tend to use it too obviously. Sinatra, characteristically, has used it more subtly. The variance from true pitch is microtonal, and, because it is so slight, the average listener may be unaware of any variance at all. But he reacts to it. It may be worth noting that Nelson Riddle, the most consistently congenial of Sinatra's conductor-arrangers, began his musical career as a trombonist.

Where Sinatra, after Bing Crosby, was most original—and it had a great deal to do with the shaping of his mature style—was in his use of the microphone. It was his constant companion. Even as a young singer doing obscure and ill-paid club dates in his native North New Jersey, he carried his own sound system with him. One remembers him from his earliest photos, "the hands tightly gripping the microphone," as E. J. Kahn noted, "as if too frail to stand alone." Frank did not need the mike to hold him up. He may not even have needed it in order to make himself heard. To him it was, or became, an instrument on which he played as an instrumentalist plays a saxophone, or a trombone—in other words, an electronic extension of his own vocal instrument.

That, at least, is the way he thought of it. I have heard Tony Bennett speak of it in the same way. As Frank and Tony saw it, where Bing Crosby had seemed to be *overheard* by the microphone, they played, or sang, on it, developing great skill in moving toward it, or away from it, learning to turn away when snatching a breath, avoiding popping consonants, and so on. With the development of the hand mike with lead wire, they could make the mike do the moving and use it more effectively than ever.

I know that they, and doubtless other singers, think of the mike as an instrument. They may be deceiving themselves. I tend to think that the mike, because it hears more acutely than the unassisted ear, simply revealed to them more of their own vocal instrument than had ever been revealed to singers before. The mike picks up otherwise unheard minutiae of the sounds made by the passage of breath over the vocal cords. A singer as sensitive to timbre as Sinatra is hears them, knows instinctively what to do with them, and learns to create and control them. It may not, in other words, be so much a matter of "playing" upon the mike as of being guided by the mike's "ear," of learning to hear as the mike hears, and of producing the voice and shaping the phrase accordingly.

This would help to explain some singularities in Sinatra's vocalism. He never had any formal training and never wanted any, just as he never learned to read music or wanted to. He knew from the beginning that he had something unique to offer. He didn't want to jeopardize that something by conventional schooling. He was probably right. As a vocalist, too, he "did it his way."

Outstanding about that way was the lightness of the breath on the vocal cords, which contributed to a markedly "forward" production, to his exemplary enunciation, and probably to a vocal longevity astonishing in a singer who, by his own admission, drank too much, smoked too much and slept too little. What was most singular in Sinatra's vocalism, however, was his handling of the tricky "passage" from the middle to the higher register, in his voice the pitches C sharp, D and E flat.

The voice itself was a typical Italian light baritone with a two-octave range from G to G, declining, as it darkened in later years, to F to F, and with greater potential at the top than he was commonly disposed to exploit. He could, and sometimes did, depress the larynx and "cover," as classical singers do, to sustain a full, round tone in moving up the scale. On his recording of "Day by Day," for example, he gives out with full-voiced, admirably focused E flats and Fs, and even lands a briefly held but confident high A flat just before the end. His high Fs at the close of "Ol' Man River" were also conventionally and successfully "covered."

But more usually he didn't cover, or covered only partially. He probably wished to avoid any semblance of art or artificiality in the vocal sound, or any suggestion of vocal vainglory. He perceived, if I hear him correctly, that the slight evidence of strain audible when these critical pitches are approached openly and lightly, as picked up and amplified by the mike, suggested innocence and sincerity, and, in a song of loneliness or longing, a sense of pain. The way he sings the D on "if only she would call" in "In the Wee Small Hours" is, as I hear it, a charming example.

The absence of any impression of art was imperative to his style. His accomplishment in avoiding it was the most compelling evidence of his stature as an artist. He was not presenting himself as an artist. He was presenting himself as a person, as Frank Sinatra, the skinny, hollow-cheeked kid from Hoboken, with a lot of hopes, a lot of problems—ethnical, social, physical and sexual—and a lot of frustrations, disappointments and hangups. More than most singers, he has lived the life he sang about.

There are many who have loved and admired Sinatra as a singer but who have been put off by his lurid, widely and wildly publicized personal life—the marriages, divorces and affairs, the Clan, the entourage, the brawls, the gambling, the big-wheeling. His generosity and charity, his loyalty to family and friends, and his genuine concern for the underdog could not obliterate the image of one whose own behavior has too often been both ill-considered and inconsiderate.

But in his case, I am satisfied, there was no separating the art from the artist, despite the fact that in musical matters his performance was always characterized by fastidious taste. A different upbringing or a successful psychoanalysis might have made him a happier man, an easier man to live with and be with. But it would have destroyed what Arnold Shaw has described so aptly as "that constant counterpoint of toughness and tenderness." It would have destroyed him as an artist just as formal musical education would have destroyed him as a musician.

> Being an 18-karat manic depressive, and having lived a life of violent emotional contradictions [Sinatra said in a *Playboy* interview in 1963] I have an overacute capacity for sadness as well as elation. . . . Whatever else has been said about me personally is unimportant. When I sing, I believe, I'm honest. . . . You can be the most artistically perfect performer in the world, but an audience is like a broad—if you're indifferent, Endsville!

It was this sense of a personal relationship between singer and listener that distinguished him from any other singer of his generation. He was superior as a technician, too, and notably original. But other singers could ape his technical accomplishments and innovations, and just about every male popular singer of the past quarter of a century, barring rock singers, has done so. They couldn't duplicate the man. They could not speak to you and of *themselves*, as Sinatra did, simply because they were not Sinatra.

For one who has spent as much time with singers and singing as I have, for one who has thought so much about singing, who has read so much and written so much, it is difficult to preserve a seemly detachment when it comes to Sinatra. I dislike hyperbole and usually manage to avoid it. But with him I cannot restrain myself from saying that I rate him with the greatest singers of my experience, especially with John McCormack and Richard Tauber, and well above any other American popular singer. I have heard most of them and admired many.

Benny Green in a tribute to Sinatra in the London *Observer*, following the announcement of his retirement, summed up Sinatra's position and significance about as explicitly as possible:

> What few people, apart from musicians, have ever seemed to grasp is that he is not simply the best popular singer of his generation, a latter-day Jolson or Crosby, but the culminating point in an evolutionary process which has refined the art of interpreting words set to music. Nor is there even the remotest possibility that he will have a successor. Sinatra was the result of a fusing of a set of historical circumstances which can never be repeated.

Frank was never happier, it has been reported, nor had he, in his own opinion, ever sung better, than in the series of charity concerts he gave in London in May and October of 1970. Single seats were priced at more than $100. Even at that price there was a lively black market for tickets. Guy Roberts, in the *Guardian*, wrote that "the man produced a distillation of excitement, a combination of vocal ingenuity, Schmaltz, insolent self-confidence and sheer theatricality which no other popular singer could match." Remembering a scalper who had offered him $240 for his ticket, he concluded, "That tout really had no chance. Some things money can't buy."

Not even such perceptions, however, get to the core of the matter. A letter from Mrs. Edna Haber, 8 Alverstone Road, Willesden, London N.W. 2, to the London *Evening Standard* did:

> Sad, sad, sad to learn that the prodigious, phenomenal Frank Sinatra has called a halt. I was one of those adoring teenagers many years ago, and now, as a grandmother, I feel he is still the greatest. With the announcement of his retirement I begin to realize how quickly the years have passed. The time I had his pictures pinned on my bedroom walls, owned his every record, are the memories of those youthful teenage years which suddenly, today, seem a little more distant. Never can there be another Frank Sinatra. My collection of his records is even more treasured now. Thanks, Frank, for wonderful memories and the pleasure you have given me until this day.

Old Pier Francesco Tosi knew what he was talking about: *Oh! How great a master is the heart!*

11

Mahalia Jackson

The one other great American singer who comes instantly to one's mind when listening to the records of Mahalia Jackson, the Gospel Queen, in her prime is Bessie Smith, the Empress of the Blues.

It seems paradoxical. Mahalia never sang the blues. To the black congregations for whom she sang in the formative years of her professional life, the blues were synonymous with sin. A gospel singer who sang them did so at her own risk, as Sister Rosetta Tharpe learned to her sorrow.

Many students of Mahalia's singing have expressed the opinion that she could have been a great blues singer had she chosen to sing the blues. I doubt it. The blues were inimical not to her voice, but to her nature. "Blues are the songs of despair," she used to say. "Gospel songs are the songs of hope. When you sing gospel you have a feeling there's a cure for what's wrong. When you're through with the blues you've got nothing to rest on."

Nor did Mahalia take gospel music into theaters and nightclubs as younger gospel singers have done. She would not even take herself into a theater or a motion-picture house as a member of the audience, let alone a nightclub. Her nearest brush with the theater occurred in 1938, when she tried out for the Federal Theater Project production

199

of *The Mikado* (which inspired Mike Todd's *The Hot Mikado*), singing "Sometimes I Feel Like a Motherless Child." According to her own account in her autobiography, *Movin' On Up*, she won, but her husband got a job the same day, and that was that. She could put the devil behind her. According to Tony Heilbut, in *The Gospel Sound*, "she quit in mid-audition, swept by guilt."

But the juxtaposition of Mahalia and Bessie is not so paradoxical as it must seem. It would have been paradoxical had Mahalia been Bessie's contemporary. Until close to the end of Bessie's career and life, the music of the black churches had little in common with the blues, least of all that of the Baptist church, which was Mahalia's denomination. Beginning in the early 1930s, however, a blues beat became a prominent and attractive element of black church music. The singer primarily responsible for putting it there was Mahalia.

Her inspirational sources were Bessie Smith and the Holiness Church next door to her own Mount Moriah Baptist Church in the neighborhood between the railroad tracks and the river in New Orleans. She was born in that city in 1911, daughter of a stevedore who moonlighted as a barber and preached on Sundays. There was show-business blood in the family. Two cousins, Jeanette Jackson and her husband, Josie Burnette, toured with Ma Rainey. But her mother, who died when Mahalia was five, would have no truck with the blues, still less her Aunt Duke, who took charge after Mahalia's mother's death.

Another cousin brought her jazz and blues records. Mahalia listened to them while Aunt Duke was away cooking for her white employers. Thus she was nurtured, musically, on Bessie Smith, Mamie Smith and Ma Rainey. "Bessie was my favorite," she remembered, "but I never let people know I listened to her. Mamie Smith had a prettier voice, but Bessie's had more soul in it. She dug right down and kept it in you. Her music haunted you even when she stopped singing." Much the same would be said of Mahalia in her prime.

Her singing always had a lot in common with Bessie's. They had, to begin with, similar voices—big, rich, full-bodied, full-throated contraltos, strengthened and ripened in public places before the days of electronic amplification. Both were belters, or, in their own jargon, shouters, never happier than when pouring it on and out, the breath heavy on the vocal cords, extracting every decibel of chest and head resonance. Mahalia was the more resourceful in achieving contrast by a sudden lightening of the breath, probably because she churned up greater rhythmic propulsion and momentum than Bessie did. Contrast, with Mahalia, was the more easily achieved, and the more effective, because it could be introduced suddenly, in full career, so to speak, when the listener least expected it.

Both were limited in range, or never learned to extend their vocal compass beyond what came naturally. Their ranges were about the same—an octave and a fourth, from the A below to the D above, give or take a pitch or two. Within that range each had a richness and eloquence, a warmth and intensity never to be forgotten by those fortunate enough to have heard them in the flesh.

Above all, they were fervent. Mahalia in full cry was ecstatic. Her description of how Bessie "dug right down and kept it in you" is apt, and it aptly describes her own singing. Both women believed in what they sang, or they made the listener think they did, which is what art is all about. They wanted you to believe it, too, which accounted for the sense of intimacy and immediacy they inspired when working before an audience.

Limited range—and fervor, too—probably had much to do with their way with a song. Problems of range could be resolved by melodic compromise and adjustment, and, in Mahalia's case, by recourse to falsetto. But more importantly, no mere melody, no mere text, could contain or convey what they wished to project. They would burst through the confines of tune and text, elaborating, reshaping, bending, improvising, embellishing. In this kind of inspired and inspirational deviation and elaboration, Mahalia was the more inventive and the more adventurous. She would land on a note or a word she particularly liked, or wished to emphasize, and mouth it, or repeat it, or repeat parts of it, or shake it, or bite into it in a manner which often reminded me of a terrier puppy playing tug-o'-war with an old sock or shoe.

Tony Heilbut noted, not long before her death, her way of ending a song:

Mahalia frequently twists to the side, as if hit in the belly. Some of her gestures are dramatically jerky, suggesting instant spirit possession. They often combine with her multiple endings, as when in New York's Mount Morris Park she closed the song "I Have a Friend" with "His love is deeper and deeper, yes, deeper and deeper, it's deeper! and deeper, Lord! deeper and deeper, Lord! it's deeper than the se-e-e-e-a, yeah, oh my lordy, yeah, deeper than the sea," breaking up the last word into a dozen syllables.

The uninhibited fervor which in Mahalia Jackson's singing found expression in an extravagant dispensation of textually, emotionally and melodically inspired fragmentation and embellishment was undoubtedly encouraged by her attendance, as a girl, at Holiness Church services, as was also an initially unresisted compulsion toward the physical involvement and participation in the making of music and the celebration of the glory of God characteristic of her public performance in the early years of her career.

Those who remember the ample (she once weighed 260), matronly, dignified, even sanctified image of her performances before largely white audiences later in her career may find it hard to credit contemporary descriptions of her routines in the days when she was "movin' on up." She was not only a handsome but also a sexy performer, known for her snake hips, for her hollering, for getting happy and lifting her robe an inch or two. "Mahalia was our original belly dancer," says one of her early accompanists. It was a natural impulse, as reflected in a significant observation in her autobiography about her reaction to music in her own Baptist church:

> I loved best to sing in the congregation. All around me I could hear the foot-tapping and hand-clapping. That gave me the bounce. I liked it better than being up in the choir singing anthems. I liked to sing songs which testify to the glory of the Lord. Those anthems are too dead and cold for me. As David said in the Bible: "Make a joyous noise unto the Lord." That's me.

That's what she found in the Holiness Church:

> These people had no choir or no organ. They used the drum, the cymbal, the tambourine and the steel triangle. Everybody in there sang, and they clapped and stomped their feet, and sang with their whole bodies. They had a beat, a rhythm we held on to from slavery days, and their music was so strong and expressive. It used to bring tears to my eyes. We Baptists sang sweet. . . . Where these Holiness people tore into "I'm So Glad Jesus

Lifted Me Up!" they came out with real jubilation. I say: Don't let the devil steal the beat from the Lord! The Lord don't like us to act dead. If you feel it, tap your feet a little—dance to the glory of the Lord!

What Mahalia was hearing there, and what she found so irresistibly attractive, compelling and rewarding, was a music which, in its secular manifestation as rhythm-and-blues, would shortly become the musical vernacular of the younger black people of urban America, then, as rock 'n' roll and, ultimately as "soul," the characteristic music of young people, both black and white, throughout a great part of the world.

It may be doubted that Mahalia Jackson was fully aware of the seminal phenomenon represented by the music she sang and the way she sang it. Not until the publication of Tony Heilbut's The Gospel Sound in 1971 had anyone explored thoroughly and exposed definitively the origins of rhythm-and-blues in gospel, although other writers had noted the significant number of rhythm-and-blues headliners whose formative musical experience was gained in the church. Younger gospel singers, however, have pointed to the irony implicit in the universal dissemination of an idiom once scorned as primitive, vulgar and low-down even by middle-class church-going blacks. Marion Williams, former lead singer of the Clara Ward Singers, told Heilbut:

> Most of what they're doing, key changes and way-out beats, the Kings of Harmony was doing when I was a girl. Anything I hear, jazz, soul, rock, they got some gospel snuck up in them somewhere. They used to call us crazy and clowns and Holy Rollers, and now all these white children are carryin' on worse than we ever did. . . . I'm looking for them to start speaking in tongues next.

To most Americans—and to many Europeans, too—gospel music has meant, first, Mahalia Jackson, and after her, and to far fewer people, the Clara Ward Singers, the Staple Singers and, thanks to "O Happy Day," the Edwin Hawkins Singers. Few have heard of Roberta Martin, whose remains were viewed by 50,000 in Mount Pisgah Baptist Church, Chicago, in January 1969. That is about the same number that filed past Mahalia's open coffin in Chicago's

Clara Ward
Marion Williams

Greater Salem Baptist Church in January 1972. Mahalia's death was noted with extensive obituaries in the national and international press, and the services in Chicago and New Orleans received worldwide coverage. There was a tribute from the President of the United States. But there was no obituary for Roberta Martin in *The New York Times,* nor, according to Heilbut, was her funeral reported even in *Jet,* although it may have been the largest ever held in Chicago.

Nor have many heard of the Reverend Thomas A. Dorsey (whose "Precious Lord" was sung by Mahalia Jackson at the funeral of Dr. Martin Luther King and by Aretha Franklin at Mahalia's funeral) and his one-time partner, Sallie Martin; of James Cleveland (the "Crown Prince of Gospel"); of Clara Hudmon (the "Georgia Peach"); of Queen C. Anderson (the "Queen of the South"), whom the young Elvis Presley heard at the East Trigg Baptist Church in Memphis; of Ernestine Washington (the "Songbird of the East"), or of Willie Mae Ford Smith, whose singing inspired the young Mahalia Jackson to say, "Willie Mae, I'm gonna leave this beauty shop and be like you."

All of which is just another way of saying that gospel music is still a pretty well-kept secret. Even Mahalia, the Mahalia, that is, whom white folks knew at the height of and toward the end of her career, had drifted, if not from her faith, then at least from her idiomatic moorings, into a repertoire referred to by gospel connoisseurs as pop-gospel. Nor does the stereotyped ecstasy of gospel groups in nightclubs and on television expose to white listeners the fervent heart of gospel song in its native storefront-church setting.

Gospel music, as a distinctive style, dates only from the 1930s, but it goes back to the spirituals and, beyond them, to the eighteenth-century revivalist hymns of the white settlers, notably to the hymns of the Reverend Dr. Isaac Watts, whose "Amazing Grace" (the music by an English composer, John Newton) survives to this day as the most famous of all, equally beloved of both white and black fundamentalist congregations. What the blacks did, in Heilbut's words, was "combine the revival hymns of eighteenth-century England with an African song style to create our greatest national music." Consistent with the pattern of an increasing dominance of African over European elements, gospel music is blacker than the spirituals.

It is fashionable nowadays to speak in accusatory tones about white artists growing rich on black artists' music, and about black artists compromising to reach the larger white audience. It is an emotive subject. In the long view, the process of give and take, of learning from one another, however mercenary the motives, has enormously enriched the contemporary treasure of Western music, and it can now be seen to be working in favor of the black musician.

To put it crassly, the diluted drink has stimulated an appetite for the stronger potion. B. B. King would hardly enjoy his present success with white audiences had the way not been prepared by Elvis Presley and the Rolling Stones. Nor should one discount, in contemplating the artistic and financial prosperity of such black artists as James Brown, Roberta Flack, Aretha Franklin and Tina Turner, the preparatory work accomplished by Mahalia Jackson, even if it did include mixing authentic gospel with pop-gospel and accepting the plush instrumental backings of Percy Faith.

Mahalia was universally acclaimed as the Gospel Queen, just as Bessie Smith, in her own time and ever since, has been the acknowledged Empress of the Blues. There have been other gospel queens, but their titles have all carried regional associations, and their fame has been regionally, even denominationally, limited. Mahalia's supremacy and celebrity were literally worldwide.

She traveled extensively, although her tours abroad were continually plagued and curtailed by ill health in the later years of her career. She sang for the Empress of Japan, for the Prime Minister of India and for John F. Kennedy at his inaugural as President of the United States. From the steps of the Lincoln Memorial, in August 1963, flanked by the Reverend Dr. Martin Luther King, she sang "I Been 'Buked and I Been Scorned" to an assembly of 200,000 civil rights workers who had "marched on Washington." She sang at Dr. King's funeral. Among the great musicians of the Afro-American idiom, white and black, only Louis Armstrong and Duke Ellington have enjoyed a comparable celebrity and prestige.

But she was more than just a gospel queen. She was, as Heilbut put it, "all by herself the vocal, physical, spiritual symbol of gospel music. Her large, noble proportions, her face contorted in song into something resembling the Mad Duchess, her soft speaking voice and huge, rich contralto, all made her gospel's one superstar." Even this accolade does not quite take her measure, not at least in a musico-historical sense. If she was certainly the embodiment of gospel, she was also one of its founders.

Robert Anderson, her contemporary, and himself a great gospel singer, has said of Mahalia that "she was the first to bring the blues into gospel," which was what has distinguished gospel, as we know it today, from the spirituals or from earlier black congregational and group singing. Such an attribution is arguably an oversimplification, although probably admissible if one is speaking only of singers. But it overlooks the role played by the Reverend Thomas A. Dorsey in Chicago in the early 1930s.

It was he, with a new kind of hymn and, more importantly, a new way of swinging hymns, who laid the foundations of a gospel-music movement, centered in Chicago. It was he who, according to his own account, actually coined the term. As a music publisher and an impresario, he made touring professionals—and hymn pluggers— out of choir singers. Dorsey, in an earlier incarnation as "Georgia Tom," a blues pianist, had played for both Ma Rainey and Bessie Smith, possibly even at a time when the young Mahalia was listening to them on records in New Orleans.

He was born a Southern Baptist in Atlanta in 1899, and despite a long career as blues and jazz pianist and composer—among his secular songs was "Tight Like That"—he never left the church. Characteristically, he divided his enthusiasm and allegiance between Bessie Smith and the Reverend Dr. C. H. Tindley, founder of the Tindley Methodist Church in Philadelphia and author of many church songs.

Dorsey was also much taken with Billy Sunday, whom he experienced in a circus tent in Atlanta on "colored night," and with Sunday's singer and trombone player, Homer Rodeheaver. He was "saved" at a Baptist convention in 1921, and from about 1929 on he devoted his considerable creative, organizational and commercial talents to gospel music, acknowledging, however, that "blues is a part of me, the way I play piano, the way I write." Among his most familiar compositions, in addition to "Precious Lord," previously mentioned, is "I'm Gonna Live the Life I Sing About in My Song," later to become a favorite in Mahalia Jackson's repertoire.

Timing is ever a factor in the phenomenon of great musical careers. One thinks of Duke Ellington, Louis Armstrong, Benny Goodman, Bing Crosby, Frank Sinatra, Elvis Presley and the Beatles. They have all been uniquely gifted. It may be doubted, however, that they would have played so vital a role in the evolution of Afro-American music, or even in the social history of the Western world in the twentieth century, had they not happened along at the right time and in the right place. For they have all been reflections of social as well as of musical forces.

Mahalia Jackson, too, arriving in Chicago in 1927, aged sixteen, found herself in the right place at the right time, on a Chicago South Side already conditioned by Dorsey's blues-tinged gospel songs to the even bluer cadences and inflections that she brought with her from New Orleans. It was also a Chicago teeming with black immigrants from the South, for whom Mahalia's fervent "shouting" was a voice from down home, much as Bessie's rustic blues had been for older blacks in the North in the previous decade, and, indeed, as the voices and songs of Hank Williams and other hillbilly singers would be for transplanted Southern whites during and just after World War II. "Gospel music in those days of the early 1930s was really taking wing," Mahalia recalled in her autobiography. "It was the kind of music colored people had left behind down South, and they liked it because it was just like a letter from home."

Not all Northern blacks were equally or similarly moved by Mahalia's uninhibited vocalism and deportment, any more than the sophisticated middle-class blacks had been charmed by Bessie Smith's ebullient and earthy candor. "Most of the criticism of my songs in the early days," Mahalia remembered, "came from the high-up society Negroes." But she, a strong-willed woman with a firm dedication both to "her own people" and to their music, was not about to mend her ways to meet the requirements of Northern fashions.

At what she described as her "one and only singing lesson," her teacher, Professor Dubois, a black tenor, told her, "You've got to learn to stop hollerin'. The way you sing is not a credit to the Negro race. You've got to learn to sing songs so that white people can understand them." In the early 1940s, when she toured with Dorsey, he attempted vainly to polish off the rough edges. "I tried," he has recounted, "to show Mahalia how to breathe and phrase, but she wouldn't listen. She said I was trying to make a stereotyped singer out of her. She may have been right."

Like the young Frank Sinatra at about the same time, Mahalia seems to have understood instinctively that she had something precious, that it was uniquely her own, and that it was not subject to assessment by, or adjustment to accord with, conventional criteria.

She did accept some modification later on, probably as a result of modification of repertoire. By then she was singing largely for white audiences. She always retained enough of her rougher characteristics to preserve a vivid identity. As with all great performers, she made it her business to know her audiences.

She began learning to know them almost immediately upon her arrival in Chicago as lead singer with the choir of the Greater Salem Baptist Church, singing for the joy of it while supporting herself as a maid and laundress. Out of this choir association came her first professional experience with the Johnson Gospel Singers, led by the son of her church's pastor and reckoned by some to have been the first professional touring gospel group. By the mid-1930s she was touring as a single, and in 1937 she made, for Decca-Coral, her first records, including the immediately successful "God's Gonna Separate the Wheat from the Tares." In the early 1940s she joined Dorsey and traveled all over America. In 1946 she signed with Apollo Records. One Apollo side, "Move On Up a Little Higher," sold more than a million copies. It established her as the Gospel Queen, and also provided the title for her autobiography.

The decisive breakthrough out of race records and the black gospel circuit came in the early 1950s. A forecast of things to come was her Carnegie Hall debut as soloist with the National Baptist Convention on October 4, 1950. Two years later, her Apollo recording of "I Can Put My Trust in Jesus" won a prestigious French award and led to her first European tour. In 1954 she had a weekly television program on Chicago Station WBBM, a CBS network outlet. Also in 1954, she left Apollo for Columbia Records. This must have been a difficult decision. Certainly it was portentous, as reflected in this account by John Hammond, talking to Chris Hodenfield, associate editor of *Rolling Stone*, after Mahalia's death:

> I first knew about Mahalia when I got out of the Army in '47 or '48. I was terribly excited about gospel, and of course she was one of the best, along with the Clara Ward Singers and the Dixie Hummingbirds. Mahalia had Big Bill Broonzy on guitar then, and that was really a nice set-up. . . . At that time, though, gospel was a dirty word amongst a lot of black people. It was associated with screaming and fainting, and people looked down on it as if it were lower class.

So Mahalia was recording for Apollo Records and getting gypped, like all the artists. She called me in the early Fifties to tell me that she had got an offer from Columbia. This was before I was working at Columbia. I told her: "Mahalia, if you want ads in *Life*, and to be known by the white audience, do it. But if you want to keep on singing for the black audience, forget signing with Columbia, because they don't know the black market at all."

She took up the offer from Columbia then . . . and she lost the black market to a horrifying degree. I'd say that by her death she was playing to a 75 percent white audience, maybe as high as 90 percent. Columbia gave her the fancy accompaniments and the choirs, but the wonderful drive and looseness from the Apollo recordings was missing. Did Mahalia miss the black audience? Mahalia was only interested in money, to be specific with you.

Only may be putting it too strongly. But there is no question about her concern for cash, or about her ability to handle it when she got it. Very early in her career she took a course in beauty culture and opened Mahalia's Beauty Salon in Chicago. To this she added a florist shop and, much later, Mahalia Jackson Chicken Dinners. She also invested heavily and wisely in real estate. In Los Angeles, she always stayed in an apartment which was one of sixteen in a house that she owned. She may not have been much of a reader—and she couldn't read music at all—but she never had any trouble with sums. "I'm a mathematics," she used to tell an audience. "I can look out and tell just how many of you here!"

Those born and raised in poverty, as Mahalia Jackson was, tend to become, when they begin to earn big money, either spenders or misers. Mahalia had little taste for extravagant luxuries. But in her were combined a good business sense with a requirement for security. She left an estate of just over a million dollars. It would doubtless have been twice that had her career not been curtailed by diabetes and heart disease.

Joe Goldberg, who produced her television show, recalled for *Rolling Stone* his first meeting with Mahalia, at the Garrick Theater in Chicago, where the show originated:

I expected some sort of Daddy Grace routine, with the Rolls Royce and the ermine and the entourage. There was no one in the theater except a big woman in an old overcoat sitting and eating a bag of popcorn. I asked her if she knew where I would find Miss Jackson. "I'm Mahalia, honey," she said. "Are we gonna work together?"

When she sang at the Albert Hall in 1969, she told Max Jones, of London's *Melody Maker*, that she liked to get paid for her work, as anyone did, and enjoyed living in reasonable comfort. "But," she added, "I don't work for money. I sing because I love to sing. I don't care for luxuries like jewelry. This is the only diamond I ever kept. . . ." And she showed him a ring that he had first seen on her hand when she visited London in 1952.

Gospel devotees never quite forgave her for the compromises she made to earn that kind of money, although they salute the unique artist she was in her Apollo recording prime, and they acknowledge the role she played subsequently in opening the ears of a wider public to the sound, if not quite the inner soul, of gospel music. Tony Heilbut said of her: "The musical daughter of Bessie Smith was effectively modified into a black Kate Smith. . . . One regrets the transmutation of Mahalia Jackson from shouter to huckster."

And John Hammond:

> I grew very disenchanted with Mahalia. She was more talented than anybody, but she wanted to do that phony religious stuff that white folks like, the Thomas A. Dorsey things. Then she lost her great accompanist, Mildred Falls, and that was gone. Mildred was probably the greatest gospel accompanist that ever lived. . . . I was kind of turned off. I'd rather go to a store-front church to hear gospel music than to Carnegie Hall.

Such observations, purely as music criticism, are unexception able. One hears the same thing—and as criticism it is valid—from country-music devotees who cannot forgive Eddy Arnold for not having stuck to the idiom of Jimmie Rodgers. But it reminds me of a conversation I had many years ago with a Swiss aristocrat. We were speaking of illiteracy in Switzerland's mountain cantons. "It's almost vanished," he said. "Isn't it a pity!" Tony Heilbut's book is subtitled "Good News and Bad Times." The bad times belonged to those who stuck to the storefront churches.

Mahalia Jackson was no music critic. She was an unlettered

singer, who brought something of her own great voice and musicality even to "Danny Boy," "Silent Night," "Trees," "Summertime" and "The Lord's Prayer." She wasn't always happy with the requirements or with the result. She fretted under the limitation of time on television, and she did not like the backings, "jazzed up and doped with a heavy beat," of some of her later records, or the choral groups and strings "cut into the tapes after I had recorded them."

She seems to have known more than the studio engineers about the problems of recording a voice such as hers, especially a voice geared to large congregations rather than the microphone. "It's harder to hold a big voice to get the beauty out of it," she noted wisely in *Movin' On Up*, "than it is to magnify a small voice. If you get an engineer who squeezes your voice, he can leave out all the depth. Some of those studio engineers have made me sound like a pig squealing under a gate."

But she was apparently unaware of any fundamental conflict between her religious faith and her pursuit of earthly reward, nor is she likely to have reflected at any length on such a matter as the integrity of idiom and style. There may have been no conflict. Her earthly rewards made it possible for her to live decently and comfortably, and to establish the Mahalia Jackson Scholarship Foundation. No storefront-church fame would have got her to the Holy Land and to the Holy Sepulchre where

I knelt down and stayed there alone, trying to find the words for a prayer of thanks. My dreams had come true. With my own eyes I had seen the place where Christ was born, and with my own hands I had touched the Rock of Calvary. Everything was drained out of me. In the old Hebrew of the Bible my name, Mahalia, means "Blessed by the Lord," and truly, it seemed to me, I had been blessed.

So were those to whom she sang!

12

Nat King Cole

I heard Nat Cole in person only once. That was in Frankfurt am Main in 1960, when he was touring Europe with a big band led by Quincy Jones. He sang, of course, but he played, too, taking piano choruses between the vocals, exuberantly but casually, not bothering to sit down. Recalling his early records with the King Cole Trio, where the star had been, initially at least, the pianist rather than the vocalist, I thought to myself: This guy can play more piano standing up than most pianists can play sitting down, and he can do more singing sitting down than most singers can do standing up!

He didn't sing sitting down in Frankfurt. The vocalist rather than the pianist was the star. But in assessing Nat Cole as a singer it is important, I think, to bear in mind that he began his professional career as a pianist. He is remembered to this day as one of the greats, certainly as one of the potential greats, among the jazz pianists of his generation. The world of jazz, ever jealous of its claims to a status separate from, and superior to, the vulgar, commercial world of popular music, has never quite forgiven him his subsequent unique success as a vocalist. It has been similarly reluctant to forgive Billy Eckstine, second only to Nat Cole as a black balladeer, whom it prefers to remember as leader, from 1944 to 1947, of a band that included at one time or another Art Blakey, Miles Davis, Kenny

Dorham, Dizzy Gillespie, Budd Johnson, Fats Navarro, Charlie Parker and Lucky Thompson, and as the discoverer and sponsor of Sarah Vaughan.

To a dedicated jazz musician, jazz critic or jazz fan, there was a suggestion of apostasy about Nat King Cole's career. The more than promising jazz pianist, winner of the *Esquire* Gold Medal as pianist in 1946, the heir apparent to the mantle of Earl "Fatha" Hines, as whose youthful reflection he had emerged in the Chicago of the late 1930s, achieves fame and fortune as a pop singer! That's putting it crassly, to be sure. He was more than that. Even as a pop singer he was an original. No one had ever sung quite like that before. He and Billy Eckstine, three years his senior, were, moreover, the first black male singers to hit the top in "the white time."

Louis Armstrong had been ahead of them. But Louis, for most of his career, was primarily a jazz trumpeter, his singing a happy and profitable means of giving his chops a rest, of adding variety to a concert format that needed it. There was about Louis' singing, furthermore, an element of clowning. Or so it seemed to lay listeners. They rejoiced in the grotesque sound of the voice, and in the exaggerated articulation of phrase and text, little noting the nuances perceptible to other singers, white and black. Singers exploited the nuances while leaving to Louis the engaging eccentricities that were his and his alone. Nat Cole was never a clown. He made it as a singer, with no assets other than an unquenchable musicality and a hauntingly lovely sound.

His defection to popular music has been spoken of in the jazz world more in sorrow than in anger, especially after his untimely death in 1965. As jazz critic Ralph J. Gleason put it in his contribution to a booklet accompanying Capitol Records' retrospective *The Nat King Cole Story*, ". . . the hard-core jazz fan like myself may regret that, while success has not spoiled him, it has lured him away from what we, selfishly, have always wanted him to stay in exclusively. But who can blame him?"

Leonard Feather, in *The Book of Jazz* (1957), probably reflected a more typical point of view in describing Nat as a singer "whose singing and setting have drifted further and further from jazz in late years, though he remains a thorough craftsman, and continues to instill a jazz beat into his fast-tempo performances." Writers not so close to the scene, or to Cole himself, could be less charitable. André

Nat Cole with Nelson Riddle ▶

Hodeir, the French critic, for example, in *Toward Jazz*, made no secret of his feelings when he referred to "the bleary-eyed young ladies who swoon when they hear Nat King Cole."

But regret—respectful, even affectionate—was the more common reaction, and not only because it is hard to take a young man to task for pursuing and achieving, as a singer, a renown and prosperity beyond the dreams of even the most prosperous of jazz pianists. Nat's personality, too, had a lot to do with the jazz world's indulgence. In a community of professional musicians not always notable for amiability, he was notably amiable. According to just about everyone who knew him or ever worked with him, or was otherwise associated with him, he was a born gentleman, just "one hell of a nice, decent guy."

He was more than that. As George T. Simon in his contribution to *The Nat King Cole Story* wrote of Nat's reaction to success:

It's been coming to him for years and years; and for years and years he has remained the same sort of unspoiled person. Cocky he has never been; but neither has he ever been afraid to stand up for what he believes is morally right, as witness his own strongly expressed convictions and actions regarding the rights of his people to live in a free and equal society. What he has done he has always done with dignity and with a calm serenity that can come only from deep and honest convictions. And through it all, one has always sensed a basic love for all his fellowmen. "Some people are so busy stewing in their own hate," he says, "that they can't do anything—even for themselves!" For himself, for his family, and for all who have come in contact with him, Nat Cole has done a great deal—a great deal of good!

Beyond these more or less sentimental considerations lies the fact that his contribution to jazz in the early stages of his career remains historically imperishable, and not just as a pianist. Almost obscured by his subsequent fame as a singer is his accomplishment in establishing a precedent, with the King Cole Trio, for the small jazz combo. According to Gleason, writing in 1961:

His was the first small group to become commercially successful. Up to that time [1939] the whole world of booking agents and promoters thought in terms of large bands exclusively. Nat Cole made the small group possible, and thus opened the door to the commercial prosperity that has blessed the jazz small group in the past decade.

From the point of view of the vocal student and historian, there are other, more immediately pertinent reasons for remembering that Nat Cole began as a jazz pianist, that he became a singer, if not entirely by accident, certainly not in response to any sense of vocation, and that, when he first started singing, he played while he sang. That was in Hollywood, in 1937, when he was already twenty, with several years of professional experience as pianist and band leader behind him.

He had been born Nathaniel Coles (he dropped the "s" to become King Cole) in Montgomery, Alabama, in 1917, but the family moved to Chicago in 1921, his father responding to a call to become pastor of the Truelight Spiritual Temple on the South Side. By the time Nat was twelve, he was playing organ and singing in the choir of his father's church. But his heart already belonged to jazz. "I was always crazy about show business," he told an interviewer shortly after attaining national celebrity, "and I was particularly crazy about bands. Why, I used to stand in front of the radio and lead bands all the time."

He was, from the start, a natural pianist. He took lessons, but only, he used to say, in order to learn to read. He could already play more piano than his teacher. But he began his professional career as leader of his own band, the Rogues of Rhythm, teaming in duo novelties with his brother Eddie, a bass player with Noble Sissle. With the band, he worked around Chicago for three years, in clubs and dance halls, and he listened to the older men, especially to Earl Hines and Jimmy Noone, the New Orleans clarinetist whose theme song, "Sweet Lorraine," would subsequently become one of Nat's own first big hits with the King Cole Trio.

The band joined a *Shuffle Along* road company during its run in Chicago and stayed with it when it moved on to the Coast, although without brother Eddie, who preferred to remain in Chicago. Nat was attracted not only by the work, but also by a chorus girl, Nadine Robinson, whom he shortly married. The show folded in Los Angeles and the band broke up. Nat worked as a single until, in 1939, a nightclub owner named Bob Lewis told him to form a trio and come into his Hollywood club, the Swanee Inn. Nat recruited Wesley

Prince, on bass, and Oscar Moore, on guitar, and the King Cole Trio was born.

According to Phil Moore, the veteran composer, arranger and vocal coach, who was in Hollywood at the time, Nat came to him one day and said that he was about to lose his job. "The man," he told Moore, "likes my playing, but he wants a singer." "That's easy," Moore remembers telling him. "Sing!" This was presumably while Nat was still working as a single. His vocals, often shared with his companions, were an attractive feature of the King Cole Trio from the very first. The trio did well, but it was not until 1944, when a Decca contract lapsed and they were signed by Capitol and scored a national hit with Cole's own "Straighten Up and Fly Right," that they became a household word.

The time they had put in "paying their dues" on the nightclub and theater circuit now stood them in good stead. They had both routine and repertoire, and were able to follow through with one hit after another, notably "Frim Fram Sauce" and "Route 66." By 1947 the trio, or the Fiddlers Three, as they were often called, had made five movies, had contracts for two more, and had signed a long term contract with the Kraft Music Hall on NBC.

Ralph Gleason, in a feature on the trio in *Esquire*, January 1947, summed it up:

> And lastly, the Fiddlers Three are about to make their logical debut in answer to King Cole's summons. A special record of a new tune, "The Christmas Song," has been recorded for Capitol with violins. "That'll surprise some of our friends," Nat says. It probably will.

It did. Along with a trio recording of "For Sentimental Reasons," it launched Nat Cole, as a singer, into the mainstream of American popular music.

"The Christmas Song" and "For Sentimental Reasons" revealed a singer strikingly different from the exuberant vocalist of "Sweet Lorraine" and "Straighten Up and Fly Right," a singer closer to ballad than to blues. Not that Nat was ever a blues singer in the Southern tradition, or even a gospel singer, despite his early experience in his father's church. He could approximate both styles, but he was neither musically nor emotionally rooted in them. He grew up in the black entertainment world of Chicago's South Side, and his state-

The King Cole Trio with, left to right, Oscar Moore, Johnny Miller and Nat Cole

ment, "I was always crazy about show business," provides a clue to his subsequent development as a singer.

His early musical exposure was to jazz and to rhythm-and-blues, the latter just beginning to emerge as the music of the young urban black subculture. But the young black performer, in those days even more than now, had to win acceptance from the white public if he was to achieve a more than local or even national celebrity. Black jazz instrumentalists had achieved that success, or were beginning to achieve it, pretty much on their own terms. But what they played in the 1930s was no longer the music of young blacks, unless the young blacks were themselves jazz musicians. Rhythm-and-blues was the new thing. It would not penetrate white consciousness for another fifteen years, and then only as a raunchy variant of country music, exemplified in the uninhibited performances of such white singers as Elvis Presley, Carl Perkins and Jerry Lee Lewis.

But while white audiences were now susceptible to the gutsy attacks and slurring cadences of black jazz, and while white jazz musicians were gaining fluency and virtuosity in a kind of jazz closer to black example, there was a less hearty welcome for black singing. Some black women had got through to white audiences, but only by adopting many of the vocal and stylistic characteristics of white singers and by singing white songs. Even then, success was limited. The singing of an Ethel Waters, the most successful of them all, was, for example, a far cry from Bessie Smith, and even Ethel, it should be remembered, achieved her greatest success as an actress.

Billie Holiday was enjoying an early, and modest, celebrity when Nat Cole began with his trio, but she was singing mostly songs that whites knew and liked, if in a way that was all her own. Ella Fitzgerald had arrived, but with Ella it is essential to recall that her first model was Connee Boswell. Even the success of such white singers as Mildred Bailey, Lee Wiley and Connee Boswell was probably inhibited by the evidence, in their singing, of an early and enduring infatuation with Ethel Waters and Bessie Smith. Less distinctive white singers of that period achieved greater fame and a commensurately greater prosperity with a kind of singing closer to European vocal tradition.

It may be doubted that Nat King Cole ever made a conscious decision to tailor his singing to white taste. It is possible, I grant, to see in the progress of his career a steady and profitable drift from black jazz and early rhythm-and-blues to white pop. The operative word is *drift*. Nat's singing, as I hear it, simply reflected an instinctive vocal and stylistic adjustment to the kind of song he sang and to the kind of arrangement provided him. He was an assimilative musician, with an acute appreciation of the characteristics of a variety of Afro-American styles. This is illustrated vividly on the three discs of *The Nat King Cole Story*, which have, for the student, the advantage of presenting the singer in dramatically contrasted material, covering, in style if not in date of performance, every phase of his career. Here, for example, are some of my notes, jotted down as first impressions on an initial hearing of the anthology:

> "Straighten Up and Fly Right"—Sort of R&B-ish.
> "Sweet Lorraine"—Black, velvety sound, curious mixture of black and white. A bit of Billie, but very little of either Bing or Frank. That talking, fall-away cadence of the blues singer!
> "Route 66"—Nice, swinging, black. Again, rather more than a touch of R&B.
> "For Sentimental Reasons"—A bit of Sinatra here. In fact, a lot, especially of the Frank of that period. The voice doesn't have the round warmth and richness of Frank's in the upper middle—or maybe he didn't try for it. A beautiful record.
> "The Christmas Song"—Now with strings. Again, a lot of Frank. But more open above. Mostly very white.
> "Nature Boy"—A sort of slow Ben Webster or Billy Eckstine wide vibrato. Wider than Frank's. Lovely record.
> "Calypso Blues"—What did Harry Belafonte get from him? A very good and very original track. A long way from his ballad work. Very musical!
> "Orange Colored Sky"—Watch out for flying glass! Frank there. Nice swinger. Fast patter with a lot of words. Good record.
> "Looking Back"—Country/R&B. Nice country feel.
> "Oh, Mary, Don't You Weep!"—Gospel, unauthentic and unconvincing.
> "Ay Cosita Linda"—Harry? Another example of Nat's versatility. Nice.

Those songs going back the farthest in this collection are remakes of earlier records, and the singer is the Nat Cole of 1961. But the purpose in remaking the earlier numbers was to duplicate the originals, insofar as possible, under the superior technical circumstances of the early 1960s. A comparison of the remakes with the earlier records confirms the success of the enterprise, although some of the jaunty, insouciant ebullience of the originals has been sacrificed to the inescapable professionalism of the singer of 1961, along with some of the sprightly swing of the young Nat King Cole.

Comparison with the earlier records also confirms Nat's vocal versatility as being something he had from the start. It is hard to think of another singer who could shift gears stylistically so fluently, so securely. The explanation may be found, as I have suggested earlier, in the fact that he was not initially a vocalist at all, but a pianist who also sang. Most singers approach a song from the point of view of the vocalist. Nat, in the beginning at least, did not.

William E. Anderson, editor of *Stereo Review*, has suggested a connection between Nat's piano playing and his singing:

> A piano, even at its most legato, is a percussion instrument, and my sense of Cole's singing, even at *his* most legato, is of isolated, crystalline tones, linked only in the aural imagination of the listener, and not in breathed slurs by the performer.

Certainly he sang without first learning to sing. In the course of his career he learned a lot about singing, not all of it congenial to his native musicality. He became a better vocalist, not perceiving, probably, that the improvement, in conventional terms, was achieved at a loss of some of those endearing characteristics and idiosyncrasies that set him apart, as a younger artist, from any other singer.

No awareness is indicated in his statement to a collaborator during the assembling of *The Nat King Cole Story*:

> I find that I'm singing out more than I used to, holding back less. I can belt when I want to, and give a song more impetus. A foxy old music teacher once told me: "You've got a lot of voice you haven't used yet." Then I had the stage experience when I did the show, *I'm With You*, in 1960, and I found out he was right.

That foxy old music teacher was right, and I, for one, wish that Nat had never found it out. Nat did, indeed, have a lot more voice than he used until late in his career. It was a good voice. But it

Harry Belafonte
Billy Eckstine

was not, when he let it out, and least of all when he belted, an especially distinctive voice.

It was, as I hear it, a light bass-baritone. I infer as much from the richness and warmth of the tone in the area between the low G and the C a fourth above, an area similarly congenial to the mature voices of both Bing Crosby and Frank Sinatra. A bass-baritone disposition is further suggested by the fact that the "passage" in his voice, as he moved up the scale and out of his natural range, would appear to have lain around D flat or D, a semitone or two below the corresponding ticklish area in the voice of a true baritone.

Nat rarely ventured beneath that low G, and he had little to show for it when he did. Nor did he have any upward extension to speak of. On the records I have checked he never sings above an E. Both the E flat and the E, while secure enough, were consistently uncharacteristic in timbre, not thin and tenuous as the voices of Ethel Waters and Bessie Smith were when they sang beyond the "passage," but somehow ill-matched to the rest of the voice and rather conventional in sound, recalling from time to time the sound of the young Bing Crosby in the same area.

Big, wide-ranging voices are a dime a dozen—better voices than Nat Cole's, or, at least, voices of more lavish endowment. But a lavish vocal endowment does not make a great singer. The trick lies in determining, or sensing, where the gold lies in the vocal ore, and in mining it expertly and appreciatively. Or one can think of the vocal cords as violin strings, of the resonating properties of throat, mouth and head as the violin, and of the breath as a bow. In Nat Cole's case, the strings responded most eloquently to a light bow. The tone coarsened under pressure, or when urged, either upward or downward, beyond the G–D range of an octave and a fifth.

At his best and most characteristic, Nat Cole was not so much a singer as a whisperer, or, as one might put it, a confider. Barry Ulanov, in A History of Jazz in America, put it as perceptively as anyone has done when he described him as "a singer of intimate conversations." Ralph Gleason has given us the characteristic picture: Nat Cole singing "in a soft, intimate, insinuating voice, flashing his white teeth and sitting sideways at the piano."

It is my own guess that the piano, as well as a unique, if less than sumptuous, voice, accounted for this characteristic intimacy. Nat, when he first started singing, was a pianist, seated at the piano, a microphone stuck in his face, articulating the lyrics of the songs he and the trio were singing. It is not easy to sing sitting down. The singer's breathing, and the diaphragmatic support and control of the emission of breath, are inhibited. It is even harder to sing while playing, especially when one is doing as much playing as he did. Even with his facility at the keyboard, his attention must have been divided, his concentration diffused.

It is pertinent to note in this connection a paradox about Nat Cole. Of a singer more deeply rooted in jazz, probably, than any other except Louis Armstrong and, possibly, Billy Eckstine, one would expect an extraordinarily improvisatory approach to singing, a wealth of melodic invention and great variety of ornamentation. Nat Cole, in all these matters, was less lavish, less inventive, than many popular singers who have never played an instrument.

He could, and did, handle most of the improvisatory and ornamental devices that had become stock in trade for most of the better popular singers. His 1958 recording of "St. Louis Blues," a souvenir of his performance as W. C. Handy in the moving picture of that name, is sheer improvisation. But as a rule he used these devices sparingly. The *appoggiatura* was the only embellishment he employed consistently. There was always the nicely turned mordent here or there, but almost none of the slurring that other singers, both black and white, had picked up from the best black singers and jazz instrumentalists of the preceding generation, and no recourse at all to the modified *portamento* so artfully exploited by Frank Sinatra.

Again, his being a pianist may have had something to do with this. Black musicians, other than pianists, all tended to make slurring instruments out of trumpets, trombones, clarinets, saxophones, basses and guitars, seeking to coax their instruments into talking in the gliding cadences of black American speech. But a piano, a fixed-pitch instrument, cannot slur. Nat Cole, as a singer, could have slurred had he chosen to. Since he was essentially a pianist, it may not have occurred to him to try.

He was inventive as a pianist. But it seems reasonable to assume that he thought of invention and ornamentation pianistically, or at least instrumentally, and that, as a singer, he left such matters to the instrumental backing, whether his own or that of other instrumentalists. What mattered to him as a singer, when he sang, were the tune and the words—especially the words. As a fashioner of melodic line he was not in Sinatra's class, nor, despite his jazz background, was he in Frank's class as a propellant force in up-tempo, swinging, big-band jazz. As a fondler of words he was in a class by himself.

I write "fondler" advisedly. All the great American popular singers have had an affinity for words, but their approach to words, to enunciation and articulation, has varied from singer to singer. Al Jolson and Louis Armstrong loved them to pieces, took them apart and did—or did not—put them together again; or they smothered them with affection. Bing Crosby treated them affectionately, too, but gaily and casually. Sinatra showed more concern than other singers for their meaning, and was a master at wedding their sentimental implications and associations to an Italianate appreciation of melodic line.

Nat Cole had a way of caressing a word, of wrapping his voice around it. So close, so intimate was this identification with the music implicit in language that I, for one, cannot evoke the memory of his voice without the words to go with it. One doesn't hear that voice simply as sound. One hears "A blossom fell," or "Sweet Lorraine," or "Darling, Je vous aime beaucoup." There were, moreover, certain inherent distinctive characteristics of pronunciation. His speech, even in song, was not conspicuously black, except in out-and-out rhythm-and-blues numbers. But there were certain delightful idiosyncrasies, notably the open sound on the short e in such words as "fell," "ended," "forget," and "loneliness," by which he can always be identified on records within a measure or two, and which sometimes give his sung English the "correct" flavor of a learned language.

I have just said that such idiosyncrasies were delightful. It is an appropriate summary word for an appreciation of Nat King Cole. Everything about his singing was delightful, except when he belted or squandered his endowment on unworthy material. He was a delightful singer, a delightful pianist and, according to those who knew him, a delightful man. The memory of his singing, his playing and his person will be treasured accordingly in the annals and archives of American music.

13

Hank Williams

When I listen to Hank Williams' records I am reminded not of Nashville and Grand Ole Opry, nor of Shreveport and Louisiana Hayride, but of Albufeira, a fishing village and beach resort on the southern coast of Portugal.

It was an April afternoon in 1968. A week's vacation behind me, I had stepped into a bus for the drive to the airport at Faro. The bus was empty. The driver had gone into the hotel to round up other passengers, leaving his radio on. I listened. Portugese music? Not a bit of it. From that radio issued the banshee wail of Hank Williams singing "Your Cheatin' Heart"!

Or I am reminded of Wexford, on the southeast coast of Eire, birthplace of Commodore John Barry, a founder of the United States Navy. Wexford is famous now for its annual opera festival, whose visitors, after dutiful attendance upon Rossini and Donizetti, refresh themselves with beer and ale in pubs where local choral groups offer Irish songs as an added attraction. But life goes on as usual among the young in Wexford, festival or no festival, and the meeting place for drinking and dancing is a public room in the rambling old hotel where I was staying. The music was rock, and it was inescapable. One tune had me puzzled. I knew it but couldn't place it. I kept

humming it, and suddenly the words came to me: "Your Cheatin' Heart." The rock setting had thrown me off.

I remember Easter 1971, and an International Country Music Festival in the enormous Empire Pool at Wembley, London's equivalent of Madison Square Garden. A planeload of Nashville's elite had been flown over: Hank Snow, Roy Acuff, Lee Conway, Waylon Jennings, Johnny Cash's kid brother Tommy—and Hank Williams, Jr. The occasion itself seemed incredible. Here were 10,000 people from all over the British Isles dedicating an Easter weekend and a great deal of money to an *ad hoc* caravan of American country singers!

The veteran Hank Snow was so moved by his affectionate reception that he could barely enunciate his folksy "Friends and neighbors" salutation. But sentiment ran highest when Hank Williams, Jr., came on and did a medley of his father's songs, supported by Jerry Rivers, Sammy Pruett and Don Helm from his father's backing group, the Drifting Cowboys. The British audience knew every song by heart. It recognized and responded to the old Hank Williams wail, catch and tear in young Hank's voice.

That festival at Wembley—it has been duplicated in other cities all over the world—was a symbol of the extent to which American country music has burst its rural American South and Southwestern regional bounds to achieve something close to universality. The man largely responsible for that explosion, as suggested by what I had heard in Albufeira and Wexford, is Hank Williams. One says *is* advisedly. He died twenty-one years ago at the age of twenty-nine. But his records have survived reissue after reissue. The songs are as fresh, as delightful and as moving, the voice as haunting as ever.

Measured against any conventional criteria either of songwriting or of singing, Hank's appeal makes no sense. Take the voice itself, for example. Words have failed just about everyone who has tried to describe it. The most successful effort I have seen came from a writer in the Alabama *Journal* who suggested, when a $1,000 music scholarship was established in Hank's memory at the University of Alabama, that among the qualifications of a recipient should be a voice "like the whine of an electric saw going through pine timber."

The writer may have been referring to sounds Hank's voice makes on certain closed vowels as they occur in such words as *could, would, look, love, me* and *see.* Those vowels emerge as though they had become lodged between the vocal cords en route from lungs to throat. Or one thinks of a man trying to sing with a fishbone stuck somewhere between pharynx and larynx. Then there is the nasality in such words as *down, town, around, want, die, cry, when, then, heart, part, shame, name,* etcetera, not to mention a curious and characteristic quaver, not quite vibrato and not quite tremolo, suggesting a kind of feedback from overloaded muscles in the throat, which is probably what it was. Play any Hank Williams record to opera buff, or even a Frank Sinatra fan, and you will clear the room.

Hank was musically illiterate and no more than barely literate when it came to reading and writing. The only musical schooling he ever had was from a black street singer, Rufe Payne, nicknamed Tee-tot, in Greenville, Alabama. That schooling did not include notation. "I have never read a note or written one," Hank told Montgomery *Advertiser* columnist Allen Rankin in 1951. "I can't. I don't know one note from another." His literary reading was confined to comics, which he called "goof books." His vocabulary was small. He knew nothing of grammar. His spelling was atrocious. He dropped out of high school in his sophomore year—when he was nineteen!

It was similar with Hank Williams as a poet. He has been called a hillbilly Shakespeare. He was a hillbilly, all right, in the generic country-music sense of the term. His language, not to speak of his versification, was anything but Shakespearean. Those simple, home-spun ditties about cheating hearts, cold hearts, honky-tonks, dog-houses and hobos, with their dubious rhymes and faulty, faltering meter—is one to take this as poetry, as Shakespearean?

It is tempting to suggest that it was precisely these deficiencies that accounted for his greatness. But they have been shared by millions of young men, including country singers and songwriters. One might, however, put it the other way around and suggest that he would never have achieved greatness without the deficiencies. Lack of schooling did not inhibit his poetic imagination. It simply kept him down to earth, where his listeners lived. Hank knew it. "You write just like Shakespeare," he once told an aspiring lyricist, "and if you don't watch out you'll be buried in the same grave with him."

Roger Williams (no relation), in his biography of Hank Williams, *Sing a Sad Song,* dug up a verse Hank wrote when he was about twelve:

Hank Williams with Hank, Jr.

Hank Williams, Jr.

Hank Snow

> *I had an old goat,*
> *She ate tin cans.*
> *When the little goats came,*
> *They were Ford sedans.*

"Doggerel," observes Roger Williams, "but with a certain imagination. Perhaps a great songwriting career is evident in those four lines."

Not the career is evident, but the talent, and, more importantly, a gift of imagery and a habit of observation. Hank grew up with old goats and tin cans, little goats and Ford sedans. He wrote about them because he knew about them. Later on, he would learn about honky-tonks, dating couples, unrequited love, deceived wives, husbands and lovers, broken hearts and broken homes. He would write about them with the same effect of something intimately and sympathetically experienced.

The subjects are not novel in literature or music. What distinguished Williams' verses and singing was the lack of pretension and an extraordinary perception of event and feeling, articulated in a vernacular as picturesque as it was ordinary and simple. "If you're gonna sing a song," he used to say, "sing 'em somethin' they can understand."

Within the limits of a rudimentary vocabulary he was linguistically both inventive and resourceful. A delightful example is "Move It On Over," a song about a man who comes home late, finds that he has been locked out (his wife has even changed the lock), and crawls into the doghouse, telling the occupant to "move it on over." Hank uses twelve synonyms for *move*, two to a verse: *get, scoot, ease, drag, pack, tote, scratch, shake, slide, sneak, shove* and *sweep.* One should say, perhaps, that he uses twelve words as synonyms. The distinction between a synonym and a word simply pressed into service as a synonym is not one that would have troubled him.

As a songwriter he was always more concerned with words than with melody. If he got the words he wanted, the melody seemed to take care of itself. He was not a distinguished or even a particularly inventive melodist. The tunes are as simple, even primitive, as the conventional tonic-subdominant-dominant chords that support them. One remembers them only in association with the words—and with the way he sang the words. That is what is remarkable about them.

Hank's melodies were the music of language. His singing issued from the same linguistic source.

Formal vocal cultivation would have been as disastrous to his singing as formal literary schooling would have been to his writing. Having none, and having no vocal pretensions or vanity, he was free to match voice to song without worrying about conventionally accepted criteria of what constitutes an admissible vocal sound. That his voice was capable of adaptation to a remarkable variety of songs and subjects makes it difficult to describe, simply as a voice. One feels that he had a different voice for each song, or as if versification and vocalization sprang from the same lyrical impulse, as they almost certainly did.

On a song like "Ramblin' Man," for example, with its long, mournful, upward glides, he stays in the lower register and sounds almost like a basso—and quite a lot like a distant train whistle. On bright up-tempo numbers such as "Hey, Good Lookin' " and "Settin' the Woods on Fire," he elects a higher area of his range and sounds like a tenor. Actually, the voice was a light baritone, with an unexceptional range of about an octave and a sixth, from an A below to an F above.

Within that range he could achieve an extraordinary variety of character and color. Some of this variety is illusory, deriving from imaginative and resourceful ornamentation rather than from alteration of timbre. In his use of ornamentation, and in the kinds of ornament he used, he was unique among country singers. It is of no little significance that in nothing I have ever read about him is there any mention of ornamentation at all. His ornaments grew so naturally, apparently so inevitably, out of word, context and phrase that they do not emerge conspicuously as ornaments. They are not, strictly speaking, ornamental. They are organic.

This is almost true even of so prominent a device as falsetto. Hank Williams could, and sometimes did, introduce yodeling breaks in the manner of Jimmie Rodgers, and as carried on after Rodgers' death by Ernest Tubb. His "Long Gone Lonesome Blues," for example, comes close to being a prototypical twelve-bar blue yodel in the Rodgers style. But more characteristic of Williams is the rapid yodeling alternation of falsetto and normal voice within the phrase, or even within the time span of a single note, the effect being that of

Charley Pride

a birdlike warble, its function at once ornamental and expressive. A spectacular example is his recording of "Lovesick Blues."

Possibly because this song was not his own, but an old vaudeville number from the 1920s, he indulged in something closer to sheer vocal virtuosity than was his wont in music of his own inspiration. He simply drenched it with falsetto cascades, leaping back and forth easily and accurately over a wide variety of intervals. It is a rollicking display of vocal agility, unprecedented, in my experience, in the work of any other singer, but reproduced nowadays with astonishing fidelity by that admirable black country singer Charley Pride.

An important difference between falsetto as used by Jimmie Rodgers on the one hand and by Hank Williams on the other is the area of the vocal range in which it is employed. With Rodgers it was almost always an upward extension of his natural range, taking him up to the D flat above high C. With Williams it was produced within the natural range, which probably accounts for the ease with which he shifted back and forth between falsetto and normal voice, achieving an effect rather like a weathercock in a whirlwind.

He turned this facility into an important and distinctive device. That crack, or catch, which gave a mournful, soulful, sometimes lugubrious inflection to so much of his articulation and phrasing—a kind of tearjerk, as it were—was accomplished by attacking a note in falsetto, then switching instantly to normal voice. Most singers of any category would find this difficult, if not impossible. To Hank Williams it seems to have come naturally. Probably because it came naturally, he never abused it.

But it was not alone his gifts and accomplishments as vocalist, lyricist and public performer that gave to his art those special qualities which have kept his memory and his music alive over a score of years spanning the most explosive era of stylistic evolution—and revolution—in the brief history of Afro-American music. With him more than with most singers, even the finest, the music was the man. That is probably why, as he matured, he ever more rarely sang anyone else's songs.

Music, it would seem, was not so much an extension of his personality as a personal fulfillment, inevitably transitory. Except in the creative act of fashioning the song and performing it, and in the flush of an audience's—or record producer's—response, it was also unsatisfactory. The adjective most commonly employed by those who knew him is "lonely." Another, significantly, is "bitter."

It may well have been just this element of bitterness that excluded, in his songs, the sentimentality characteristic of much country music. Certainly it distinguished his special vein of lyricism from that of Jimmie Rodgers, whose voice and songs, on records and radio, were Hank's earliest musical inspiration. There was nothing of the "dear old South," or "dear old pal of mine," or "dear Mother of mine" in Hank Williams' repertoire, and probably nothing of it in his nature, either. Jimmie Rodgers was an amiable fellow. Hank Williams wasn't—except on stage.

No one seems ever really to have known him, least of all, probably, Hank Williams himself. Jim Denny, until his death in 1963 the general manager of *Grand Ole Opry*, and head of its Artists' Service, who experienced much of the best and the worst of Hank, once said of him, "I never knew anybody I liked better than Hank, but I don't think I ever really got close to him. I don't know if anyone really could."

His audiences, maybe. Only to them could he, or would he, reveal himself. Says Allen Rankin:

> He didn't have much personality except when he was singing. That's when his real personality came out. He'd come slopping and slouching out on stage, limp as a dishrag. But when he picked up the guitar and started to sing, it was like a charge of electricity had gone through him. He became three feet taller.

As with Jolson and Frank Sinatra, so with Hank Williams, too, the life of a public performer was the only one he knew or ever wanted to know. He worked for a year and a half (in 1942–44) for the Alabama Drydock and Shipbuilding Company in Mobile as a welder. Even then, at nineteen, he already had six years of public performance behind him, and while working at the shipyard he moonlighted as a musician in the Mobile area. After that, he never earned another nickel or dime that he didn't sing for, play for or write for.

Various circumstances of his birth and upbringing throw light on the man and the musician. He was born on September 17, 1923, in Mt. Olive, Butler County, Alabama, and grew up, after a fashion, in a number of small communities in the vicinity of Georgiana, including Georgiana itself, which Roger Williams, in *Sing a Sad Song*, places "sixty miles south of Montgomery and 115 miles north of Mobile, meaning practically nowhere."

His father, Elonzo Williams, drove locomotives for the W. T. Smith Lumber Company. Lon Williams had worked for many other lumber companies before Hank was born. "I had a lot of jobs," he says today, " 'cause that's the way I wanted it. A company gets to feel it owns a man. I always felt I was a free man and could go off and work somewhere else." Can his father have been the inspiration of Hank's "Ramblin' Man," one of his finest songs and, on the recording, one of his finest vocal performances?

The family, if hardly affluent, was not too badly off at the time of Hank's birth. But the depression was on the way, and in 1930 his father entered a Veterans Hospital in Biloxi, suffering from the after-effects of gas, or from shell shock, or both. Responsibility for the maintenance of young Hank and his sister, Irene, fell upon their mother, Lilly. A decisive, resilient, resourceful woman, she managed—as a nurse, as a factory worker in a WPA cannery, and as proprietress of her own boardinghouses.

She had apparently been the dominant member of the household even before Lon Williams' admission to the Veterans Hospital. As young Hank began to be active as a country singer, she played a significant role as promoter and administrator of his professional affairs. It would seem to have been a mother-son, man-woman relationship with which Hank was never quite able to come to terms, imposing and cultivating a dependency which, at his tender age, he could hardly escape—or do without. From it evolved patterns of ambiguity in his emotional relationships with other women that would color both his character and his music, especially his lyrics, and eventually help to shorten his life.

Reminiscences of Hank as a boy, solicited by Roger Williams from those who "knew him when," suggest some degree of alienation at an early age. A cousin, J. C. McNeill, for example, remembers him as "a real loner. He never was a happy boy, in a way. He didn't laugh and carry on like other children. He'd go along with the gang, but he never would get interested in nothin'. Say a baseball game. That's a boy's pride and joy, but Hank didn't much care about it. It seemed like somethin' was always on his mind."

Nor was he physically strong. A Georgianan recalls him as "a little bitty feller, with legs no bigger'n a buggy whip." Another says: "A thin boy with legs that looked like pipestems." And still another: "He was a li'l old boy, kinda like you'd throw away." From these and other first-hand sources, Roger Williams contrives a composite picture of Hank at the age of about twelve: "A tall, painfully thin boy with a shock of brown hair, a sad mouth and sadder eyes, and ears that stuck out much too far, a quietly happy boy, but content to go his own way at his own pace."

What made Hank "quietly happy" at that age was almost certainly music. Although his experience of music began in his infancy at Mt. Olive, where his mother played organ—that is, she accompanied the hymns—in the local Baptist church, and although he tooted on a harmonica when he was six, a potentially intense interest in music dated from the year 1934–35, which he spent with his McNeill cousins—Mrs. McNeill was his mother's sister—in Fountain, in neighboring Monroe County.

The McNeills lived in a camp car near a lumbering operation where Walter McNeill was employed. Young Hank, then eleven, was exposed to the music of Saturday-night dances, and it stuck to his ribs, as Roger Williams puts it, "like Mrs. McNeill's fried chicken." He heard the hymns every Sunday at Mrs. McNeill's Methodist church, and they must have made an indelible impression. Although he never became much of a churchgoer, his "sacred" songs, innocently and forthrightly fundamentalist in their diction and imagery, would number among his best and most popular. He did some hunting and fishing. He also did some drinking.

It was at Fountain, apparently, that he had his first taste of public performance, humming into a jazz horn, a kind of kazoo, at logging-camp dances and at the Fountain railroad station, where he would serenade incoming passengers. It is not certain whether he did this for money or just for the hell of it. The former seems likely, as he was an enterprising and industrious boy, ever willing to earn a bit of pocket money by selling peanuts and shining shoes.

There are conflicting stories about how he first came to take up the guitar. All that matters is that he had an instrument by the time he was twelve, and had learned the basic chords that would serve him the rest of his life. He had also, in Georgiana, encountered Tee-tot, the black street singer from Greenville, who included Georgiana on his minstrel circuit. In 1935 the Williamses moved to Greenville, the county seat of Butler County, and there Hank's work with Tee-tot began in earnest. The relationship became so close that Tee-tot used to worry about it. "Little white boss," he would say, "these here white folks won't like me takin' so much keer of you."

Tee-tot was a professional, if illiterate, entertainer. It was from him that Hank first learned the rudiments of establishing contact with, and appealing to, an audience, probably more by watching him at work than by specific and explicit instruction. He learned much, too, about matching accompaniment to song. He certainly learned the importance of establishing and maintaining a steady, swinging beat. He may have picked up some repertoire. There are those who attribute Hank's celebrated "Bucket's Got a Hole in It" to Tee-tot. It's an old song, but Hank probably got it from Tee-tot.

In July of 1937, when Hank was not quite fourteen, the family moved to Montgomery, where his mother opened a new boarding-house and where Hank, shortly thereafter, equipped with a new Gibson guitar and appropriately attired in boots and cowboy hat, entered an amateur contest at the local Empire Theater. He sang a song of his own, "WPA Blues," and won. He also won fifteen dollars, which he promptly, and prophetically, blew. He never learned to handle money or liquor. In the years to come he would run through prodigious quantities of each.

Back in Montgomery in 1937, rejoicing in the first taste of success as a performer before a paying public, he was still a long way from the big time and the big money. When he landed a twice-weekly fifteen-minute spot as "The Singing Kid" on Station WSFA, he was paid fifteen dollars for the two shows. It wasn't much, even by the standards of the time and the place. But the station covered most of southern Alabama. Before long Hank had his own band, the first version of the Drifting Cowboys, and was launched into that life of the itinerant musician, playing schoolhouses, granges, hoedowns, honky-tonks and barbecues, that would lead him eventually to Nashville, to *Grand Ole Opry*, to fame, to fortune and to ruin.

It was the best of all possible schooling—and the roughest and toughest. There were drinking and brawling. Drifting Cowboy Don Helm reminisces today about the kind of joints "where they sweep up the eyeballs every morning." He remembers how, when he and some other teenagers joined Hank in 1941, the young leader took them to a pawnshop and bought each of his new men a blackjack.

"You'll need these," Hank told them. Hank himself broke at least two guitars over the heads of backwoods roughnecks. But guitars were expensive, and Hank found the steel bar used to fret the steel guitar both more economical and more effective. Roger Williams gives this account of a typical outing:

On another occasion, the steel bar let him down to a point where it cost him a chunk of his eyebrow. As Hank told the story years later, a guy at a dance hall who'd been baiting him all night finally grabbed him, and the two of them tumbled onto the dance floor. Hank had been playing steel guitar, so he still had the bar in his hand. "I was poundin' him on the head with the steel bar, and he was about to go under. One more good blow woulda done it. But he reached out and bit a plug outta my eyebrow, hair and all." Hank bore the scar from that little tiff for the rest of his life.

There were more troublesome scars. He was already an alcoholic while still in his teens, given to periodic and incapacitating benders succeeded by stretches of varying length on the wagon. His mother was much in the picture, and often in the way. She and Hank fought continually and violently, just as Hank would later fight with Audrey Sheppard, a farm girl and would-be singer whom he married in 1944, when he was twenty-one. Many of Hank's songs may be heard as a chronicle of his life with Audrey, including one called "Mind Your Own Business," directed at those who gossiped about what went on in the Williams home. "Me and that sweet woman," the song says, "got a license to fight."

Hank's apprenticeship ended in 1942. He and his band, while regionally successful in a modest way, were not truly getting anywhere. The war was making it difficult for him to hold on to personnel for the Drifting Cowboys. He was himself rejected by the Army because of a back injury suffered during a brief and ill-advised flirtation with rodeo. There followed the year and a half with the Alabama Drydock and Shipbuilding Company. The interlude was probably good for him. When he quit the job and re-formed the Drifting Cowboys in 1944, things began to turn his way. Sammy Pruett joined the group as lead guitarist. Don Helm, released from the service, was back on steel guitar. Most importantly, Hank was beginning to mature and to find himself as a songwriter.

It was as a songwriter rather than as a singer that he presented himself to Fred Rose, of the then newly formed Acuff-Rose Publishing Company in Nashville in the fall of 1946. Fred Rose and his son, Wesley, heard Hank's songs and liked them. They signed him to a contract and bought the songs he had sung for them. It was a good day both for Acuff-Rose and for Hank Williams. The association would continue as long as Hank lived, with Fred Rose, a professional songwriter—among his songs was Sophie Tucker's hit, "Red Hot Mama"—providing the professional and commercial know-how required to put the final polish on the product of an unlettered, untutored country genius.

But if Fred Rose was attracted by the poet, Wesley remembered the singer. When a call came from Sterling Records in New York for a country singer, six months later, Wesley said to his father, "Hey, how about that skinny kid who came in with the songs? I liked his singing." "Okay," said Fred Rose. "Let's call him." Hank recorded "My Love for You [Has Turned to Hate]," "Never Again," and two of his sacred songs, "Wealth Won't Save Your Soul" and "When God Comes and Gathers His Jewels." In a subsequent session he cut four more sides, including "Honky-Tonk Blues," the first, and one of the best, of those up-tempo songs that provided a delightful contrast to the doleful ditties in the repertoire of Hank's best years.

Fred Rose was so impressed by these sessions—among the first, by the way, to be held in Nashville itself—that he negotiated a contract for Hank with Frank Walker, head of the recently founded M-G-M label, with which Hank was to remain for the rest of his brief career. He did almost all of his recording, however, in Nashville, and all of it under the guidance and supervision of Fred and Wesley Rose. His first record for M-G-M was "Move It On Over." It was an immediate hit.

Hank was not yet a big enough name for *Grand Ole Opry*, Mecca for country singers since 1926, and he needed a more indicative success as a public performer than was represented by his following in the Alabama boondocks. Fred Rose, accordingly, had him taken on by Station KWKH in Shreveport, whose weekend *Louisiana Hayride* was to that station what *Grand Ole Opry* was to Station

WSM in Nashville. Like *Grand Ole Opry* at that time, it ran an artists' service, booking its radio stars throughout western Louisiana and East Texas.

Hank matured as a singer and showman at Shreveport. He made of the Drifting Cowboys, with special emphasis on the fiddle and the steel guitar, the ideal setting for his songs and his singing. He wasn't an "arranger" in any conventional sense of the term. But he knew what he wanted from his backing group, and he got it by trial and error, by practice and repetition. Bob McNett, who joined the Cowboys as lead guitarist while Hank was working out of Shreveport, has recalled some of his habits, methods and characteristics as a leader:

> He got the musicians to work behind him just as he wanted. Nothing complicated, just plain and simple. He was a nut about rhythm. It had to be right and kept right. If one of us got a little hot on the instrument, he was quick to tell us to cut it out. He wanted the stuff played straight. He liked it that way, and he was convinced the public did, too. People still tell me, "You had the best band I ever heard," so he must have known what he was doing.

A typical Williams set, according to Roger Williams,

> would open, minus Hank, with a couple of instrumental numbers. Then the emcee, Bob McNett, after he joined the band, would introduce Hank with appropriate fanfare. Hank would come on, sing a song without saying anything, then introduce each of the band members. He always got some humor into his introductions, and the boys in the band led the audience in yukking it up over the jokes. The body of the show was Hank's singing. The band provided the accompaniment, with intermittent instrumental solos and a bit of vocal work on the choruses.

It was probably the most satisfactory period in Hank's life. The circuit operated by the *Louisiana Hayride* was a considerable cut above what he had known in the Alabama honky-tonks. He was a success on the air and with his audiences on the road. His records and his songs were selling, and they drew attention to him far beyond the area covered by the *Hayride*. He was making enough money, and he

Ernest Tubb

Red Foley   Roy Acuff

was drinking less. His eye, of course, was on *Grand Ole Opry*, and he knew that *Grand Ole Opry*, well aware of his reputation for "unreliability," was keeping a weather eye on him.

His ticket to the *Opry* turned out to be, curiously enough, "Lovesick Blues," a song, as noted earlier, that was neither his nor typical of the songs he sang. No one seems to know just how he came upon it. He introduced it at Shreveport, and it immediately became his biggest number. Wesley Rose went to Shreveport to hear it. A recording was made and it shot right to the top of the charts. At the end of 1949 it was voted Best Hillbilly Record of the year in the *Cash Box* poll of jukebox operators, and was Number 1 in *Billboard's* listing of country-and-western records.

Grand Ole Opry had already got the message. Hank was given a guest slot on the night of June 11, 1949. He sang "Lovesick Blues" and brought down the house. Within a matter of months he was the brightest star country music had ever known. He was also the most erratic and the most miserable, as unable to handle success and prosperity as he had hitherto been unable to handle whiskey and women.

The refuge he sought in liquor and drugs became a private prison, a private hell and a public disaster. As time went on, he ever more frequently failed to show up for his scheduled engagements. He was sometimes too drunk to remember even the words of his own songs when he did. Three and a half years after that memorable debut at *Grand Ole Opry* he was dead in Oak Hill, West Virginia, in the back seat of the car taking him to a New Year's Day engagement in Canton, Ohio.

He was buried in Montgomery on January 4, 1953. It was fitting that both Roy Acuff and Ernest Tubb, as well as Red Foley, should sing at the funeral. In the chronology of country music they occupy an intermediate station between Jimmie Rodgers and Hank Williams, and they were, after his initial exposure to Jimmie Rodgers, Hank's early models. He used to say that his own style was a cross between them, a combination of Acuff's wail and Tubb's phrasing.

Tubb sang "Beyond the Sunset." Acuff sang Hank's "I Saw the Light," joined on the choruses by Foley, Carl Smith and Webb Pierce. Then Foley sang the traditional "Peace in the Valley," choking up as he did so. The Reverend Henry L. Lyon, pastor of Montgomery's Highland Avenue Baptist Church, said sensibly, "I

Minnie Pearl

Kitty Wells   Loretta Lynn

can't preach Hank's funeral. He preached it himself in song. He had a message written in the language of all the people. His life was a real personification of what can happen in this country to one little insignificant speck of humanity."

A monument marks the grave. Nothing wrong in that. But as a memorial it seems a puny thing beside the songs and the records. No other singer has left quite so eloquent or explicit a self-portrait. Play "Ramblin' Man," or "I Feel So Lonesome I Could Cry," or "You Win Again," and then remember Minnie Pearl describing Hank's features: "Especially his eyes. He had the most haunting and haunted eyes I'd ever looked into. They were deep-set, very brown and very tragic."

Or remember the valedictory Hank himself used to offer at the close of his concerts, promising to see the folks again, "if the good Lord's willin' and the creeks don't rise. Don't worry about nothin' 'cause it ain't gonna be all right nohow!"

It wasn't, under the circumstances, a good joke; it was, rather, a wry statement of fact. But as Eva Weissman, president of the Hank and Audrey Williams International Fan Club, has put it, "If he wouldn't have been the way he was—would we have these songs today?"

14

Ray Charles

The first lesson to be learned by anyone coming from the European world of opera and art song to the Afro-American world of contemporary popular singing is that there is more than one way of phrasing and more than one way of producing the voice. And in the hundreds of records cut by Ray Charles in a career already spanning more than a quarter of a century, one can hear instructive if not invariably successful examples of most of them.

No other singer has dipped into so many styles. He began in 1949, when he was nineteen, on the obscure Swingtime label, both as singer and pianist, imitating the light-fingered, light-voiced, jazz-tinged rhythm-and-blues stylings of early Nat King Cole. After signing with Atlantic Records in 1954, he moved to an earthier, rougher, urban blues idiom more congenial to his native musicality and to an essentially unlovely voice. This soon gave way to a manner of singing and phrasing, and to a type of semichoral arrangement in which a gospel feeling was prominent, often dominant. He also favored a kind of blueslike utterance harking back to the older idioms of the rural South. He could always play and sing jazz. And however he sang, he always sounded like Ray Charles.

He forsook Atlantic for ABC-Paramount in 1959 and experimented with popular ballads in the style of the later Nat Cole and

even of Frank Sinatra. Thereafter came a series of country-and-western records, when he sang the songs of, among others, Hank Williams and Eddy Arnold. In the late 1960s he was trying his hand at Beatles numbers, notably "Yesterday" and "Eleanor Rigby." It has been an extraordinary stylistic odyssey, especially for a singer of such meagre vocal endowment.

Or maybe not. Singers with beautiful voices tend to find and stay with the style that shows off the voice to the best advantage. They become, in a sense, prisoners, first of their own voices, then of the devices they have evolved to give their use of the voice a distinctive character. With Ray Charles it has been the other way around. Rather than seek a style congenial to a beautiful voice, he had to find a style compatible with his want of one. He found it in gospel, becoming, paradoxically, one of the greatest of all gospel singers without ever singing gospel! Not being bound to the church, or to its music, he was free to lend a gospel fervor to many other kinds of music.

He was not, certainly, the originator of what is now called soul singing. But he was a singer who translated soul, or gospel, into secular terms. He released it, as an idiom, from the confines of storefront Holiness and Sanctified churches, introduced it to a wider secular public, both black and white, and prepared the way for the subsequent secular success of many singers reared in gospel, among them Ruth Brown, Sam Cooke, Aretha Franklin, Wilson Pickett, Lou Rawls and Dionne Warwicke.

Of the many kinds of singing that have evolved in the roughly fifty years of Afro-American popular singing, soul falls least engagingly upon ears attuned to European concepts and notions of what constitutes good or even acceptable singing. Those concepts and notions, embodied in the term *bel canto*, envision, as I have noted earlier, a vocal tone well rounded and modulated, covering a range of about two octaves without discernible register breaks, without audible or perceptible stress and strain, and, above all, without any suggestion of screaming, shouting, shrieking or yelling. And it is precisely screaming, shouting, shrieking and yelling that soul is all about—or so it seems to the European-oriented ear.

There is a lot of that in opera, too. American blacks, not brought up on opera, hear it. I am thinking of a passage in Pearl Bailey's memoirs, *The Raw Pearl*, describing a visit to the opera in Rome: "I

Sam Cooke

Ruth Brown

didn't know what they were talking about anyhow, the singing, you know, the screaming. . . ." She was right. But in opera the screaming occurs in a dramatic, rather than an ecstatic or orgiastic, context; and it has, moreover, crept into the idiom slowly, gradually, almost imperceptibly, as a result of larger houses, larger and louder orchestras, a rising pitch and the heavier vocal requirements of Meyerbeer, Verdi, Wagner, Puccini and Strauss. Opera-goers today accept without indignation vocal emissions that would have been roundly and rightly denounced as bawling by eighteenth-century connoisseurs of *bel canto*.

But they will not, as a rule, accept the sounds of soul. The reason, I suspect, is not so much that those sounds are felt to be ugly as that they are felt to be primitive. This was certainly the motivation behind much of the violent rejection of jazz by European-oriented musicians and music lovers in the 1920s and 1930s. Jazz eventually prevailed—not with every European-oriented listener, to be sure— because subsequent generations found in its primitiveness a vitality long since refined out of European music. Similarly, the sounds of soul (rhythm-and-blues and gospel), originally rejected by Europeanoriented listeners (and jazz musicians and jazz lovers too) are now enjoyed by a subsequent generation for a vitality long since refined out of jazz. Ray Charles already begins to appear, in retrospect, to have been to soul what Louis Armstrong was to jazz—the herald of a new style.

Actually, as with jazz, the soul sound is not so far removed from European precedent as it must seem, on first encounter, to the uninitiated. Three elements, especially, it shares with seventeenth- and eighteenth-century European vocal practice: *rubato*, falsetto and melismatic ornamentation. And for each of these elements even more striking parallels may be found in European conventions dating from medieval times and earlier, derived, significantly, from Hebrew and early Christian liturgical practice. All three elements are common in the vocal music of Asians and Africans.

Those who reject soul singing out of hand are guided, as an earlier generation was guided in rejecting jazz, by the assumption that the performance conventions of nineteenth-century Europe represented an esthetic peak of musical accomplishment in terms of creativity, virtuosity and taste, from which any deviation or retreat

into earlier practices must seem a betrayal of Bach, Beethoven, Brahms, Wagner and comparable European masters. Such deviation or retreat, especially if thought to reflect atavistic tendencies, seemed to be a defiance of civilized accomplishment, a willful abandonment of high standards of human conduct.

In some respects, with jazz, as now with soul, this is true. But it is also true that European (classical, or serious) music had, in the course of harmonic elaboration and expressive refinement, drifted too far from its roots in song and dance. Excessive intellectualization had sapped its physical and emotional vitality. Jazz, despite its prevailingly instrumental character, was distinguished by a type of phrasing shaped by the contours and inflections of Afro-American speech, a heritage of the blues. Soul goes even further back, beyond language to expressive vocal sound. Sinatra, and before him Bing Crosby, had been a master of words. Ray Charles is a master of sounds.

His records disclose an extraordinary assortment of slurs, glides, turns, shrieks, wails, breaks, shouts, screams and hollers, all wonderfully controlled, disciplined by inspired musicianship, and harnessed to ingenious subtleties of harmony, dynamics and rhythm. What he sings, whether his own songs or those of others, begins as text. But whereas a Sinatra, or even the less tuneful Billie Holiday, would find and illuminate the music inherent or implicit in a word, Charles finds in the word, or the textural phrase, little more than a springboard for sonorous excursion.

It is the singing either of a man whose vocabulary is inadequate to express what is in his heart and mind or of one whose feelings are too intense for satisfactory verbal or conventionally melodic articulation. He can't *tell* it to you. He can't even sing it to you. He has to cry out to you, or shout to you, in tones eloquent of despair—or exaltation. The voice alone, with little assistance from the text or the notated music, conveys the message.

The esthetic danger implicit in soul singing, and all too often explicit, too, is its easy susceptibility to abuse. The line separating true ecstasy and empty, dreary, vulgar, tiresome exhibitionism, as in much pop-gospel and in much soul-derived modern jazz, is too thin. The fervor of soul singing at its best cannot be evoked or aroused at a moment's notice night after night by artists doing two shows a night, and only the very greatest artists can simulate it satisfactorily. There

◀ José Feliciano

is the further hazard of exhaustion common to any art form dealing so nearly exclusively in superlatives. The superlative, as Hanslick noted wisely of Wagner, has no future.

But it can have a compelling present, and no artist has revealed it in soul more vividly and consistently, outside of church, than Ray Charles. In the process he has accomplished miracles of vocalism, feats that leave the traditionally trained singer shaking his head in disbelief. It belongs to the very nature and purpose of soul singing that the singer appear continuously to be under pressure, to be straining at the limits of his vocal range. It is not easy.

Ray Charles is usually described as a baritone, and his speaking voice would suggest as much, as would the difficulty he experiences in reaching and sustaining the baritone's high E and F in a popular ballad. But the voice undergoes some sort of transfiguration under stress, and in music of a gospel or blues character he can and does sing for measures on end in a high tenor range on A, B flat, B, C and even C sharp and D, sometimes in full voice, sometimes in a kind of ecstatic head voice, sometimes in falsetto.

In falsetto he continues on up to the E and F above high C. On one extraordinary record, "I'm Going Down to the River," my favorite among all the Ray Charles records I have heard, he hits an incredible B flat. He has no lower register to speak of, and uses it rarely, although there are instances on records where he sings down to the low A and A flat, giving him an overall range, including the falsetto extension, of at least three octaves.

To the classical singer it seems a wonder that a voice could survive such treatment for more than a year or two, let alone the twenty-five years that Ray Charles has been singing in this fashion without apparent vocal damage. Other soul singers, both male and female, have similar histories of vocal survival, including such white offshoots as Elvis Presley and José Feliciano. Ray Charles often sounds hoarse, but then he always did. And the hoarse sound is singularly appropriate to his manner of vocal utterance.

I can only guess at an explanation. As a starter, I would suggest that the soul singer's ignorance or avoidance of the classical singer's technique for disguising or covering the upper-register break may be his salvation. Covering the register break, as classical singers do it, involves considerable muscular exertion, imperceptible as this may be to the listener. The natural tendency of the voice to break as it moves upward toward the limit of the normal range has to be frustrated and suppressed. It seems inevitable to me that the muscles concerned in this exercise become less malleable, less responsive, with age, and rebel, thus shortening the vocal life of many classical singers, especially opera singers.

The soul singer sings with little wittingly imposed laryngeal discipline up to and through the breaking point, actually making expressive use of the break, and he continues on into head voice or falsetto, rather than into an upper register, without embarrassment. The use of falsetto was common in European music until about the middle of the nineteenth century, when it was found to be inappropriate for the later melodramatic requirements of grand opera and Wagnerian music drama. It was probably also felt to be effeminate, or at least lacking in virility. Black blues and gospel sin, ers, even black popular singers, both male and female, have always used it effectively and without inhibition. Classical singers could learn a lot from their example.

It is a matter of some curiosity as to how Ray Charles, born Ray Charles Robinson to poor parents in Albany, Georgia, on September 23, 1930, black, and blinded by glaucoma at the age of seven, should have drifted into and mastered a style of singing we now think of as "soul." It was, when he was a boy, still essentially a church style, and although brought up in the Baptist faith, he seems never to have felt a vocation to be a church singer.

Like Nat King Cole, he was originally an instrumentalist, playing both piano and alto saxophone. Also like Cole, he seems to have had both a remarkably assimilative musicality and a widely ranging interest in music, his enthusiasms extending from classical music—which he learned to read from Braille while a student at the St. Augustine School for Deaf and Blind Children in Orlando, Florida—through rural blues and jazz to country-and-western.

> I was an exellent musical student [he told Whitney Balliett in a *New Yorker* Profile]. I studied Chopin and Mozart and Bach. Beethoven had a lot of feeling, but Bach was nervous, with all those lines running against each other. Classical music is a great foundation for playing jazz. You play correctly, with the right fingering. With classical music you play exactly what the man wrote, but in jazz, when you get rid of the melody, you put yourself in. So, every time I thought my teacher wasn't listening,

I played jazz. And I listened to Goodman and Basie and Ellington and Erskine Hawkins and Andy Kirk and Lunceford and Tiny Bradshaw and Artie Shaw. Shaw got me interested in clarinet, so I took it up with the alto saxophone and a little trumpet. . . .

In speaking of influences he has also mentioned Charles Brown (whose Three Blazers followed in the footsteps of the King Cole Trio in the mid-1940s), Nat Cole, Big Boy Crudup, Blind Boy Phillips, Tampa Red, Washboard Sam, Art Tatum, Joe Turner, Muddy Waters, Sonny Boy Williamson and—Grand Ole Opry, which he started listening to on the radio when he was eight.

It is a protean assortment, curiously lacking in gospel names. But Tony Heilbut, in The Gospel Sound, quotes Alex Bradford, one of the greatest of gospel singers and composers, as saying: "Ray Charles told me I was his ideal as a gospel singer." Further, according to Heilbut, Charles was influenced by a gospel quintet, the Five Blind Boys. It seems noteworthy, in view of Charles's predilections and accomplishments as a falsettist, that Alex Bradford as a young man used to sing up to the A above high C.

But the ultimate emergence of a vocal and musical style so clearly derived from early blues and gospel may probably be attributed most reasonably to musical sensibility, strong character and good sense. Ray listened, learned and experimented. When he encountered the style that suited him he recognized and pursued it, even if it meant composing most of the music himself, as he had to do in the absence of any established secular repertoire in the gospel idiom. His good sense, combined with a considerable fund of business acumen, told him that he would have to adapt it to other idioms if he would break out of the circumscribed market for race records.

In a Playboy interview some years ago he was asked, "Why do you think the top black female vocalists, such as Ella Fitzgerald, Sarah Vaughan, Carmen McRae and Nancy Wilson, have been striving over the past generation for a more 'legitimate' sound than the Bessie Smiths, Ma Raineys, Nellie Lutchers and Dinah Washingtons had?"

And Ray replied: "I'd say that singers like Carmen and Ella and Sarah are trying to get to as many people as they can—and not just for the sake of money, either. When the President makes a speech, he wants to speak to all Americans. These girls obviously reach more

Carmen McRae

Nancy Wilson

people than they would if they only sang blues. I sing in more than one way for the same reason."

For Ray Charles, singing in "more than one way" has not been so simple as it sounds. Ella, Sarah, Carmen and Nancy all have had a vocal equipment and a vocal technique compatible with the requirements of singing the songs of the American popular-music mainstream, and they could sing them idiomatically, the performance rendered the more attractive by just the right touch of African exoticism. Ray has had neither the lovely voice nor the musical predisposition to excel consistently in that repertoire, which demands, above all, the ability to sustain a given melody.

He has always been more talker, or shouter, than singer in any conventional sense. He finds mere melody inhibiting, as witness his statement to Balliett: "In jazz, when you get rid of the melody, you put yourself in." Elsewhere he has said that melody is "your guideline, or radar." It was probably the awareness of his own predilections and limitations that guided him into country music, in which, as in gospel, melody takes second place to oratory. He had, of course, a lifelong liking for the country idiom and a shrewd appreciation of its market.

Ray's records and interviews reflect a constant preoccupation with such problems of style, repertoire—and market. He has tried just about everything except spirituals. He has had his failures—I would reckon "Eleanor Rigby" and "Yesterday" among them, although they did well for him—and he has usually recognized them. He is no Sinatra, nor even a Nat Cole. He hasn't the big, robust voice of a Joe Turner or a Jimmy Rushing to belt out the jazz-tinged blues of early Count Basie (compare his recording of "How Long?" with Joe Turner's).

He can handle early rural blues. He was born for gospel. He is at home in the urban rhythm-and-blues idiom of the 1940s. He finds country music congenial. Some popular songs lend themselves better than others to his voice and personal style. "Georgia," for example, is one of the finest records he ever made. And he has sought out songs like these.

> I'm not even sure I'm a singer [he told Whitney Balliett].
> I've been able to take a pop song, and it paid off, and a country-
> and-western, and a blues, and standards like "Old Man River"

and "Georgia," and they paid off. But I've tried to find songs I can get the feeling of. I must please myself before I sing a song in public. The song must strike me some way in my heart. Now, I love "Stardust," but I'll never record it. Every time I sing the song to myself, I can't get the feeling out of it. The same with the national anthem and Nat Cole's "Nature Boy." I loved that record, but I can't sing it to sink.

Charles is today a millionaire, president of R.P.M. (Recordings, Publishing and Management), with headquarters in Los Angeles; owner (not pilot, contrary to scary legend) of two airplanes (a Viscount four-engine turboprop and a twin-engine Cessna 300), and squire of a $300,000 home in nearby View Park for his wife and three boys. "It's all a matter of zeros," he told *Playboy*, "whether you're talking about ten bucks or $100,000. Since I'm in business to make an honest dollar—because I'm too chicken to steal—I figure I might as well make two or three while I'm at it."

He started picking up an honest buck or two when he was fifteen, suddenly not only black and blind, but also orphaned. He quit school, went to live with family friends, and jobbed around Florida as a pianist, saxophonist, singer and arranger (dictating the notes). One of the groups he worked with was a white hillbilly group called the Florida Playboys, whose pianist had dropped out. From them he learned to yodel. It wasn't easy sailing. "Times and me got leaner and leaner," he recalls today, "but anything beats getting a cane and a cup and picking out a street corner."

He seems always to have been both adventurous and decisive. His quitting school at fifteen and starting to earn a living as a musician was an initial example. Another was his decision, as soon as he had saved some money, to go to Seattle.

I decided I wanted to get out on my own [he told Balliett], go to a nice-sized city the furthest from where I was. I was afraid of New York and Chicago. I had a friend, and we took a map of the country, and he traced a straight line diagonally as far as it would go, and it hit Seattle. I didn't know anybody there, and nobody had sent for me, but I got on the bus. . . .

He made contacts in Seattle, formed his own trio, modeled on the King Cole Trio, and worked the local clubs. Quincy Jones, who many years later would do the arrangements for a Charles recording with the Count Basie Band, *Genius Plus Soul Equals Jazz*, met him there. Ray was seventeen, Quincy fifteen. "He was like forty years old, then," Quincy recalls. "He knew everything. He knew about ladies and music and life, because he was so independent." Curiously, many listeners to Ray's earliest recordings have heard in them the voice of "an old man."

He went to Los Angeles in 1949, toured the West with blues man Lowell Fulson, and went with Fulson to New York, where he appeared at the Apollo Theater and was signed by the Shaw agency. After a considerable and, for a singer still far from established, hazardous hassle about the kind of musicians he was getting to work with, he was allowed to form his own backing band, and he worked for a time with Ruth Brown, a gospel-reared rhythm-and-blues singer from whom, as from Fulson, he probably learned a lot about the rudiments of showmanship. In 1954 he had his first record hit with "I Got a Woman." It established a precedent of success that continues to this day.

Reviewing Ray Charles's extraordinary career, it is difficult, but important, to place his many accomplishments in perspective. The manner in which he has prevailed over blackness, blindness and a long siege of drug addiction excites admiration. The breadth and depth of his musicianship, and his achievement in secularizing a style hitherto confined to gospel, are matters of far-reaching musico-historical significance. The pleasure he has brought to millions all over the world, on records and in personal appearances, is a heart-warming fact.

But in terms of the evolution of Afro-American music and the part played in it by black Americans, there is more to it than that. Ray Charles was not just the first singer to secularize gospel music. Far more importantly, he was the first black singer to win acceptance by a large national and international public, largely white, without whitening his music, or without having sung white music in a fairly white way from the beginning.

Not that he willed it so. He tried everything, and in trying he discovered that a gospel style was what came naturally. It was the later, 1940s gospel style, to be sure, with its mixture of blues, rhythm-and-blues and jazz. In it he found everything congenial to his own oratorical and musical predilections, including the call-and-response (antiphonal) devices of black church services. He has exploited these consistently and successfully with the girl quartet, the Raelets, backed by a wailing big jazz band. Thus surrounded and supported, he can sit down at the piano, turn to an audience, rock to a slow beat or jump to a fast one, right leg pounding, swaying wildly from side to side, and pour his heart out.

The timing was a factor. He anticipated by only a year or two the rock explosion heralded by Elvis Presley and Carl Perkins, which launched something close to gospel into the mainstream of American music. Charles may have contributed to its acceptance. But he spoke to a more varied audience. The Charles fans were not limited to restive teenagers, nor was there in his lyrics anything akin to the brash, acerbic, defiant social attitudes that sparked a generation—and a race—gap in the assertive and irreverent imagery of the songs of Chuck Berry and Bo Diddley. Ray Charles did not incorporate a message. He incorporated—Ray Charles.

"Do you think there is any element of your style," he was asked by *Playboy*, "that is essential to your continued popularity?"

Ray, characteristically, knew the answer.

"Yeah," he replied. "*Me.*"

15

Elvis Presley

During the lunch hour, one day in the summer of 1953, Elvis Aron Presley, then eighteen, and driving a truck for the Crown Electric Company of Memphis, Tennessee, dropped in at the Memphis Recording Service, put four dollars on the line, and recorded the Ink Spots' "My Happiness" and a sentimental ballad, "That's When Your Heartaches Begin." He accompanied himself on his own beat-up guitar, sounding, as he said years later, "like somebody beatin' on a bucket lid."

The Memphis Recording Service was a profitable adjunct of Sam Phillips' Sun Record Company. Sam was out of the shop, and Elvis was greeted by Marion Keisker, his office manager. She, not long ago, gave Jerry Hopkins, Elvis's biographer, this account of that first recording:

"While he was waiting his turn, we had a conversation. He said he was a singer. I said, 'What kind of a singer are you?' He said, 'I sing all kinds.' I said, 'Who do you sound like?' He said, 'I don't sound like nobody.' I thought, 'Oh, yeah, one of those!' I said, 'Hillbilly?' He said, 'Yeah, I sing hillbilly.' I said, 'Who do you sound like in hillbilly?' He said, 'I don't sound like nobody.' "

Elvis, in that last simple, ungrammatical declarative sentence, was offering an incomplete but otherwise impeccable definition of his

263

uniqueness as a singer. He did not sound like anybody else then, and he does not sound like anybody else now. Nor does anybody else sound much like him. The Welshman Tom Jones has mastered the style and the stage format. But he does not sound like Elvis.

The great singers are always unique. Louis Armstrong, Nat Cole, Bing Crosby, Al Jolson, Frank Sinatra and Ethel Waters have been imitated. The best of their imitators have sung well. But there have been no duplicates. One recognizes and acknowledges the original in the first eight measures.

It is not merely a matter of timbre, of the quality, color or size of the voice as it is heard on any single pitch, or even as it might be heard in a vocal exercise. The sound becomes fully alive and distinctive only in the articulation of the musical phrase as shaped by the text and by the singer's identification with language. Elvis Presley's enunciation has not always been immaculate, although it can be as distinct as anybody's when he wants it to be. But he has never sung a phrase whose contours were not derived from his own native Southern American speech.

His musical upbringing, if such it may be called, began with the white gospel music of the First Assembly of God Church in Tupelo, Mississippi, or rather in poorer East Tupelo, where he was born on January 8, 1935. Elvis' mother tells how "when he was just a little fellow, he would slide off my lap, run down the aisle, and scramble up to the platform, stand there looking up at the choir, and try to sing with them. He was too little to know the words, but he could carry the tune."

It was not just the singing. Even in the Pentecostal denominations, white congregations were less given to exuberant vocal exaltation and incantation than the black. The preachers were another matter. As Elvis has since told it:

We used to go to these religious singin's all the time. There were these singers, perfectly fine singers, but nobody responded to them. Then there was the preachers, and they cut up all over the place, jumpin' on the piano, movin' ever' which way. The audience liked them. I guess I learned from them.

He was given a $12.95 guitar when he was about ten, a substitute for the bicycle his family could not afford. With a little help from his uncles, he taught himself to play it. He started, sensibly, listening to the radio, copying what he heard. The principal musical fare in East Tupelo was, predictably, hillbilly, not yet upgraded to a more decorous categorization as country-and-western. He heard the big names of the time: Roy Acuff, Jimmie Rodgers, Ernest Tubb and Bob Wills, among others. But he was also listening to music originating from Station WDIA in Memphis, a black station broadcasting such up-and-coming Delta blues singers as Arthur (Big Boy) Crudup, Arthur Gunter, B. B. King, Junior Parker and Muddy Waters. Some of their songs would later become Elvis Presley hits. As Elvis himself has told it:

> I'd play along with the radio or phonograph, and taught myself the chord positions. We were a religious family, going around together to sing at camp meetings and revivals, and I'd take my guitar along with us when I could. I also dug the real low-down Mississippi singers, mostly Big Bill Broonzy and Big Boy Crudup, although they would scold me at home for listening to them. "Sinful music," the towns folk in Memphis said it was. Which never bothered me, I guess. . . .

According to Tony Heilbut, in *The Gospel Sound*, Elvis, after the family had moved to Memphis, also attended services at the East Trigg Baptist Church, listening to Queen C. Anderson ("Queen of the South") and the congregation's famous pastor, the Reverend W. Herbert Brewster, among whose many fine hymns was "Move On Up a Little Higher," which gave Mahalia Jackson not only one of her greatest hits but also the title of her autobiography.

Elvis' earliest records bear testimony to his affinity for black blues and gospel and to his gift for assimilating their idiomatic characteristics. On them he discloses, as Charles Gillett has put it in *The Sound of the City.*

> . . . a personal version of this style, singing high and clear, breathless and impatient, varying his rhythmic emphasis with a confidence and inventiveness that were exceptional for a white singer. The sound suggested a young white man celebrating freedom, ready to do anything, go anywhere. . . .

Even by the time he walked into the Memphis Recording Service that noontime in the summer of 1953, this black style had

Arthur "Big Boy" Crudup

Muddy Waters Big Bill Broonzy

become an indelible part of his way with a song. Marion Keisker
heard it.

> When we went back to make the record, a 10-inch acetate [she
> told Jerry Hopkins], he got about halfway through the first side,
> and I thought, "I want to tape this."
>
> Now this is something we never did, but I wanted Sam to
> hear this. He was out at the time, and the only thing I could find
> was a crumply piece of tape, and by the time I got it set up I'd
> missed part of the first song. I got maybe the last third of it and
> all the second song. . . . The reason I taped Elvis was this:
> Over and over I remember Sam saying, "If I could find a white
> man who had the Negro sound and the Negro feel, I could make
> a billion dollars." This is what I heard in Elvis, this . . . what I
> guess they now call "soul," this Negro sound. So I taped it. I
> wanted Sam to know.

She wrote down Elvis' name and address on a slip of paper and
noted: "Good ballad singer. Hold."

Of such providential coincidences is music history made. Or, to
put it more rationally, music history makes such coincidences appear
to have been providentially ordered. Sam Phillips had been introduced to the blues while sitting on the knee of a black man, Uncle
Silas Payne, on his father's Alabama plantation. Years later, recalling
how he had quit a well-paid job as radio announcer in Memphis to
pioneer in the recording of black artists, he said, "It seemed to me
that the Negroes were the only ones who had any freshness left in
their music, and there was no place in the South where they could go
to record. The nearest place where they made so-called 'race' records
—which was soon to be called 'rhythm-and-blues'—was Chicago, and
most of them didn't have the money or time to make the trip to
Chicago."

Sam began by recording local blues singers and selling the
aluminum masters to Chess and Checker Records, in Chicago, and to
Modern and RPM Records in Los Angeles. In 1953, the year Elvis
walked in, he began issuing records under his own Sun label, among
them Little Junior Parker's "Love My Baby." It would be the better
part of another year before he got around to Elvis. Early in January
1954, Elvis came again to Memphis Recording Service to cut a four-

dollar record. This time Sam was in and Marion Keisker was out. Elvis sang two country ballads, "Casual Love" and "I'll Never Stand in Your Way." Sam was impressed. He noted Elvis' name, address and phone number (a neighbor's—the Presleys could not afford a telephone), and for the time being that was that. Sam thought that Elvis "wasn't quite ready." Probably he wasn't. But he was working at it, singing at every opportunity and getting useful exposure and experience as soloist in spirituals at all-night "gospel sings" in a local auditorium, backed by a gospel quartet, the Songfellows.

Sam finally called Elvis to duplicate a demo record he had liked by a young black singer he could neither identify nor locate. Elvis' attempt was a failure, but it led to further experiments with backings by guitarist Scotty Moore and bassist Bill Black. One night, months later, Sam decided that the time had come to make a tape. Scotty Moore tells what happened:

> The first thing that was put on tape was "I Love You Because." Then Elvis did a couple of those country-orientated things. They were all right. Little while later we were sitting there drinking a Coke, shooting the bull, Sam back in the control room. So Elvis picked up his guitar and started banging on it and singing "That's All Right, Mama," jumpin' around the studio, just acting the fool. And Bill started beating on his bass, and I joined in. Just making a bunch of racket, we thought. The door to the control room was open, and when we was halfway through the thing, Sam came running out and said, "What in the devil are you doing?" We said, "We don't know." He said, "Well, find out real quick, and don't lose it. Run through it again, and let's put it on tape!" So to the best of our knowledge we repeated what we just done, and went through the whole thing.
>
> We spent three or four nights trying to get a back side in the same vein. We finally did "Blue Moon of Kentucky," and this came about the same way. We'd gone through this song, that song, and I don't think any of them were on tape. Then Bill jumped up, started clowning with his bass and singing "Blue Moon of Kentucky" in falsetto, mimicking Bill Monroe [the bluegrass musician whose song it was]. And Elvis started banging on his guitar. And the rhythm thing jelled again. That was the first record.

Says Jerry Hopkins:

What had been cut in the tiny studio was in many ways historic. Not only were Elvis and his two back-up musicians combining the sounds of white country and black blues to form what would be called "rockabilly," but on "That's All Right, Mama," the blues song, the instrumentation gave the version a country sound, while on Bill Monroe's bluegrass hit Elvis was singing the blues. Scotty says he and Bill shook their heads as they listened to the playback, agreeing that, yes, the sound was exciting enough, "but good God, they'll run us outa town when they hear it." Mixing black and white music wasn't as acceptable then as it would be just a few years later.

Hopkins' "in many ways historic" is, if anything, an understatement. Those two sides were just what he says they were, but they were more than that. They heralded a metamorphosis of popular music, a new phase in the interaction of white and black musicality that had already given the world ragtime, jazz, swing and bop. They represented the convergence in one small-town boy, born at the right time, in the right place, in the right environment and under the right circumstances, of all the musical currents of America's subcultures: black and white gospel, country-and-western, and rhythm-and-blues. Within two years Elvis would be the talk of the nation. As with Louis Armstrong's "West End Blues," recorded in 1928, popular music would never be the same again.

A phenomenon common to all the most original and the most influential of the great American popular singers has been the animosity they have aroused. It is not quite the right word. Loathing probably comes closer, or contempt. They have been enormously, prodigiously popular, and they have earned a lot of money. (Elvis' earnings have been reckoned at upward of fifty million dollars.) Had the singers been less popular, they would have been less intensely rejected, less cruelly, mercilessly ridiculed. Jolson was put down for his brashness and sentimentality, Bing Crosby for what seemed to many, when it was new, his blubbery crooning and his obtrusive ears, and the young Sinatra for his gentle sighing—callow and gutless it seemed to the older folks back in the early 1940s. But none, probably, has been so severely anathematized as Elvis Presley.

There was always, to be sure, something in his appearance and performance that invited caricature, that seemed preposterous and outrageous, and so he had to endure Elvis the Pelvis, and such jokes as the one to the effect that what so disturbed his mother about Elvis the Pelvis was that Elvis had a younger brother named Enos (he doesn't). Even after his re-emergence on an NBC-TV special in 1968, and at Las Vegas in 1969, critics by now well disposed could not resist descriptions as unflattering as they were picturesque.

Albert Goldman, for example, reviewing the NBC-TV special for *The New York Times*, spoke of "novocaine lip, hormone hair, pale poached face dripping into black leather." Robert Shelton, reviewing the same show, also for *The New York Times*, referred to "a twisted smile suggesting a cross between George Wallace and Richard Burton." To Alexander Walker, movie critic of the London *Evening Standard*, he was "a mascot dolly jigging in a car window," and for Richard Goldstein, again in *The New York Times*, he was "a white boy with black hips."

It was, initially, pretty much a sexual thing. As Jerry Hopkins has put it:

> Until rock 'n' roll (and Elvis) came along, "popular music" was 100 percent White Bread America—starch with no nutriments but lots of added preservatives. There had been a total embargo on sex in pop music. Teenagers were worrying about saltpeter in their school cafeteria lunch. . . . Could Rosemary Clooney and Eddie Fisher mean anything to them? So along came rock 'n' roll, dealing with sex point-blank. And along came Elvis, putting action to the words he sang.

As Ray Connolly, pop feature writer for the London *Evening Standard*, expressed it, many years later, Elvis' guitar was "a sort of phallic tommy-gun." Another English commentator, Tony Palmer, of the London *Observer*, summed it up as succinctly as anyone. Elvis, he said, was "the first teenage symbol that grown-ups couldn't possibly share."

How little they could share it, or wanted to, was reflected by Jack Gould, television critic of *The New York Times*, reviewing Elvis' appearance on the Milton Berle show on June 6, 1956:

Mr. Presley has no discernible singing ability. His specialty is rhythm songs, which he renders in an undistinguished whine; his phrasing, if it can be called that, consists of the stereotyped variations that go with a beginner's aria in a bathtub. For the ear, he is an unutterable bore, not nearly so talented as Frank Sinatra back in the latter's rather hysterical days at the Paramount Theater. Nor does he convey the emotional fury of a Johnnie Ray.

From watching Mr. Presley it is wholly evident that his skill lies in another direction. He is a rock 'n' roll variation of one of the most standard acts in show business: the virtuoso of the hootchy-kootchy. His one specialty is an accented movement of the body that heretofore has been primarily identified with the repertoire of the blonde bombshells of the burlesque runway. The gyrations never had anything to do with the world of popular music, and still don't.

A paradox about Elvis is the fact that he has never, in his social conduct and behavior off-stage, represented or embodied the defiant, disaffected, liberated attitudes which he came to symbolize for his contemporaries. Something of such attitudes may have been latent. He was given, as a youngster, to loud, rather offbeat attire, and he was wearing sideburns and having a pompadour with ducktail fashioned at a beautician's at a time when, and in a community where, such affectations were hardly typical of a young, presumably red-blooded middle-American boy. For the rest, he was closer to the mother's boy and teacher's pet than to the angry young man. He was an average student and a sometime football player. "Sweet" was a word used by some of his elders to describe him. He was polite and deferential, saying "Yes, sir" and "No, ma'am" and rising when older people entered a room, as he does to this day.

Certainly he was not, initially, wittingly offensive. In an early interview, released on a 45 rpm record in cooperation with *TV Guide,* he had something to say about those corybantic gyrations:

The very first appearance after I started to record, I was on a show in Memphis where I started doin' that. I was on the show as an extra added single . . . a big jamboree in an outdoor theater . . . uh . . . outdoor auditorium. And, uh, and I came out on stage and, uh, uh, I was scared stiff. My first big appearance in front of an audience. And I came out and I was doin' a fast-type tune, uh, one of my first records, and everybody was hollerin' and I didn't know what they was hollerin' at. Ever'body was screamin' and ever'thing, and, uh, I came off stage and my manager told me they was hollerin' because I was wigglin'. Well, I went back for an encore and I, I, I kinda did a little more. And the more I did, the wilder they went.

Elvis said, on another occasion: "I'm not kiddin' myself. My voice alone is just an ordinary voice. What people come to see is how I use it. If I stand still while I'm singing, I'm dead, man. I might as well go back to drivin' a truck." He was thinking of his gyrations apparently in terms of their effect as a stage act. They were more than that. He was gyrating long before he had any inkling of the effect it had upon an audience. Bodily participation in the music he made would seem to have been instinctive, an integral element of his musicality.

James Blackwood, leader of a male quartet with whom Elvis sang spirituals at gospel sings when he was about eighteen, recalls how he used to sing with his eyes closed, "moving his hips in a manner not wholly suited to spirituals." Steve Sholes, who was head of Artists and Repertoire for RCA when Elvis began recording for that label, has told how Elvis "danced" even in the studio. This was disturbing to the engineers, as his movements tended to take him off mike. But when Sholes asked him if he couldn't stand still, Elvis would reply, "No, I can't. I'm sorry. I start playing, and the movements are involuntary."

He was not the first popular singer, certainly, to help a song along with a bit of body English. Al Jolson and Sophie Tucker were vividly physical performers, and their song routines could be thought of as choreography. Jolson even spoke of "dance steps," and there is a brief sequence in *The Jolson Story* where Jolson himself appears. He was convinced that Larry Parks, who played the Jolson role, could not "do the steps." But with none of the earlier singers had bodily movement seemed to be so blatantly, so explicitly sexual.

Nor was it the exuberant sexuality alone that excited indignation. There were social, intellectual and even racial implications, too. Adult white Americans who can have had little, if any, knowledge of the black origins of Elvis' songs, or of his way with them, sensed an exotic, alien, atavistic presence, something from outside their own culture and traditional environment. They reacted instinctively, just as their own parents had reacted to jazz and their grandparents to ragtime. They felt their values threatened. From this description by Jerry Hopkins of an early Elvis outing, it is not hard to understand why:

> Draped in black slacks with a pin stripe down the sides, a pink shirt with collar turned up, catching the ends of his longish hair, and a pink sports jacket with big black teardrops on the front and back, he was the Hillbilly Cat, he was the King of Western Bop. He leaned forward, legs braced, guitar hung around his neck, hands clutching the stand microphone. He looked at the girls in the front row with lidded eyes, eyebrows forming a loving and woeful arch. During the song's instrumental break he gave them that lopsided grin and maybe twitched one leg. Once.
>
> The next song might be a rocker, giving Elvis a chance to show the folks what they had come to see. Now both legs were twitching—jerking and snapping back into that original braced position. It's not likely that Elvis was thinking of the Pentecostal preachers of his Tupelo childhood at moments like this, but it was apparent he hadn't forgotten them. . . . His arms flailed the inexpensive guitar, pounding the wood on the afterbeat and snapping strings as if they were made of cooked spaghetti. From one song right into another. Country songs. With a beat. The girls began to squirm and move; it was music that made their behinds itch.

It was not music designed to beguile the girls' parents—or their boyfriends. But not all the boys were resentful. Many of them, sensing the vitality of this new idiom and rejoicing in their parents' horror of it, were delighted with the opportunity it offered to thumb their noses at a complacent society and all its works. Among them were Bob Dylan and, in England, Tom Jones, John Lennon, Paul McCartney and Tommy Steele.

Jackie Gleason sensed the young people's mood of the time. Elvis was, as Gleason described him, when he booked him for a television show in 1956, "a guitar-playing Marlon Brando." Others thought of James Dean and Robert Mitchum. Unlike them, Elvis was not, wittingly, at least, a rebel. He just did what came naturally. But he was a phenomenon of social significance. This mother-loving boy, who seemed, as one perceptive critic put it, to be sneering with his hips, symbolized the generation gap that has plagued America and most of the Western world ever since.

In terms of a general appreciation of his musical and vocal gifts and accomplishments, Elvis' history has been very much that of the great innovative singers who came before him—Jolson, Crosby and Sinatra. What was new in their work, or what seemed new to the unsophisticated, was so at odds with conventional criteria that it was simply dismissed out of hand, the dismissal rendered the more emotional by the social implications manifest in popular acceptance of an "unacceptable" approach to music, and especially to song.

A phenomenon common to all these singers has been the charge that they were voiceless, that they could not sing, that the adulation they earned had nothing to do with voice or song, not to speak of art. The explanation may lie in the fact that the unsympathetic were so put off by what they heard that, after a few measures, they did not listen. All but diehards now agree that Bing Crosby had a beautiful baritone and was a master phraser. The same is largely true of Sinatra. But that is not what was being said of them in the 1930s and 1940s when they were arousing the same hysterical enthusiasm Elvis was to arouse a generation later.

It would be harder today to find similarly amiable opinions of Elvis' voice and art. His vogue is still too close to us, as are the implications evident in the work of those who came after him. But he has a voice. He has an art. He has always had them. No singer survives for nearly twenty years without them. There have been some more-or-less voiceless and artless wonders. But they have not lasted long. Elvis has plenty of voice. For the student of vocalism, his use of it is quite as fascinating as the vocalism of Crosby and Sinatra. Vocalism, with such innovative artists, is, of course, inseparable from style. Since Presley has worked most distinctively in a style wholly foreign to that of Crosby and Sinatra, his vocalism is radically and dramatically different from theirs.

Elvis has been described variously as a baritone and a tenor. An extraordinary compass and a very wide range of vocal color have something to do with this divergence of opinion. The voice covers about two octaves and a third, from the baritone's low G to the tenor's high B, with an upward extension in falsetto to at least a D flat. His best octave is in the middle, from about D flat to D flat, granting an extra full step either up or down. In this area, when he bears down with his breath on the cords, the voice has a fine, big, dark baritone quality. When he eases off, as he often does in ballads, he achieves a light, mellow, seductive sound reminiscent of Bing Crosby, if rather breathier, with a wide vibrato that he may have got from Billy Eckstine. Elvis' vibrato, however, is faster and less conspicuous. Call him a high baritone.

The voice has always been weak at the bottom, variable and unpredictable. At the top it is often brilliant. His upward passage would seem to lie in the area of E flat, E and F. On E and F particularly, there is almost always the telltale evidence of strain common to singers who have not mastered the transition from one register to another. On his very first records he made distressing sounds on these pitches. They were open, callow, sometimes nasal, and utterly unrelated to the round baritone timbre of the middle voice. As early as 1959, however, he seems to have gained some measure of control, or accommodation. Even today it is not an entirely congenial area any more than it is for singers better schooled than he.

From there on up, what Elvis does with his voice depends upon what he is singing. He has always been able to duplicate the open, hoarse, ecstatic, screaming, shouting, wailing, reckless sound of the black rhythm-and-blues and gospel singers. But he has not been confined to that one type of vocal production. In ballads and country songs he belts out full-voiced high Gs and As that an opera baritone might envy. While he has not learned to sing comfortably and predictably in the "passage," he learned early how to focus his voice when he got above it. For those who have any doubts about this, I suggest that they listen to the 1960 recording of "It's Now or Never" (an English version of "O Sole Mio"), where he ends on a full-voiced cadence, A–G–F, that has nothing to do with the vocal devices of rhythm-and-blues or country. That A is hit right on the nose. It is rendered less astonishing only by the number of tracks where he lands easy and accurate B flats.

Elvis' is, in a word, an extraordinary voice—or many voices. In classical singers a multiplicity of voices is commonly the result of a singer's failure to achieve a uniform sound as the voice moves up and down the scale and through the register breaks. It is counted a fault unless the variety of color is related to characterization.

In Elvis' early records, the multiplicity of voices is often clearly faulty, especially in ballads. The 1956 recording of "I Want You, I Need You, I Love You," for instance, sounds as if it had been made by two different singers, one a booming baritone, the other a raw, tentative, nasal country tenor, while "Love Me Tender," recorded a few months later, is uncertain in intonation and uncouth in sound. Both performances, however, are disarming for their innocence of affectation. Elvis sounds like a country boy singing for friends and neighbors on the front porch. That was part of his appeal.

In later years, the vocal multiplicity has been rather a matter of idiom, with Elvis producing a sound for country, a sound for gospel, a sound for ballads, and a sound for rhythm-and-blues. He would seem always to have been a naturally assimilative musician, with an acute sense of style. The black rhythm-and-blues style, he has had in hand—and in throat and body—from the very first, along with the heavy breathing, urgent, exuberant vocalism and verbal articulation that goes with it, and a natural feeling for appropriate embellishment. Gospel music, and the gospel sound, are second nature to him, too, along with the gospel singer's affectionate mutilation of words. There are songs where he lays into them in a manner worthy of and reminiscent of Mahalia Jackson.

There is less of the typical country singer in Elvis than one would expect from a young man born in rural Mississippi and raised in urban Tennessee. But it helps to remember that Elvis' musical roots were nurtured in Memphis, a blues town, rather than in country music's capital in Nashville. Although he commands the country idiom and can color his voice to suit the country cadences, he never sounds to me quite like a country singer. With ballads, he was uncertain at first, and one hears echoes of many other singers as he felt his way from ballad to ballad. He gained confidence subsequently, as he learned to suit voice to song and to exploit the rich middle area of his range, untapped, as a rule, when he was surging through rhythm-and-blues numbers using more breath than voice. "Now or Never" ("O Sole Mio"), mentioned previously, is a stunning example of his sense of style. In this famous Neapolitan air he suddenly sounds for all the world like a Neapolitan tenor. And on "That's Where Your Heartaches Begin" he goes into a talking chorus typical of Al Jolson, and even rather like Jolson, if closer in its inflections to the fervent oratory of a country preacher.

Elvis' career has been as unique as his voice and his vocalism. He served a valuable apprenticeship, combining country schoolhouses and rural jamborees with regular radio exposure on Shreveport's *Louisiana Hayride*. Then he hit—and went into the U.S. Army. Thereafter, thanks to the promotional genius of Colonel Tom Parker, who has brilliantly played P. T. Barnum to Elvis' Jenny Lind, he withdrew to Hollywood to make some thirty-odd deplorable—and deplored—pictures at a million dollars a picture, plus 50 percent of the gross, and to run up record sales estimated to be in the neighborhood of 250 millions. He re-emerged in 1968 on television, and in 1969, in Las Vegas, with his talent intact, if only, as Richard Goldstein has suggested in *The New York Times*, "because it had remained unused."

Nothing much had changed, certainly, except the backings. Elvis, when he surfaced in Las Vegas, sang the old songs pretty much as he had sung them fifteen years before. The voice, on his most recent recordings, insofar as it can be heard through the muck of studio orchestra and heavenly choir, is darker, the phrasing, on ballads, more professional, more assured. But there has been no significant stylistic change. In this he reminds one of Louis Armstrong. Louis' contribution to the evolution of Western music was complete by the time he was thirty, Elvis' by the time he was twenty-two. Neither of them has had anything further to offer, but no others have influenced the course of popular music so profoundly.

Elvis' contribution has been, in some respects, the more remarkable of the two. Louis documented the black musician's importance and won him status in the evolving new Afro-American idiom. But he was outstanding among many—Sidney Bechet, Duke Ellington, Earl Hines, King Oliver, Bessie Smith and Ethel Waters, to name only a few. And Louis was black. Elvis introduced young white America to the music that had been fermenting in the black subculture since Louis' prime. He stimulated in an enormous young white public an appetite and a readiness for the real thing. Elvis was white, and he was, at that time, pretty much alone. What he accomplished has been neatly and accurately summarized by Jerry Hopkins:

> He wasn't the first to record songs written or originally recorded by Negroes, but most of *that* action, in the middle fifties, came when somebody like Bill Haley "covered" Big Joe Turner's "Shake, Rattle and Roll," or Georgia Gibbs took "Jim

Dandy" from LaVern Baker. Those singers were taking established rhythm-and-blues hits and cleaning them up for the white pop market. Elvis may have wanted to cover some rhythm-and-blues songs he heard while at Sun, but he never did. And when he included songs by Little Richard and Ray Charles and others on his RCA albums, it was long after the originals had been hits. Elvis wasn't snagging songs from the black for gain, but because he honestly dug the music. And so others began to show respect.

It is tempting to suggest that Elvis has paid heavily in terms of a personal life for fame and fortune and a secure place in the history of music. The adulation of his fans has driven him into seclusion behind the walls of his Graceland Mansion, near Memphis, or into isolation with his retinue of Memphis buddies in hotel suites in Hollywood or Las Vegas. But he seems never to have complained. Despite social amiability as a boy and young man, despite his exemplary conduct with his fellow GIs in the Army, he may have been, inwardly, a loner all along.

In music, especially, he knew what he wanted, or recognized it when it came his way. While deferring to Colonel Parker in promotional matters, he has been in charge of his own music-making.

An observation by his friend Johnny Rivers sticks in the memory: "He had created his own world. He had to. There was nothing else for him to do."

16

Judy Garland

Pearl Sieben, in *The Immortal Jolson*, quotes an unidentified critic: "God made Al Jolson, then he made Judy, and then he broke the mold."

As observation, commentary or criticism, this may seem, at first glance, glibly extravagant. But just follow the lives and careers of Al Jolson and Judy Garland. Listen carefully to their records. Note the devotion they inspired in the hearts of millions. Note, too, what the devotion meant to Jolie and Judy. You may, then, agree that it represents a flash of perceptive appreciation.

Certainly Jolie and Judy had much in common, as persons and as performers. Pearl Sieben said of Jolson that he was born at the age of eight, singing with his brother Harry for congressmen and senators in front of the Hotel Raleigh in Washington, D.C. Judy used to say of herself: "I was born at the age of twelve on the Metro-Goldwyn-Mayer lot." They both experienced little of either childhood or adolescence. One could say of them that they were born grown-up, or, probably more accurately, that they never grew up.

Ray Bolger, who was Judy's Scarecrow in *The Wizard of Oz*, has said: "Judy was a child who never had a childhood." Mickey Deans, her fifth and last husband, in his affectionate memoir, *Weep No More, My Lady*, quotes a friend: "The trouble with Judy was

that she had no adolescence. She went from child to woman." Deans adds: "The missing link nearly destroyed her." One questions only the *nearly*.

Show business, *i.e.*, the business and the exhilaration of singing for people, was the only life Jolie and Judy ever knew. Judy was born into it, in Grand Rapids, Michigan, in 1922. Jolson was drawn to it. Only an audience's love, responding to their own love for an audience, could create, for an exciting hour or two, a satisfactory emotional relationship for either of them. Life off-stage was a losing battle with loneliness, emptiness, insecurity, anxiety, fear, even terror. They had many acquaintances, few friends. Marriage was no help; it was rather a complication, possibly felt almost as infidelity to the audience. Nor was an audience, as lover, entirely satisfactory. It may have offered approval, admiration and love. But it could not provide companionship. The fall of the curtain spelled separation, frustration, exasperation and despair.

To those who knew them well there always seemed to be two Judys and two Jolies: the on-stage star, radiantly happy, and happily in command, and the off-stage waif, homeless, restless, fearful, suspicious, devious, forever vacillating irrationally between a too exuberant amiability and undisguised petulance and irascibility.

"I never got used to the difference between the Judy waiting in the wings and the Judy Garland making her entrance," Mickey Deans remembered. "You wouldn't know it was the same person. Her trembling vanished. The joy of being with an audience transformed her." One recalls Pearl Sieben on Jolson: "He needed applause the way a diabetic needs insulin."

Judy knew all about that, and she talked about it to Deans: "Whenever I'm on stage I have a love affair with my audience. But there's too much of a gulf between the love of an audience I've just sung to and the awful silence of a hotel room. Maybe I've got a hangup about silence. But it makes me feel as though I hadn't been born."

To a friend in London, during the last months of her life, she said: "Professional happiness doesn't last through the night. You can't take it home with you after the curtain rings down. It doesn't protect you from the terror of a lonely hotel room. And, in a way, it destroys your soul to feed off applause. I know. I've tried to draw strength and security from it. But in the middle of the night applause becomes an empty echo, and you think, *God, how am I going to make it until morning?*"

She didn't always make it until morning. Sometimes she didn't try, preferring to do a round of clubs and bars with more-or-less congenial companions until well after dawn. At other times, racked by insomnia and jitters, she would be on the telephone, just chatting, or begging the person at the other end of the line, if he or she was within commuting distance, to come on over and keep her company. Mel Tormé, arranger of special material for her 1963–64 television series, has told, in *The Other Side of the Rainbow*, how the show's producers maintained what came to be known as the Dawn Patrol.

One cannot help wondering what kind of life Judy might have led, what kind of grown-up she might have become, had she not spent the most hopeful and the most vulnerable years of a girl's life singing not for live audiences of unexacting admirers, but for relentlessly exacting producers, directors, arrangers, coaches, cameramen, costumers, accountants and dietitians on the lot at M-G-M. Between 1935 and 1951, between the ages of thirteen and twenty-nine, she made thirty-odd pictures. They made her famous and rich. Estimates of her lifetime earnings agree on a figure of about ten million dollars.

But the grind of making pictures left her no time to savor the fruit of her success, or to learn how to conserve it. She died broke. Besides, for a girl who had first experienced the intoxication of applause from a theater audience in Grand Rapids at the age of two, neither an ecstatic press nor awareness of stardom was an adequate substitute for a live audience's demonstrative affection and adoration.

She had been from early childhood not so much a person as a property, controlled, directed and exploited first by a stagestruck mother, subsequently by Louis B. Mayer, with her mother's connivance. Judy's parents, Ethel and Frank Gumm, were small-time vaudevillians, he a singer, she a pianist who also sang. Their three children, Suzy, Jimmy (a girl) and Frances (the future Judy Garland), became members of the family act, with Frances the best part of it. The parents withdrew in due course, and the family act became the Gumm Sisters. A notice in *Variety* (December 6, 1934), covering their appearance at Graumann's Chinese Theater in Hollywood, tells the story:

As a trio it means nothing, but with the youngest, Frances, 13, featured, it hops into class entertainment; for, if such a thing is possible, the girl is a combination of Helen Morgan and Fuzzy Knight. Possessing a voice that, without a p.a. system, is audible throughout a house as large as the Chinese, she handles ballads like a veteran, and gets every note and word over with a personality that hits audiences.

The Gumm Sisters were on the West Coast because that was where their mother wanted them to be: either in Los Angeles or Hollywood, or anywhere else within hearing distance of the movie studios. This was the age of the child actors: Freddie Bartholomew, Deanna Durbin and Shirley Temple were the big names, heady examples of gold that might be romping in the nursery or kindergarten. Ethel Gumm was vaudevillian enough to recognize talent when she saw it. In Frances she saw it in her own household, a promise of vicarious fulfillment of her own theatrical ambitions and of a financial security she had never known.

The first break came at Cal-Neva Lodge on Lake Tahoe in 1934, where Judy was heard by Al Rosen, a Hollywood agent, Louis Brown, casting director for Columbia Pictures, and Harry Akst, Al Jolson's songwriter and accompanist. They were favorably impressed. But it did not prove easy to interest the studios in a girl, however talented, who was no longer a child and not yet a woman. It was Rosen, eventually, who set up an audition at M-G-M. Judy sang "Zing! Went the Strings of My Heart!" Louis B. Mayer himself was summoned. She sang it again. Two weeks later came the contract.

What Judy could not have foreseen was that the coveted contract, viewed in retrospect when she was fired seventeen years later, would appear as a prison sentence, her firing as a parole. That, at least, is the way Judy saw it when she returned joyfully to vaudeville at the Palace in New York in 1951 and to a reunion with a live audience. But the damage had been done. As early as 1939, when The Wizard of Oz made her a star among stars, the little Dorothy who gazed wistfully at the rainbow was already living in "the valley of the dolls."

A tendency to put on weight was fateful, eventually fatal. The camera magnifies pudginess, especially in a girl only five feet tall. Judy, accordingly, was held to a near-starvation diet. Pills were pre-

scribed to still the hunger and to provide energy for an undernour-
ished body already overtaxed by the daily routine of picture making.
Other pills were prescribed to bring her down from the elation of
successful rehearsal and performance and to put her to sleep.

As Mickey Deans put it:

> As the expensive star-mounted musicals came off the studio
> assembly line, elevating Judy's professional status, her insomnia
> worsened, and she was existing on a schedule of Ups and
> Downers. She was overstimulated, underfed, overworked, and
> nobody worried about killing the young Golden Goose.

The metaphor is apt. Judy was overdosed, overworked and
underfed for stardom just as a goose is overfed and underexercised for
pâté. "Sometimes," Judy used to say, "it seems as if I've been in
bondage since I was a fetus."

The termination of her bondage to M-G-M brought only a
contractual release. The bondage not only to pills, but also to the
frustrations, anxieties and loneliness accumulated from sustained
deprivation of normal emotional experience, aggravated by unremitting hard work under the tensions of high expectations, could not be
shaken off.

That bondage—to pills, sometimes to alcohol, often to fear, to a
sense of personal inadequacy—would persist as long as she lived. But
between 1951 and 1969, when she died in London, aged forty-seven,
she made her finest picture, A Star Is Born (1954), and, as a concert
and club singer and recording artist, she delighted hundreds of thousands on stage and millions on television and records with some of
the loveliest singing ever accomplished by even the greatest of the
American popular singers. Our remembrance of the luster of those
performances in the 1950s and early 1960s has been blurred by the
sordid, much-publicized disasters of her declining years.

The latter inspired vivid commentary. "A raffish sequin-sprinkled
Lazarus" was the way Vincent Canby described her in The New
York Times when she returned to the Palace in 1967, "the voice now
a memory, her presence colored by those sad and forlorn tales of her
personal life, but still one of the most remarkable personalities of the
contemporary entertainment scene." An unidentified friend is quoted
as saying of her singing during that engagement: "It sounds as

though she's playing her old records through her body, which is simply no longer a good phonograph."

Derek Jewell wrote, in London's *Sunday Times*, when Judy appeared at The Talk of the Town in 1969: "She walks the rim of the volcano each second. Miraculously she keeps her balance. It is a triumph of the utmost improbability." She didn't always keep her balance. It was presumably her singing at that period of her life that prompted Oscar Levant to hear in it "a vibrato in search of a voice." This would not have been a perceptive observation of Judy's singing in better times.

Opinions as to what constituted her best years and her best work may differ according to what one looks for. To my ears, and for my taste, based on the records—I never heard her in person—she reached her peak as an artist after the break with M-G-M, in the decade between 1951 and 1961. What may have been a summit is happily preserved on the Capitol recording of her concert at Carnegie Hall on April 23, 1961. All that was most admirable in her singing flourishes here in untroubled full blossom, with little of the un-tutored stridency that sometimes blemished her singing on sound tracks in her M-G-M days, and without a trace of the tremulous uncertainty, the shortness of breath, the memory lapses and occasional vocal refusals of the last years.

Some will always prefer the carefully nurtured innocence of the M-G-M days. It was appealing, especially in a voice that seemed at once to ask for and offer affection in tones uncompromised by any suggestion of sophistication. This innocence became a problem for the older Judy. She used to say of "Over the Rainbow": "That song has plagued me all my life. You know, it's hard to be remembered by a song you first sang thirty years ago. It's like being a grandmother in pigtails."

Not even Judy could escape the fascination of her teenage image. When the producers of her television series suggested a parody of "Over the Rainbow," Judy would have none of it. "There will be no jokes of any kind about 'Over the Rainbow,'" she said. "It's kind of . . . sacred. I don't want anybody anywhere to lose the thing they have about Dorothy or that song!" As Mickey Deans observes: "I believe that in her mind she still saw herself in starched organdy and Mary Jane slippers." Appropriately, "Over the Rainbow" was the last song she ever sang in public.

She might have gone on being, or sounding like, the Dorothy of *The Wizard of Oz* or the Betsy Booth of the Andy Hardy films. But reunion with a live audience, beginning with her appearances at the Palladium in London and at the Palace in New York in 1951, made a truly professional singer of her. It was only then, in public performance, that she could complement, with the radiance of her physical presence in a theater or a club, the professional tutelage absorbed as a by-product of her marriages to David Rose and Vincente Minnelli.

It was a hazardous growth. The secret of Judy's art was its artlessness. For her to have sung with the sophisticated virtuosity of an Ella Fitzgerald or a Peggy Lee would have been disastrous. She must have sensed as much. As an artist, if in no other respect, she was surefooted. She learned much about what to do with her voice, and what to do with a song, when she ventured forth as a concert singer, but she never made a display of it. Least of all did she ever tamper with the sound, as innocent in the wreckage of 1969 as in the budding promise of 1939.

She had the most utterly *natural* vocal production of any singer I have ever heard. Probably because she sang so much as a child, and learned to appreciate the appeal of her child's voice, she made no effort as she grew older to produce her voice in any other way. It was an open-throated, almost birdlike vocal production, clear, pure, resonant, innocent. One keeps coming back to that word *innocent*, again and again. It was not just an innocent sound. More importantly, it was a sound innocent of anything that smacked of artful management.

This almost certainly explains a conspicuously limited vocal range that must have made problems for her arrangers, especially for Tormé when he was matching her with other singers appearing as Judy's guests during that ill-fated television venture. I can think of no other singer whose top was so low. One reads of Judy's occasional troubles in reaching for high notes. Those notes were not so very high, no more than Cs and Ds, and not a soprano's high Cs and Ds at that, but the Cs and Ds an octave lower. She never extended that range by recourse to head voice or falsetto as other popular singers have done. She just sang naturally and purely as far as she could go without vocal expertise, and that was that.

She hadn't much at the lower end of the range, either. She could always sing down to the contralto F or E, but there was not much to it below the A flat. Between that A flat and the C or D an octave and a third or fourth higher, all was in order, the voice strong, clear, warm, vibrant and susceptible of an infinite wealth of shade and nuance. These refinements, too, she achieved in a seemingly artless manner. All she did was vary the weight of breath on the cords.

Any track from any recording of Judy in her good years, but especially any ballad track, will serve ideally to illustrate the familiar analogy between singing and playing the violin. In this analogy the passage of breath over the vocal cords is equated with the drawing of a bow across the strings of a violin—or any other instrument of the viol family. All schooled singers are aware of it, and all schooled fiddle players, too. But I can think of few other singers in whose work I have been so continuously aware of the singer's breath being used as a bow.

The quality, or character, of the voice itself had something, possibly everything, to do with this. It was a viola-like voice that responded almost electrically to every variation in the weight of breath imposed upon it. This may have been due as much to the absence of any muscular restriction or pressure as to the intrinsic timbre of the voice, fine as that timbre was. Judy sang freely, which is why she could sing as many as twenty-five songs a night without developing any symptoms of vocal fatigue.

The voice responded more amiably to light than to heavy bowing, and most amiably to the lightest. Or maybe it was just that Judy did not always know how to channel the response when she bore down. I suspect the latter, for there was less open stridency in her belting in the 1950s than there had been when she sang at M-G-M. She must have listened critically to those M-G-M recordings, or she may have profited by advice and coaching. She learned, in any case, to cover the tone just enough to round off the strident edges, to build without bawling. The lesson has been lost on many subsequent singers, who have mistaken bawling for building. The Judy Garland of Carnegie Hall in 1961 was a shrewd and successful builder.

Another natural phenomenon that she exploited skillfully was vibrato. It could become obtrusive when she was not in good shape. In the precarious circumstances of her last public appearances it was more tremulous than vibrant. When she was at her best, however, it contributed importantly to the heart-throb quality of her singing. It was, if I hear it correctly, a controlled vibrato, the control possibly intuitive rather than witting. Certainly she could widen it toward the end of a sustained tone, not so spectacularly as Billy Eckstine and Sarah Vaughan, but probably the more effectively because it was done so moderately.

Judy would seem to have spent a lot of time listening to other singers. Although she was always unmistakably Judy Garland, there are echoes of many other singers on her records, the other singer determined largely by the material at hand. When she sang "Swanee," for example, or "Rockabye Your Baby with a Dixie Melody," there was a lot of Jolson, including the nasality and the sliding major third descending terminal cadences. In a song such as "Who Cares?" or "Come Rain or Come Shine" one hears Lena Horne in her pronunciation of such words as "together" and "care."

She could sound like Ethel Merman when belting, like Sinatra in a nostalgic song such as "Last Night When We Were Young," and like Bing Crosby on "Play That Barber Shop Chord." Privately, she was a good mimic, and the predilection for mimicry surfaced from time to time in public performance, notably, I am told, in an imitation of Marlene Dietrich, just as it had surfaced many years earlier in the singing of Ethel Waters sending up Rudy Vallee and Josephine Baker.

Judy's enunciation was exemplary. She knew it and cultivated it, which may be why in ballads she tended to favor very slow tempi, giving herself and her listeners time to savor not only the words, but also the delicate shading she could achieve with the bow of her breath. On up-tempo numbers she could swing lustily. I find her at her most delightful, however, in lilting tempi. With hard-driving songs like "The Trolley Song" she could sound a bit hectic.

She was not the most melodically inventive of the great popular singers. As was also true of Sinatra, she was essentially a tune singer, usually sparing in her deviations from the notes as written, and little given to extravagant ornamentation. When she did embellish, as in her 1938 recording of "Bei Mir Bist Du Schoen," one suspects an arranger's hand. Also like Sinatra, she was a master—or mistress—of *rubato*. She relished and managed well the light blues-derived trail-offs to unidentifiable pitches at phrase endings, where the singing voice merges with the speaking voice to sustain the narrative character of song.

None of these physical and technical gifts and accomplishments goes very far toward explaining the Judy Garland phenomenon. She might well have been equally appealing had she sung less well, as indeed she did toward the end of her career and life when both body and spirit were failing. Of many singers one can say that it has been not so much what they had by nature that accounted for their success as what they did with it. Of Judy Garland one is tempted to say that it was not so much what she did with it as what she had, and what she was, or seemed to be.

There was, to begin with, the voice itself—not its extent, which was modest, but the sound: the warmth, the tenderness, the radiance, the exuberance. Then there was the image, or images: Dorothy, Betsy Booth, Esther Blodgett (in *A Star Is Born*). Finally, there was the real person, the fearful, insecure, erratic, floundering female, the girl-child unable to achieve any but a physical maturity, terrified and resentful of the responsibilities that adulthood imposed, haunted by the inevitability of middle age and beyond.

Other singers, notably Frank Sinatra, Ella Fitzgerald and Peggy Lee, have been able to accommodate their images to their advancing years. Judy could not. The youthful, vernal image was too deeply engraved both upon her own conception of herself and upon the memories of her fans. Judy Garland at forty-seven was a contradiction in terms, a natural catastrophe—almost, one is tempted to say, an indecency. She felt it and exposed the feeling. Her audiences felt it, too, and their hearts went out to her. That is why she could sing, as a composer who worked with her once expressed it, "not to your ears, but to your tear ducts." Jerry Lewis understood. In a moment of non-clowning, he told writer Bill Davidson:

> People of all kinds, with worries and problems and heart-aches, go to see her, and they identify with her. When she sings, she is communicating with them all the emotions they can't communicate themselves. . . . The stout women in the audience identify with her, and the insomniacs in the audience, and the losers-in-love, and the alcoholics and the pill takers. All the people whose insides have been torn out by misery identify with her—and she is singing for all of them. In a way, she's singing with a hundred voices.

Judy did not have a hundred voices. She had only one. But it was a voice in which everyone could hear an echo of his own. "I can't hold a man," she used to say. "I'm nothing but a pair of lungs and a voice box." She was underestimating herself. She had the lungs and she had the larynx. But without the heart they would not have made a Judy Garland.

17

Johnny Cash

Few singers of our time have inspired such fanciful flights of descriptive prose as Johnny Cash.

The face, the six-foot-two frame, the stage costume, the voice, the characteristic movements of the body, the songs and the case history, social and pathological—each has presented an irresistible challenge to those who would explore the hearts and minds of our mid-century society as reflected in the music, the lives and the legends of its minstrels.

Johnny's face, with its scar on the right cheek—from the removal of a cyst, not a knife wound—has been pictured as "right out of Marlboro Country," or "looking as though it has been ripped from a 'Wanted' poster." The nose, thanks to an automobile accident, is not quite where it ought to be, and the left eyelid tends to droop when Cash is tired, a souvenir of a childhood attack of measles. His wife, June Carter, sees it, acutely, as a face that looks "lived in," and she describes his manner of singing out of the right side of his mouth as "whopper-jawed." He has also been described as a "singing John Wayne." He looks rather like John Wayne. When he speaks, he sounds like him.

The restless pivoting of the long body on its heels prompted *Life* to suggest that "he wears his clothes out from the inside." Marshall

Grant, who has played bass behind him for nearly twenty years, remembers meeting him for the first time, in an auto-repair shop in Memphis: "I saw him coming down a row of cars, and he seemed magnetic. He was tall and dark, and edgy as a cat on a hot tin roof." Cash says of himself, "I'm not nervous but I'm quick."

And that stage costume! One of his biographers, Albert Govoni, in *A Boy Named Cash*, has captured it nicely: "A frock coat out of another era, a diplomat's gray-striped trousers and a vest over a white shirt with ruffled front, variously described as giving him the appearance of a riverboat gambler, a raffish parson, a card shark out of the old west, a post-Civil War dandy, a New Orleans rakehell on his way to a duel over a woman."

"Cash," wrote John F. Szwed in *Jazz & Pop*, "is the Bad Man and the Hero together; he's cowboys and Indians, sharecropper and rancher, truck driver and laborer, soldier and drifter, and, God knows, he may be the last Grown-Up Male Singer that pop music is going to see for a long time to come!" Another writer, Tom Dearmore, in *The New York Times Magazine* (September 21, 1969), said: "It's not difficult to imagine that he is a frontiersman who took the wrong turn on a trail 160 years ago and has just now delivered his pelts to Fort Nashborough."

The voice has prompted much irreverent and bemused commentary. "It occasionally has trouble finding the middle of a note," wrote Bob Dawborn in *Melody Maker* (November 1, 1969), "and it is inclined to slip while trying to hang on to it." Rex Reed, in *Stereo Review* (March 1967), wrote: "He has almost no vocal equipment whatsoever. But he makes up for his basic cornfield twang by singing with his soul instead of his tonsils." Others have found the play on words irresistible, and have called him a "soil singer." Don Law, who produced Cash's first records for Columbia, has said: "It's a virility and a guts to his voice that he's got. He's always sung off pitch." A *Time* writer came closer to the truth about it with "a big blackstrap-molasses voice." To Dearmore it is "something like smooth and mellow thunder . . . earthy-deep, ominous sometimes, resonant, virile, untrained, unconventional. . . ."

I have no quarrel with what has been written or spoken about the face, the figure, the comportment and the costume. It reflects vividly the sense of *presence* which is an essential ingredient of the magic Johnny Cash works upon a live audience. I would add to any

Tennessee Ernie Ford

Tex Ritter

appraisal of his magnetism in public performance only the handling of the guitar, held high and proud, the right hand far up the fingerboard, about an inch from the left.

Those sudden, swift, challenging thrusts and swerves and lunges are more important to his stage image than any music he draws from the instrument. He reminds me of Chuck Berry and the late Jimi Hendrix, who have also used the guitar as a dynamic symbol, proclaiming virility, toughness and defiance, although Berry and Hendrix have been more accomplished pickers. For Johnny Cash the guitar is hardly more than a stage prop, and his exploitation of it is at once masterly and masterful.

But what has been said of his voice and his singing, while not untrue, is, I think, inadequate. Only Rex Reed's "He has almost no vocal equipment whatsoever" is lamentably wide of the mark. The judgment is noteworthy, however, as a significant repetition of derogatory vocal estimates of many other great popular singers, notably Bing Crosby and Frank Sinatra. They, too, have been derided as no-voice freaks even by critics who assessed them justly as artists. Both had, in fact, exceptionally fine voices, as has Johnny Cash today. But they, like Cash, have worked more from language than from notation. The listener is so engrossed in the song and its substance as to overlook the singing.

To my opera-oriented ears, Cash's voice is both marvelous and delightful. What has thrown some critics off is, I think, its lie. Johnny is usually referred to as a baritone, occasionally as a bass-baritone. He is neither. He is a true bass, singing easily—as do Tennessee Ernie Ford and Tex Ritter, by the way—in a subterranean area hostile to even the deepest of opera basses. Play "I Walk the Line," and you will hear, on that fifth and last chorus, a low C, sung so easily, so nonchalantly, that it passes unnoticed.

Things do not always go so easily for him at the other end of the scale. The most comfortable area in his voice would seem to range from the low E to the A or B flat an octave and a fourth or fifth above. Beyond that, there are likely to be signs of distress. He can, and sometimes does, sing on up to the high F, giving him an overall range of well above two octaves, although from about C on up it tends to be heavy going.

But if he has a lot more voice than he is commonly credited with, and of finer quality, there is no getting away from the vagaries of his intonation. Bob Dawborn put it well: "His voice occasionally has trouble finding the middle of a note, and it is inclined to slip while trying to hang on to it." I hear him somewhat differently. The trouble, to my ears, is usually his failure to reach up to a note. There are many examples on records, including "I Walk the Line," where he fails to reach the same note again and again, and always by about the same margin.

The failures usually occur just where one would expect them, especially in a singer whose breath on the cords is as heavy as his. They occur at the upper end of his normal range, at that point, or pitch—in his voice at about the B flat, sometimes lower—where singing ceases to be easy, but before it has become so difficult as to make the necessity of extra effort obvious. He could correct it easily enough—if precise intonation were on his mind. It is not. In my notes on "I Walk the Line" I find, for instance: "He often misses, i.e., doesn't reach a pitch, because *it doesn't matter to him. He doesn't try to reach it!*"

Nor does it matter to me, as a listener. The importance of precise intonation varies in accordance with the musical context. With Johnny Cash, as with other country and blues singers, the context is oratorical rather than melodic or harmonic. The lyric is more important than the tune. Since the singer is working closer to the less precise intonation and inflections of speech, imprecision in the identification and articulation of pitches becomes, if not necessarily a virtue, at least a compatible idiosyncrasy. Another of Cash's biographers, Christopher Wren, in *Winners Got Scars Too*, has put it well: "Blues or jazz convey their emotion through music, with the words as an accessory. In country, the lyrics—blunt, direct, painful—become the expression; the tune just lubricates them."

Many of those critical of Johnny Cash's intonation may have been put off by his extensive use of the slur. It may seem to some that he is feeling his way toward a pitch when, in fact, he is gliding up to it, quite consciously—or, at least, instinctively—for oratorically expressive purposes. He is especially given to a long upward slur, usually covering approximately a major third. A familiar example is his rounding off of the word *'round* on "messin' 'round" in "Jackson."

Related to his problems with pitch—if one can call them problems, which I think doubtful—is Cash's inability—or disinclination—to sustain a long melodic line in the manner of, say, Sinatra, or Tony

Bennett. He simply is not, and never has been, that kind of singer—and he knows it. Hence his habit of speaking of himself as a talker rather than a singer.

His approach to song and to songwriting is, however, essentially and fundamentally musical. He began writing songs as a kid on the farm, before he had done much singing. During the years of his military service he whiled away dull hours writing poems, some of which were even published in *Stars and Stripes*. But Albert Govoni has noted that whereas the average poet tries to fashion a line that will scan and fall easily from the tongue, Johnny would not put a line on paper until he had sung it first. He seems always to have been extraordinarily aware of the music of words, and this is reflected not only in the purity of his Southern, or Southwestern, enunciation, but also in its musicality.

This sense of the singer's oratorical role, the requirement of seeming to be talking, doubtless explains why he is probably more dependent than others upon a backing group. Those who have heard him, on his television shows, sing an occasional song to no other accompaniment than his own guitar will have noted the inadequacy. He can sustain mood as can few other singers but he needs rock-firm rhythmic and harmonic support to sustain himself in that never-never land midway between speech and song which is his natural habitat.

He has been fortunate in his back-up musicians, the Tennessee Three, both in their grasp of what he is musically all about and in their constancy. Originally there were Marshall Grant, on bass, and Luther Perkins, on guitar, whom he met in Memphis when they were mechanics for the Automobile Sales Garage and he an unsuccessful house-to-house salesman for a firm called Home Equipment. With them he began his career as a public performer, and with them he cut his first records. W. S. Holland was added on drums in 1960, a concession to trends that had turned hillbilly into rockabilly. Perkins died from burns suffered in a house fire in 1969, and was replaced shortly afterward by Bob Wootten.

That there have been no other personnel changes speaks for the loyalty inspired by John R. Cash. His immediate sidemen—and also June Carter, the Statler Brothers, Carl Perkins, and the Carter Family, who comprise the supporting bill in a Johnny Cash Show—remained steadfast during the trying years between 1961 and 1968 when Johnny was caught in a vortex of barbiturates and tranquilizers, apparently destined to destroy himself as Hank Williams had destroyed himself a decade earlier. Their loyalty and perseverance almost certainly had a lot to do with Johnny's decision to fight free of addiction, and with his ultimate success in doing so, just as the self-effacing musicianship of the Tennessee Three has made possible his oratorical flights as a singer.

Johnny's oratorical predilections probably derive from his exposure, as boy and young man, to the hortatory rhetoric of rural Baptist preachers in Dyess, Arkansas, where he grew up as the hard-working son of a hard-working, God-fearing cotton grower. Evangelistic fervor is, moreover, in his blood. A grandfather and a great-grandfather on his father's side were Baptist missionaries, and two of his paternal grandmother's brothers were Baptist preachers. The music of the Baptist congregation in Dyess was the first he ever heard. Church hymns were the fireside music at home—until the family could afford a battery-operated radio. There was no electricity in Dyess, a Governmental homesteading and colonization project, when Johnny was a boy.

It is neither insignificant nor surprising, therefore, that when he joined forces with Grant and Luther Perkins in Memphis in 1954, their first public performances were playing a gospel repertoire for church barbecues, and that their first professional work was playing gospel music over country station KWEM. When Johnny approached Sam Phillips, whose Sun Records had just signed Elvis Presley, he presented himself and his colleagues as a gospel group. Had Phillips been interested in gospel, they might have been a gospel group to this day. Sam, fortunately, had other music in mind.

An affection for gospel music has remained with Johnny Cash to this day, as evidenced by the many sacred songs he has sung and recorded. One senses in his performances—and in the country-preacher implications of his stage getup, too—that, as with Elvis, declamation from the pulpit may have affected his innate musicality as much as the more conventionally melodious strains issuing from the organ—or piano—and from the choir and congregation.

Johnny says that there must still exist some gospel tracks that he and Elvis cut together for Sam Phillips back in the mid-1950s. There is, in any case, a strong gospel flavor in his music, and it has had, I would guess, something to do with his reluctance to be classified as a country singer. He prefers to think in terms of "Johnny Cash music."

Granting his right to the distinction, gospel is one of the strongest and most persuasive elements of that music. There are others.

The Cashes got their first radio from Sears Roebuck in 1936, when Johnny was four. He has recalled for Christopher Wren what that radio came to mean to him:

> I remember I could turn that dial and pick up WLW in Cincinnati and WCKY in Covington, Kentucky, and KOMA in Oklahoma City, WLS in Chicago, or XEG in Fort Worth, or XERA in Del Rio, Texas. I knew what time everybody came on. I knew where they all were when I was a kid. I'd listen to all those country music programs. The Carter Family. The Brown's Ferry Four. . . . Every Saturday night there would be the *Grand Old Opry* from WSM in Nashville. . . .

It is clear from the foregoing that if Johnny Cash has one foot rooted in gospel, the other is rooted in country music, and twin-rooted at that, one foot in the Southern, often blues-tinged, rural idiom of Jimmie Rodgers and Hank Williams, the other in the Appalachian ballad tradition of the Carter Family—A. P. Carter, his wife Sara (Dougherty) and his sister-in-law Maybelle (Addington) Carter. The Carter Family went to Bristol, Tennessee, from their home in Maces Spring, Virginia, to sing for Ralph Peer, representing the Victor Talking Machine Company, at the same auditions in 1927 that also discovered Jimmie Rodgers.

June Carter, Johnny's second wife—his first marriage, to Vivian Liberto, of San Antonio, ended in divorce—is the daughter of Mother Maybelle, recently installed in the Country Music Hall of Fame, and referred to affectionately as the Queen Mother of Country Music. Mother Maybelle and June's sisters, Helen and Anita, are now an integral part of the Johnny Cash Show, a symbol of Johnny's deep sense of country-music history and tradition, as indeed is his lifelong identification with the songs of Jimmie Rodgers, documented both in solo numbers and in the Rodgers railroad songs and blues he has sung on television with Merle Haggard.

For a boy who grew up surrounded by gospel and country music, and who would ultimately excel in both, he was a late starter. Both his father and mother were musical. The Cashes had a $37 piano before they had a car. Johnny's older brother, Roy, even had his own country band for a time, the Delta Rhythm Ramblers. Carrie Cash,

Johnny Cash with his parents
With June Carter Cash

their mother, bought Johnny a $6.98 guitar from Sears Roebuck and tried to teach him to play it. Johnny, according to Wren, was not interested, and eventually sold it to a neighbor.

But by the time his voice had changed, he was doing a bit of singing. He held forth at social gatherings, although the country songs he liked best were not thought suitable for respectable occasions. He sang "Drink to Me Only with Thine Eyes" at his high school graduation. There is nothing, however, to indicate that he had professional ambitions. What the record does show is that listening to the radio had done more than nourish a taste for country music. It had made him aware of a more inviting and less exacting world outside the confines of Dyess.

He had been working in the cotton fields and doing other back-breaking farm labor since he was six, and he had had enough of it. "When we grew up," he told Wren, "it was second nature that we wouldn't live in Dyess when we were grown. It was the aim of every person to get a better job. But if I hadn't grown up there I wouldn't be what I am now. It was the foundation of what I became."

After graduation from high school, he headed for Detroit, where he worked for a brief spell at the Fisher Body plant in Pontiac. He hated it, returned home, took a job in an oleomargarine factory in nearby Evadale, hated that, too, and quit. On July 7, 1950, he enlisted in the U.S. Air Force, signing up for four years. He was sent to Germany as a radio intercept operator. And there, in Landsberg, Bavaria, he fell in with a crowd of amateur singers and guitar pickers, received his first instruction on guitar, bought an instrument from a local music store and became one of an ad hoc GI country group calling themselves the Landsberg Barbarians.

Returning home when his hitch was up, Johnny still seems not to have thought seriously about becoming a professional entertainer, although he did think about becoming a radio announcer and took vocational training to that end. He settled in Memphis, married, and got a job as salesman for Home Equipment. Only his failure as a salesman and his inability to meet the financial responsibility of a wife and child, it would seem, drove him into translating his informal sessions with Marshall Grant and Luther Perkins into a full-time job. Their records with Sun caught on, their public appearances were well received, and Johnny Cash was on his way. He was twenty-three. Hank Williams, at that age, had been a professional for a decade.

There remains only one significant detail to relate of Johnny's musical development. As a salesman, working the black ghetto in Memphis' Orange Mound district, he met Gus Cannon, an elderly black singer and banjo picker. Johnny, according to Wren, used to lay out his route so that he would end up at Gus Cannon's. There, presumably, he listened and experimented much as Hank Williams at an earlier age had absorbed the musical invention and showmanly wisdom of Tee-tot. It is another example of that informal, unselfconscious interaction of black and white that has always, and again and again, enriched our American, or Afro-American, music. It has worked both ways. While white country singers were learning from blacks, they also had a large black audience, beginning with Jimmie Rodgers, and probably even earlier. Ray Charles and Charley Pride were not the only black singers to adopt and master the white country style. Chuck Berry, when he arrived in Chicago from St. Louis in the mid-1950s, was regarded by the Chicago blues men as a country singer, and his style categorized as rockabilly.

As with Hank Williams, neither the voice nor the musicality can account for or explain what it is that sets Johnny Cash apart from many excellent country singers. There have been, certainly, even in his own generation, better voices, better guitar pickers, better musicians, better poets. With Cash, as with Hank Williams and, in other categories, Judy Garland, Billie Holiday, Peggy Lee, Frank Sinatra and Bessie Smith, the phenomenon has been personal. It has been human rather than merely musical. It has been the artist rather than the art.

All these singers have been complex, and most of them have been, more or less disastrously, the victims of their own complexities and complexes. This has been true, of course, of millions of less famous mortals. But they have had neither the inclination, the talent nor the accomplishment, certainly not all three together, to find in an audience a momentarily satisfactory companion, while at the same time offering that audience an assuaging reflection of its own complexities. The operative characteristic in all these singers, and in none more conspicuously and tellingly than in Johnny Cash, is compassion. The late Peter LaFarge, whose songs about the American Indian gave Johnny, himself part Indian, his *Bitter Tears* album, including "The Ballad of Ira Hayes," once said, "I know what's wrong with him. He cares too much."

Johnny's kid brother Tommy, also an engaging country singer, has said of him, as quoted by Wren:

> He is as complex as anything God or man put on this earth. He's a man of uncommon characteristics, mentally or physically. Even though you're his brother, or his wife, or his mother, you never know him completely. I've felt myself at times trembling, because of my inadequacy around him. And there's times I feel completely at ease.

Tommy speaks from experience. In the fall of 1963, when Johnny was already well under way in his slide into amphetamine addiction, he established an office in Nashville and put Tommy in charge. Three times in the space of only a few months, Johnny visited that office and wrecked it. In 1967, gone on pills, and at what must have been the nadir of his life and his career, Johnny provoked Tommy into a brawl at the Nashville airport in front of their parents. Ray Cash, their father, had to step in and separate them.

Wren notes a disposition, or compulsion, to violence manifesting itself much earlier. While serving with the Air Force in Landsberg, Johnny once knocked out two security guards who had relieved him of a carton of cigarettes he was taking to sell on the black market. On another occasion, in his own words:

> One night, after I'd been in Germany about a year, I just got fed up. We were working on the second floor, and before I knew it I picked up my typewriter and threw it through the window. I started crying. They sent me to the dispensary and gave me a couple of aspirins. I got the rest of the night off.

During the long years of one-nighters, a grind that has proved disastrous for many country and jazz musicians—Cash estimates that by 1961 he was doing 290 shows a year and covering 300,000 miles, most of it by car—Johnny sublimated his violent impulses by joining with his sidemen in a long series of practical jokes, many of them involving the use of explosives. "There's a lot of things blamed on me that never happened," he says today. "But then there's a lot of things that I did that I never got caught at. So I guess it cancels out. I wouldn't do that now, shoot off cannons in the dressing room, and I'd throw out anyone that did."

Wren relates Johnny's explosive disposition to his Dyess childhood and boyhood. "The suffusion of old-time virtues drilled into

Johnny Cash as he grew up," he writes, "was essential to the welfare of the colony. Industriousness, thrift, honesty, religious zeal, so flourished that they were bound to constrict, breeding within Cash a latent restlessness that would erupt into rebellion years later."

One is encouraged to accept this observation by the fact that, while Johnny extols those old-time habits and virtues—"These Hands," for example—and likes to sing the old hymns and songs, the sentiment is rather acknowledgment, admiration and homage than nostalgia. He doesn't even look back upon his own rough, tough beginnings as a singer with any sense of "the good old days." "Those shows aren't pleasant memories to me," he told Wren. "They're not the good old days to me."

But for every instance of mad, thoughtless violence toward others and, during his seven years of addiction, toward himself, there is a corresponding anecdote of spontaneous warmth, generosity, affection and sympathy reminiscent of Sinatra, who has similarly teetered all his life on one side or the other of the fine line separating fulfillment and insupportable exasperation. For both men there has been no comfortable, sensible, moderate, rational middle way. There is always tension, and it is this tension, this sense of loneliness, of pent-up emotion, of a need to pour out in public the private thoughts and feelings sealed by inhibition in social intercourse, that is communicated to, and captures, their audiences. Audiences feel loved and wanted, just as the singer himself craves to be loved and wanted.

It seems almost to be a curse visited upon the greatest artists, possibly even a prerequisite for the greatest communicative artistry, that life begins, day after day and night after night, when the curtain goes up and is suspended when it comes down. It is not insignificant, nor is it surprising, that during the worst periods of Johnny Cash's pill addiction he was reliable when the shows kept him busy. It was the occasional night off that was regularly and predictably his undoing. He says now that he finds in an adoring audience an elation beyond any he ever experienced on drugs.

An essential element in the appeal of such singers is that their concern is people rather than ideas, their motivation emotional, vaguely idealistic, sometimes irrational, rather than intellectual. They tend to be gut-reactors, which easily accounts both for inconsistency and ambivalence in their behavior, and for the breadth of their appeal.

Cash is aware of his intellectual limitations, and admirably reluctant to appear as propagandist for anything more subtle, more divisive, more emotive than the plight of the American Indian and the hapless day-to-day existence of men and women behind bars within prison walls. He has said—and would that some of our younger minstrels might share his wisdom and humility—that messages should be sent by telegraph. He is also aware of his inconsistencies. "Don't ever tell anybody how John Cash feels about anything," he has said, "unless I've told you in the last few minutes."

But if in Johnny Cash the artist is the man rather than the art, an equally important element in his appeal is the image. The man—the life story, the successes, the humiliations, the disasters, the fascinating juxtaposition of the sinister and the charming, the suggestion of unpredictability—is an attractive figure. But possibly even more important is the figure he seems to represent: the frontier American. As has so often been the case with our greatest singers—with Al Jolson, for example, as with Crosby, Presley and Sinatra—the timing was right.

Johnny Cash entered upon the musical scene at a moment in history when America—and not only America—had grown unsure of itself and of its direction. It looked back nostalgically to a time when life was simpler, closer to nature, less tortured by tempo and doubt. Johnny had sprung from a backwater of that earlier environment, and he revived it in song as had no previous singer. Wren has put it well:

> Cash is the lost American, recalling some classic gunfighter or preacher (it doesn't matter which). He has walked out of yesterday at an uncertain juncture when yesterday looks very, very good. His strength is in neither the singing nor the songs, but in grass-roots credibility. He still belongs to the Dyess Colony with its weathered shotgun shacks, muddy drainage ditches and flat fields stuffed with cotton, though he left it more than twenty years ago. The land has graced Johnny Cash with a sense of its tradition.

Elsewhere, Wren has written of "the singer's revival message of the dignity of the commonplace and the redeeming grace of hard knocks."

I doubt that it can be put better than that.

18

B.B. King

B.B. King seems comfortably and securely established as "King of the Blues." The title has nothing to do with the fact that King just happens to be his real family name (his Christian name is Riley; B.B. stands for "Blues Boy"). His supremacy, both as singer and guitarist, is just about universally acknowledged. The unanimity of the acknowledgment is the more notable in view of the number of other excellent blues men more or less of his generation—I am thinking especially of Muddy Waters, ten years his senior—who might themselves have been kings in a less fertile era, or in any era that did not include B.B.

I have always counted myself fortunate to have heard him for the first time, either in person or on records, at the Royal Albert Hall in London, on April 23, 1969, following a concert the night before by Janis Joplin. It was a first London appearance for each of them. Hearing them on successive evenings offered an unusual opportunity for comparative listening. One could not have asked for a more vividly, more dramatically instructive juxtaposition of amateur and professional.

Both had enormous successes with enormous audiences [I wrote, combining the two concerts in a single review for the

307

International Herald Tribune] but B.B. King's was by far the greater and the more heartwarming. There was a standing ovation and almost delirious enthusiasm. Heartwarming it was because he is a real pro, an eloquent singer, a splendid guitarist and an engaging personality, with that certain dignity and composure almost always associated with the greatest musical artists. He has paid his dues, as they say in the trade, and it shows in everything he does.

Joplin is something else again. What King achieves through the most consummate musicianship, she attempts through sheer reckless exuberance. King never screams. Joplin rarely does anything else. At the top of her very considerable range she makes a sound that little boys of four or five produce when trying to determine just what degree of aural torture will finally drive Mummy or Daddy into giving them a smack in the teeth.

One enduring impression of B.B. King that evening was his gentlemanly deportment. There was not a trace of the brashness, the garish attire, the grotesque posturing with which so many of the young blues men of the 1950s and 1960s saw fit to call attention to themselves. Nor was it merely a matter of deportment and attire. It had more to do with manner and manners. He made everyone feel that he was proud to have arrived at the Royal Albert Hall, that he was delighted to be performing for a British audience, that he was determined to do his best, that his only purpose was to give his listeners pleasure, and to live up to their high expectations. The audience met friendship with friendship, a superlative performance with manifest appreciation. B.B. was moved. So was everybody else.

"He appeared to be as affected by the welcome as we were by his subtly controlled vocal and instrumental art," wrote the veteran jazz and blues critic Max Jones, in *Melody Maker*. "From the beginning of his 'Every Day I Have the Blues' to his final encore, B.B. and his fine, tight band projected swing, electrifying feeling, a highly professional polish and a kind of charm which is not all that common among blues artists."

B.B.'s manner did not seem, at the time, to be an act, an attitude donned for the occasion. And in fact it was not. He was just being himself as he has been described by everyone who has known him or interviewed him. Jimmy Witherspoon, a fellow blues man, calls him "the gentleman's gentleman of show biz." Harvey Siders, after interviewing him for *Down Beat*, wrote of "the gentlest, most smile-wrinkled face in show business." Stanley Dance, who interviewed him for *Jazz* in 1967, when B.B. was on the verge of an international breakthrough, remembered him as "mild-voiced and considerate." Phyl Garland, in her book, *The Sound of Soul*, says his manner "is so gentle as to seem almost apologetic." Jon Hendricks says: "He's a good man, a real nice man, which is a lot to say in this business."

Eric Clapton, British blues guitarist and onetime lead guitar of the British rock group Cream said of B.B. (in a *Down Beat* interview with Jim Szantor): "He's always been the best, always. He's the most adaptable musician I ever met. For a man who has gone unrecognized, he's paid all his dues twice over, and there's not a sign of bitterness . . . nothing, man. I've met cats that have been twice as successful that have been bitter and twisted and just angry. But he's humble . . . he just wants to please. It's really a great lesson to see someone like that."

My second enduring impression of that evening at the Royal Albert Hall was of B.B.'s ultimate professionalism. He was just off the plane from the United States. He had not slept for thirty-six hours. It was an English debut. And the Royal Albert Hall is a formidable auditorium, vast, high-domed and cavernous, its pit, stalls and soaring tiers seating 6,000 persons. B.B., keyed up and nervous, as he always is before any performance, came on with "Every Day," and right in the middle of his first guitar chorus a string broke.

He never faltered. Since everyone's attention was focused on that guitar, he decided to tell us about it, and specifically why and how it came to be called Lucille (he pronounces it Loo-*sill*). While his backing group sustained a riffing vamp, and while a new string was fetched and attached, he told us:

> I was playing a place called Twist, Arkansas, in 1949. Geographically speaking, Twist is about seventy miles northwest of Memphis. It's a little plantation town, and we used to play there every other Saturday night. Place wasn't very large. You could get seventy-five people in there—at one time. But they'd really be packed in, and some nights we got two to three hundred of what we called a "comin' and goin' crowd." You know, people would come in, stay a while, get hot or tired, and walk out.
>
> It used to get very cold there in the winter, and they had what looked like a big garbage pail half filled with kerosene or

coal, and we used that for heat. They danced around it—just like a skating rink. Well, on this particular night, two guys started fighting, and they knocked over this container of kerosene. The building, being a board building, man, it really burned. Above the dance hall was rooms where cats lived. Well, after the fuel spilled all over the floor, everybody made for the front door— including me. But when I got outside, I remembered my guitar [he pronounces it GI-tar] was *inside*.

Now, man, I used to have lots of problems with my guitars. Guys would steal 'em, they'd get busted up in auto accidents, or something like that. It was hard to keep a good guitar, and if you did have one, man, you held on to it for dear life. So I ran back to save my guitar, and I was almost burned to death. Next day I found out that two men in those upstairs rooms got burned to death. And I also found out those two guys who were fighting were fighting over a lady named Lucille. So I named my guitar Lucille to remind me never to do anything like that again. You can always get another guitar, but not another B.B. King.

It was a masterpiece of professional showmanship, and it established an immediate, warm, relaxed, friendly relationship between B.B. and his new British audience. There was more to it, however, than mere entertainment, the mere telling of a good yarn. From the story itself and its setting, and from the Southern inflections of B.B.'s speech, one could learn a lot about his background and about what is meant when people say that he has "paid his dues."

Most of the great American popular singers have achieved national recognition at a relatively early age, and often enough international recognition, too. B.B. spent twenty years singing and playing in places like Twist, Arkansas. His ultimate emergence as a national and international figure in the late 1960s was due not to the perception of American audiences and critics, white or black, but to white British rock musicians such as Eric Clapton, Rolling Stones lead singer Mick Jagger and blues devotee John Mayall.

Their original black American idols and models had been Chuck Berry, whose "Roll Over Beethoven" was years ahead of Bob Dylan's "The Times They Are A-Changin'" in heralding an adolescent cultural revolt; Muddy Waters, whose "Rolling Stone" had given a name both to a rock group and to a rock magazine; Bo Diddley, the irrepressible, flamboyant personification of black rock 'n' roll, and bassist and songwriter Willie Dixon, whose "Little Red Rooster" provided Mick Jagger with one of his early hits. The success of the British groups, in both Great Britain and the United States, opened the ears of young listeners, both black and white, to a music closer to the blues than Carl Perkins', Elvis Presley's, Buddy Holly's and Jerry Lee Lewis' had been, and stimulated curiosity and critical perception in a manner that led them inevitably to B.B. King.

No one was more surprised or more grateful than B.B. "America," he told Harvey Siders, "is basically a child of other countries. Yet it's a very hip country, 'cause we check on anything those European musicians tell us about. The British groups actually re-imported blues back into America, and I'd like to thank them for what they've done. Now they didn't have to, but they mentioned the fact that they listened to guys like B.B. King, Muddy Waters, Lead-belly [Huddie Ledbetter], etcetera. So America got hold of this; the white youth started to dig it because some of their idols dug it, so they did research on us, and I guess I happened to be one of the few lucky guys who got caught in the net."

Luck may have had something to do with it, along with the fact that the young British musicians have been, as B.B. noted, generous and candid in identifying and acknowledging their black American sources, and in giving them a career lift by taking them (including B.B.) on tour and introducing them to young white audiences. But luck is no help if one is not ready and prepared to exploit it. Nor is it any help if the audience is not receptive. It may seem a vicious irony that white musicians, both British and American, were making fortunes from the music of B.B. King and other black blues men well before the black musicians were able to enjoy any comparable prosperity. But the audience had to be prepared, just as young white musicians, British and American, had had to be prepared for the real blues by the intermediation of Perkins, Presley, Holly and Lewis.

B.B. knows all about that. "Now I was a disc jockey when Fats Domino started, same with Chuck Berry, Little Richard and all those guys," he told Tam Fiofori in a *Melody Maker* interview, "and I used to play their records on the radio station where I worked. Until Elvis Presley came out, there wasn't too much happening as to where the guys could really make good. When Elvis came out, then Fats Domino went up. Little Richard went up. Chuck Berry went up, and all of them began to be giants at that time."

By the time other white musicians, following the British lead, had found the way back, so to speak, to B.B. King a decade later, both B.B. and the public were prepared. He was already the best singer and the best guitar player of them all, probably the best in either department that the blues had ever known, and could now be appreciated as such. But what distinguishes him most importantly and significantly from his contemporaries is not, I would suggest, so much a matter of voice, virtuosity, warmth, invention and showmanship as it is a matter of style.

B.B. is not and never has been notably original, either as composer or performer. Certain of his—I am tempted to say "conversational"—devices as a guitarist may properly be termed innovative. That's about all. But in no other singer, or instrumentalist, for that matter, have I felt the harmonious convergence, the congenial absorption, the definitive summation of so many styles, and this with never a trace or suggestion of stylistic inconsistency or incongruity.

In selecting singers as chapter subjects I have looked, as a rule, for those who have been either the originators of a style (Mildred Bailey, Bing Crosby, Elvis Presley, Jimmie Rodgers, for example) or those who carried a style to its ultimate artistic and technical fulfillment (Ella Fitzgerald, Mahalia Jackson, Peggy Lee, Frank Sinatra and Hank Williams). One might see in B.B. King a fulfillment of everything implicit in the blues, but it has always seemed to me that he reflects a broader musical base, a wider historical perspective. I sense in his performance a panorama of Afro-American music, embracing all those stylistic phenomena that have for nearly a century nourished the American musical mainstream—blues, country, jazz, swing, boogie, rhythm-and-blues and gospel.

Only the mainstream itself is missing. B.B. has never been a singer of popular songs. He has the finest voice among all blues men, and he can sustain a melody more successfully than the others when he chooses to. But a prescribed melody in the form of a popular, familiar tune seems to inhibit him. He will always shake himself free of it within a matter of measures. He is rooted in the oratorical tradition of the blues. He prospers musically in that no-man's-land between song and speech which is the blues singer's most congenial habitat.

B.B. King is an articulate talker—which may have something to do with his being so articulate a musician—and in scores of interviews he has discussed his musical origins and early enthusiasms.

What one learns of the breadth of his interest, knowledge and perception gives rather more than a clue to the diversity of styles and periods reflected in his singing and playing. It is well to reiterate in this connection, however, that there is no suggestion of a stylistic mishmash in the actual music and its performance. Everything has been absorbed and, so to speak, homogenized. What one hears is all distinctively and uniquely B.B. King.

His early sources appear to have been pretty evenly distributed among gospel, blues and jazz. Gospel singers had a lot to do with shaping his vocalism, especially, according to his own testimony, Sam McCrary, tenor lead of a gospel group called the Fairfield Four. The influence has been noted by Tony Heilbut in *The Gospel Sound*. "King's vocal lines," he writes, "are more elaborate and dramatic than those of the laconic early blues singers. McCrary's quartet stylings provide the difference." They probably also guided B.B. to his mastery of falsetto.

Among the older blues singers B.B. cites Blind Lemon Jefferson and the less widely known "Doctor" Peter Clayton. But he also mentions LeRoy Carr, Leadbelly, Robert and Lonnie Johnson and Memphis Slim. Among the big-band blues shouters of the 1930s and 1940s his idols were, not surprisingly, Jimmy Rushing and Big Joe Turner. He was well aware of a newer breed of rhythm-and-blues singer, notably Louis Jordan and Charles Brown (who was also an important influence on Ray Charles).

B.B.'s affinity with jazz is more apparent in his guitar playing than in his singing. Here the primary influence, as he has said again and again, was the French gypsy jazz guitarist Django Reinhardt, especially as heard on Reinhardt's few late records with electric guitar. Charlie Christian was a B.B. idol, but B.B. does not credit him as an influence on his own guitar playing. The same is true of Wes Montgomery.

B.B. himself was guided to the electric guitar first by a guitar-playing preacher relative, then, in a blues contex, by the example of T-Bone Walker, one of the first, if not the very first, of the blues men to go electric. B.B. tried to learn the bottleneck (or steel slide) technique from his cousin Bukka White in Memphis, but found it physically uncongenial and evolved his own substitute for it in the form of a wide, slurring vibrato, and in a way of "bending" notes which he says was inspired by the saxophone slurrings of Lester

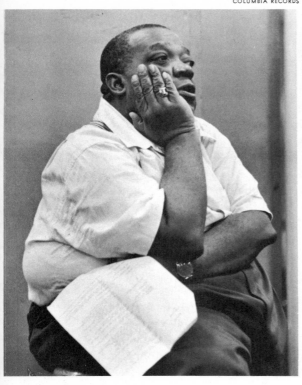

Jimmy Rushing
Jimmy Witherspoon

Joe Williams
Joe Turner

Young. For my own part, I hear a great deal of "Singing Brakeman" Jimmie Rodgers in B.B.'s use of the guitar as a complementary or supplementary singing voice, and B.B. has listed Rodgers as among those whom he heard (on records) as a boy.

B.B., like Elvis Presley, happened along at the right time and the right place. B.B. was the earlier on the scene by nearly ten years (he was born on September 16, 1925); but, like Elvis, his birthplace was Mississippi (Itta Bena, near Indianola) and also like Elvis, and Johnny Cash, too, he served a musical apprenticeship in Memphis, Tennessee. The age difference is important, because it enabled B.B. to hear the older blues men, in person or on records, while they were still relatively young, and while their music was still an integral element of Southern black plantation culture. This would explain a traditionalist flavor in his music uncommon in the work of younger men or in the work of men his own age who came from outside the Mississippi Delta (roughly Memphis to Vicksburg).

My father and mother separated when I was about four [B.B. told Stanley Dance (in *Jazz*)] and my mother carried me up in the hills of Mississippi. She passed when I was about nine, and I spent a lot of time alone then, because my father didn't know where I was. I worked for the white people my mother had worked for. I lived by myself, but they fed me and let me go to school. The school was a one-room building with one teacher and about eighty-six kids, and that was where I got most of my elementary education.

I had to walk five miles each way—ten miles a day. I didn't think much about it then, but now I wonder how I did it. I used to milk ten cows in the morning and ten cows at night. These people I worked for didn't have much money, but I got about fifteen dollars a month. Now believe me, it was one of the happiest parts of my life, because there, then, they were just simple people. Today, I find, people are different. You've got to be at a certain level to be recognized; but then, whoever you were, you were that particular person.

I had a mule and a plough when I was twelve, and we used to plough six months out of the year. On the plantation we always worked five and a half days a week, usually six, and often six and a half. I once tried to figure out how far I must have traveled in ten years of ploughing—six of them behind a mule. I never heard of a vacation until I left the plantation.

B.B.'s father found him when he was fourteen, and brought him back to the Delta. There was more of the same kind of hard work, but now there was a difference. His father had married again, and the new brother-in-law was a guitar-playing Sanctified preacher. There was also a young aunt who was a blues fan with a collection of early blues records. Young B.B. was fascinated by the guitar and the preaching; less so, at the time, by the blues records. He persuaded his plantation boss to buy him a guitar and take the cost (eight dollars) out of his wages.

> That was how my musical career began [he told Dance], but there were no teachers of music through there that I ever heard about. Four of us boys got a little quartet together, but I wasn't interested in blues then. I always thought I might be able to get somewhere in the spiritual field. The Golden Gate Quartet were our idols, and we'd hear them on the radio. I learned by just watching and listening to that preacher play. I kept fooling with the guitar, and I learned three chords. It seemed as though I could sing almost anything with those three chords, like 1, 4 and 5.

He still can. "I think a guy has a lot of work to do in twelve bars when he doesn't have but three chords," he told Harvey Siders. "To make it listenable and appealing you really got to put forth some effort. But I think it's a greater challenge than other types of music. Say you play a thirty-two-bar thing. You got a whole lot of changes that you can do things with. Of course, now you gotta be thinking of those changes, but with a straight twelve-bar thing you have the challenge of filling it up, and all you got is those three chords to work with."

But blues were in the air—or at least in the halls and joints where plantation workers gathered for drinking, dancing and gambling. B.B. ran into other boys who were playing guitar, and before long he was walking or riding the eight miles to Indianola to hear Charles Brown, Louis Jordan, Robert Junior Lockwood and Sonny Boy Williamson (actually Willie "Rice" Miller, usually referred to as Sonny Boy Williamson II to distinguish him from the more famous Lee "Sonny Boy" Williamson, although Willie was the older of the two). The names are significant as demonstrating an early exposure to both the older rural and newer urban blues styles.

The war came. B.B. was inducted, and did his basic training at Camp Selby and Fort Benning. But he was soon released as an indispensable plantation hand. It was just this short experience of army life, however, that sparked his subsequent career in music. As B.B. tells it to Stanley Dance:

It was a funny thing, but it was when I went in the army that I started singing blues. A lot of fellows seemed to get religion and sing spirituals when they got in there, but me, I didn't. When I got home I realized a lot of fellows were making a living singing the blues, but my people were very religious, and I was afraid to sing the blues around the house. My aunt would get angry with anyone singing the blues. I would have to do that away from the house, but I found later on that people seemed to like my singing and playing.

So I would work all the week and sometimes on a Saturday I would have eight or ten dollars. I would take this money and buy me a ticket to the nearest little town—me and the guitar. I would go to this little town and stand on the corners and play. The people seemed to like it, and they would tip me a nickel, a dime or a quarter. Sometimes on a Saturday I'd visit three or four towns, some as far away as forty miles from where I lived, and sometimes I'd come home with maybe twenty-five or thirty dollars. So I found I made more in that one day than I had in the whole week. The money was nice, but that wasn't all of it to me. I wanted to do it, and it made me feel good that they enjoyed listening to me.

As long as the war lasted, B.B. had to continue working on the plantation or face reinduction, but as soon as it was over, inspired by his success on small-town street corners, he headed for Memphis, picked up a job as singer and disc jockey for a new black radio station, WDIA, and a new name, the "Beale Street Blues Boy," later shortened to "B.B." The radio spot gave him a local reputation he could exploit in one-night stands in the Memphis area. In 1949 he made his first recordings. With "Three O'Clock Blues," recorded in the same year, he had his first rhythm-and-blues hit, and set forth on the travels that would lead him eventually to the Regal Theater on Chicago's South Side, to the Apollo Theater in Harlem, and ultimately to Europe, to London's Royal Albert Hall and to world tours.

The B.B. King of those early records is essentially the B.B. of today. The voice—a warm, radiant, virile high tenor—was younger and lighter. The style was closer to the rhythm-and-blues idiom of that time than to the older country blues, and he favored boogie rhythmic and chordal patterns. B.B., as he became more aware of the blues as an honorable expression of Afro-American culture, has tended to look backward rather than forward, to Mississippi rather than to Chicago, and he has eschewed any flirtation with rock 'n' roll and subsequent pop style. But his accomplishments as vocalist and guitar player were fully evident on those early records. So it seems to me, as reflected in notes I made on a first hearing:

Of "My Own Fault, Darlin'," I find: "Head voice high D (not falsetto), kind of ecstatic head voice, or walking a narrow line between head voice and falsetto in the gospel manner—guitar *talking*—tremendous vibrato (he calls it trill)—he just lives up there on that high D—call and response with himself on guitar—a wonderful record!" Of "Walkin' and Cryin'": "Lovely slow blues, more melodic, more *sustained*—beautiful guitar chorus—*talking* guitar as extension of voice—lovely melancholy sighing slurs—good enunciation—fine record." And of "Everything I Do Is Wrong": "Attacks on B natural, then B flat—high E without going into falsetto."

B.B. does not nowadays take as much voice as high as he once did, but in falsetto he sings as high as ever, and there is less evidence in his singing of disparity between normal voice and falsetto than I can remember in any other solo singer I have heard. He also colors falsetto artfully for comic effects (a female voice in disputation, for example), and he can even match it to the higher reaches of his guitar so exactly that it is sometimes difficult to tell which is which.

He has become a riper, more resourceful performer, interspersing singing with exhortatory talking bits (he could have been a great gospel preacher, and rather looks like one), and pacing himself with the alternation of voice and guitar.

Phyl Garland has put it well:

His approach is so smooth, his fire so controlled, that each performance comes across a little like a triumph of dramatic as well as of musical art. His sense of taste is so infallible that he is one of the very few around who can cry out in all passion while retaining his "cool." And this is why he is considered a master.

All this is true, and doubtless gratifying to B.B. King, especially coming from a black writer (Phyl Garland is an associate editor of *Ebony*). B.B. is well aware that the distance between Itta Bena, Mississippi, and the Royal Albert Hall cannot be justly measured in miles, and he is aware of his own accomplishment in covering that distance. But the awareness is neither the source nor the subject of his greatest satisfaction. His career as a public performer has been a fight not so much for himself as for the blues, and for his own status as a blues singer.

He might well have come to the top earlier had he wandered into a more popular, more fashionable, more lucrative repertoire. He did not, although since joining a major label (ABC) in 1965, he has accepted the string and heavenly choir backings that record-company executives seem to consider a prerequisite for reaching a numerous white, and even black, market. That aside, he has stuck to his own idiom and style. It was not so much a question of being true to himself as of being true to the blues. He has prevailed, and he sees in his personal success a victory for the blues.

Most whites think of the blues as being the music of the black American. They are not. They have been, and still are, the music of some black Americans. But black society is as stratified as white society. For many blacks, especially in the Northern cities and among those who have risen socially both in the North and in the South, the blues have been looked down upon as old-timey, old-fashioned, uncouth and non-U, a childlike reminder of a primitive, rural, shanty past, as Bessie Smith learned to her sorrow in the late 1920s and early 1930s. A legitimate parallel might be drawn with the attitude of the greater part of American white society—until recently—toward country music, formerly despised as "hillbilly." Not all snobs are white.

> When I first started [B.B. told Harvey Siders] music seemed to be really segregated—you know, clannish: all the jazz musicians would stick with jazz musicians; with the exception of a few, they wouldn't associate with blues musicians, or with guys affiliated with spirituals [B.B. seems to use the term "spiritual" where others would say "gospel"]. It seemed like musicians had little clans, and they stayed in them. Of course, being a blues singer in those days was looked down on, so when you talk about overcoming obstacles, *it was like being black twice.*
>
> I was a little bit ashamed to make myself known in the

presence of a lot of other people who was famous or popular because the first thing they would say was "B.B., that blues singer." It seemed that most people would say it in disgust. I know I don't speak good English, and I know I'm not real educated. I'm a high school dropout, because I finished tenth grade and that was that. And I didn't go to any music school or conservatory. But when I think about all these things that I *don't* have, I know that I'm *me*, and I know that I have what I do have and I'm proud of it. In other words, I'm glad today to let people hear it again, and I'm not ashamed of it.

B.B. had first encountered disdainful attitudes in Memphis, and, as he told Stanley Dance:

. . . that was when I really began to fight for the blues. I refused to go as rock 'n' roll as some people did. The things people used to say about those I thought of as the greats in the business, the blues singers, used to hurt me. They spoke of them as if they were all illiterate and dirty. It was like a kid being whipped for something he didn't do. He has no defense, and he just has to take it.

The blues had made me a better living than any I had ever had, so this was when I really put my fight on. A few whites gave me the blah-blah about blues singers, but mostly it was Negro people, and that was why it hurt. To be honest, I believe they felt they were trying to lift the standards of the Negro, and that they just didn't want to be associated with the blues because it was something still back *there*.

To me it wasn't like that. If Nat Cole could sing in night-clubs and be a great popular singer; if Frank Sinatra could sing his songs and be a great person; if Mahalia Jackson could sing spirituals and be great—why couldn't I be a blues singer and be great? Then there were so many young people who wanted to play like me and sing like me, that I wanted to bring it up to a level where they could be proud.

A word B.B. has often used in talking about the blues is *respect*. He wants himself to be respected. He has conducted himself, as citizen and performer, respectably. He has always treated the blues and other blues performers with respect. He wants others to do the same. "I don't mind being called a blues singer," he told Charles Keil (*Urban Blues*), "just so long as the tone of voice is right."

The tone of voice, these days, is right.

19

Aretha Franklin

A curious fact in the story of the blues is the fluctuation in the relative prominence and prosperity of male and female singers.

When the blues first intruded upon national and international consciousness in the 1920s, it was through the art of female singers: Ida Cox, Chippie Hill, Ma Rainey, Bessie Smith and Sippie Wallace. Theirs were the big names. No male blues singer, at that time, had achieved a comparable prominence. By the mid-1930s, however, the ladies' day was done. Jimmy Rushing, Big Joe Turner and, following them, Joe Williams, propelled by the bluesy swing and burgeoning fame of the Count Basie Band, were, as far as a wide public was concerned, the blues greats of the late 1930s and early 1940s, along with Big Bill Broonzy, whose success in Chicago, New York, London and Paris drew critical attention to a more traditional—and masculine—blues idiom.

For the next twenty-five years, in the various evolving and developing urban rhythm-and-blues styles, it was the men who broke new ground and nourished a taste among younger blacks, and among younger whites, too, for brasher, louder, more confident, more assertive sounds: Chuck Berry, Bobby Bland, Bo Diddley, Fats Domino, John Lee Hooker, B.B. King, Otis Redding, T-Bone Walker, Muddy Waters, Jimmy Witherspoon and Howlin' Wolf, right down to Jimi

Hendrix and James Brown. Then, suddenly, in the late 1960s—in 1968, to be precise—there was Aretha Franklin, and the ladies were back. Tina Turner followed, and, still more recently, Roberta Flack and Carla Thomas.

That, in broad outline, is the story as it appears to all but the most devoted and diligent researchers. It was not, certainly, that black female singers, as such, had disappeared from the scene. There were Pearl Bailey, Ella Fitzgerald, Billie Holiday, Lena Horne, Mabel Mercer, Maxine Sullivan, Sarah Vaughan, Ethel Waters and many more. It was rather that the most successful among them were not singing blues, or even the black vaudeville songs that had passed for blues in the 1920s. They were working within, or close to, the mainstream of American popular music, singing the music of white American songwriters for mostly white audiences, both American and European.

Granted, the music already rejoiced in black characteristics, thanks to the example, primarily, of Louis Armstrong and Ethel Waters, and to black influences perceptible in the singing of such white performers as Al Jolson and Sophie Tucker. But this was a long way from what could still be heard in the Mississippi Delta and other rural and small-town areas of the South and Southwest, not to mention Chicago, or the vocal music of the black fundamentalist churches.

The story, inevitably, is oversimplified. There were many male blues singers in the time of Bessie Smith and her female contemporaries. But their names, at that time, were known only to researchers. Among these singers were LeRoy Carr, Blind Lemon Jefferson, Lonnie and Robert Johnson, Leadbelly (Huddie Ledbetter) and Charley Patton. Thanks to research and record reissues, their names are more familiar today, if still hardly household words, than they were when the singers themselves were alive and in their prime.

Perhaps their obscurity in their own time was due to the fact that they had not the physical charm and show-biz allure of their blues and vaudeville sisters. Their music, moreover, was thought to be crude and old-fashioned by younger urban blacks. Thus, they never figured even in the vaudeville history that brought a national recognition to Bessie and Ethel and, in a lesser degree, to the many black female singers of the 1920s and early 1930s who worked in a style midway between blues and popular, and who are now remem-

Tina Turner   Roberta Flack
Chuck Berry   Otis Redding

bered affectionately as the "cake-walking babies." The males stayed put in their native Southern, rural and small-town environment.

Similarly, there were blues ladies during the interim separating Bessie Smith from Aretha Franklin: LaVern Baker, Ruth Brown, Moms Mabley, Lizzie Miles, Memphis Minnie, Victoria Spivey and, above all, Dinah Washington—splendid artists every one. Among them only LaVern Baker (with "Tweedlee Dee") and Dinah Washington emerged fitfully from the circumscribed world of race records and rhythm-and-blues, and they had to embrace a more widely popular repertoire and a more widely popular style to do it. For the rest, the black women either sang mainstream popular music or stayed, like Mahalia Jackson, in church.

It must be reckoned a cultural misfortune that they not only stayed in church, but that they had to. The abundantly recorded art and vocalism of Dinah Washington, who began as a gospel singer—she died in 1964—offer a taste of what a gospel-schooled singer could do when turned loose on the blues, or even on jazz and popular music. The same is true of Sister Rosetta Tharpe and, from an earlier generation, of Lizzie Miles.

But the church was jealous of its children, its music and its righteousness. It could not contain the music itself, which merged happily with blues as rhythm-and-blues in the 1940s, but it would not, until Aretha came along, and not wholeheartedly even then, countenance a flirtation by its singers with the "evil, low-down" blues. Many excellent singers chose not to defy the ban, prompted by faith or by principle or by reluctance to forsake the relative security of the church for the precarious fortunes of show business. Thus it must have seemed symbolic of a new relationship, musically at least, between the church and the secular world that it should have been Aretha Franklin who sang Thomas A. Dorsey's "Precious Lord" at the memorial services for Mahalia Jackson in Chicago.

No other singer, to be sure, not even Mahalia, had been more firmly rooted in gospel. Aretha's father, the Reverend C. L. Franklin, was, and is still, pastor of the New Bethel Baptist Church in Detroit, with no less than seventy LPs of his sermons to document his persuasive oratory. Her early environment was saturated in gospel. She was a soloist in her father's church at twelve. She developed her showmanly talents in the church, and she was already a famous gospel singer when she ventured into secular music at the Trade Winds in Chicago in 1960, when she was eighteen.

But neither had any other female singer, at the time of Mahalia's death in 1972, had so stunning a career singing the blues, or the modern approximation of the blues called soul. Yet here she was, at the peak of her secular, worldly success, singing the hymn closest to the gospel heart at the funeral of the church's hallowed "Halie." For Aretha, there was no contradiction. Only a month before Mahalia's death she had documented her determination to reconcile, by her art and example, the heretofore conflicting claims of the sacred and secular worlds by recording an album, *Amazing Grace*, live at the Cornerstone Baptist Church in Los Angeles, the enterprise blessed by the participative assistance of the Reverend James Cleveland, "Crown Prince of Gospel," the Southern California Community Choir, and her father as preacher. Aretha may have defied both convention and tradition by straying from the fold to earn a few millions and then conducting herself as if she had never left it. But she was not content to accept anathema. She is not a lady easily denied.

She would have had to accept it twenty or even ten years earlier. But by the time of Mahalia's death, gospel music was no longer the exclusive property of the church. In the chapters on Mahalia Jackson and Ray Charles I have discussed the various avenues by which it seeped out to the secular community, and the various guises it assumed. At the close of the 1960s it had already so infiltrated every constituent element of contemporary black American music and, in rock, of white American (and British) music, too, that the church would seem to have had no course other than acquiescence, however grudging that acquiescence may have been in some quarters. Aretha sang at Mahalia's funeral not because she was the greatest of all surviving gospel singers—Bessie Griffin is touted as heir-presumptive to Mahalia's mantle—but because as Lady Soul, or Queen of Soul, and as a gospel singer born and bred, she represented the triumph of a truly black indigenous American music among most Americans, black and white.

The clue to an apparent, possibly still only incipient, about-face by the black church community is to be found, I would suggest, in the substitution of the word *soul* (a satisfactorily churchy word) for *blues*, attributing to the former, for the moment, a social and emo-

Dinah Washington

Moms Mabley

Big Mama Thornton

tional, rather than merely a musically formal, connotation. Not for nothing do American blacks address one another as soul brothers. Implicit in the term is the acknowledgment of a community of interest, identity, experience, aspiration and—more importantly—self-awareness and pride, bridging former regional, economic, social and religious stratification and fragmentation. Also implicit in the word *soul* is the assumption that it is something blacks have which whites do not have—and which whites envy.

What whites envy, I suspect, is not so much the black man's—or black woman's—soul as his lack of inhibition about baring it. Centuries of Western European civilization—Western European far more than Eastern European—with its emphasis upon decorous comportment and behavior, upon the assumed virtues of restraint and moderation, and upon the assumed felicity of favoring others by keeping one's own troubles and ecstasies to oneself, have conspicuously diminished the white man's powers of exuberant self-expression. The debility has been strongly felt and deeply resented by younger whites, hence the attraction, for them, of the unembarrassed fervor of the black American's music, especially that part of it most vividly reflected in the soul-baring characteristics and devices of gospel.

Soul, or gospel, as a style, has its hazards. Nothing is more offensive to the fastidious, as I have noted previously, than exaltation feigned. What is permissible, even compelling and admirable, in an inspired performance becomes dreary, hideous exhibitionism when trotted out on schedule for an audience of voyeurs. Even in more honorable circumstances there is a temptation to uncritical self-indulgence for performers and auditors alike, aggravated by the familiar fact that where intensity of expression and experience is urged to extremes, or sustained beyond the resources of inspiration, the line separating high art from high camp, the sublime from the vulgar, becomes thin.

Both the glories and the hazards of soul and gospel are demonstrated vividly in the singing and the vocalism of Aretha Franklin. She is musical. Her voice is lovely when not pressed—I would call it an F to F mezzo-soprano—and she has a considerable sensitivity for word and phrase. But while, at her best, she reveals all that is noblest in gospel and soul, she also provides distressing examples of much that, to my European-oriented ears, is abominable. Hearing her, both in public performance and on records, I am ever reminded of Ethel Waters' recollection of her grandmother telling Ethel's gospel-shouting mother: "You don't have to holler so. God has very big ears. He can hear you even if you whisper." Aretha is most persuasive when she whispers.

That more often she hollers and shrieks and screams is not her fault alone. Everybody nowadays is hollering and shrieking and screaming. And since all are doing it into microphones, the din is appalling. It is also acoustically and artistically shortsighted and self-defeating. The microphone rendered hollering unnecessary. Such singers as Mildred Bailey, Bing Crosby, Billie Holiday and, above all, Frank Sinatra, showed how it could be made to reveal untapped, even unsuspected subtleties of vocal production and articulation. Now, in gospel, soul and rock, we are back where we were before, only worse—and amplified. The conventions of gospel singing, corrupted and carried over into rhythm-and-blues, have been largely responsible for it.

One regrets the hollering the more in Aretha's case, not only because the voice itself is so fine, so capable of warmly communicative utterance, but also because the gospel fervor tempts her to sing continually outside her normal range. This is characteristic of contemporary black singers—I have already noted it in speaking of Ray Charles—and it has to do with their compulsion to achieve, or seem to represent, a state of ecstasy, or, as in some recent secular music, anger and defiance. Mere loudness is not enough for them. Indeed, they rarely sing loudly in their normal range. They know what the microphone can do for them there. It is the sense of extraordinary exertion, emphasis and accomplishment that they want, and for this they have to appear to be going up and up, ever higher and higher, to be reaching, so to speak, "out of this world."

This is the vocal counterpart of one of the most distasteful and tedious characteristics of modern jazz: the young jazz musician's predilection for forcing trumpets, trombones, saxophones and clarinets beyond their normal range and into an area where the only product can be squealing, squeaking, squawking, screaming and shrieking. It is partly a matter of competition, the urge to play higher and faster than the next fellow. But it is partly, too, a matter of trying to make oneself heard in a world, and especially in a young world, where everyone is clamoring for attention. It is musically, artistically, esthetically deplorable. One hopes only that the outer limits may, by now, have been reached, and that young artists, instrumentalists and singers alike, may find in a return to beautiful singing and playing, to *bel canto*, a more satisfactory device for drawing favorable attention to themselves.

The squalling sounds of singers can be deceptive. Some critics have attributed to Aretha an extraordinary range of four octaves. According to my own reckoning she has about two and a half, from a low E to a high B. She rarely uses the lower fifth, which tends to be weak, and she would be better advised to approach the upper fifth only in falsetto, which she manages skillfully. But she persists in alternating falsetto with full voice right on up to the top B flat, and because of the effort audible in ascending above an F, the higher pitches seem higher than they are. They also sound thin, shrill and sometimes nasal. It is not an agreeable sound.

I first heard her in person when she made her London debut at the Odeon Theater in Hammersmith in 1968, and was greatly impressed by her strength as a performer and by her way with an audience, especially when she was working alone at the piano in one of her favorite numbers, "Dr. Feelgood." I was less enchanted by the presence of a large backing band and the vocal trio, the Sweet Inspirations. They were all expert enough. But I sensed in Aretha an artist capable of going it pretty much alone. All else, to me, seemed an intrusion between her and the audience.

I react similarly to many of her records. Arrangements by Turkish-born Arif Mardin, as well as shrewd production by Jerry Wexler and Tom Dowd, are usually credited with having had a lot to do with the sudden change in her fortunes following her move from Columbia to Atlantic in 1966. Jerry Wexler is said to have "put her back in church." For my taste, until *Amazing Grace*, he didn't put her back far enough. In the records she made for Atlantic before that, I find the backings, however skillfully conceived, played and engineered, too conspicuous.

Again, it is not necessarily Aretha's fault, if, indeed, one may speak of fault in procedures that have proved so successful. A tendency toward overarrangement has been evident in the backing for many singers in the past decade. It seems almost as if the arranger and the band were beginning to challenge the singer's predominant role, just as the composer and the symphony orchestra challenged it, and usurped it, in Europe, beginning with Mozart. I am reminded of Angelica Catalani's description of Mozart's orchestral accompaniments as being "like a police escort." Let singers beware!

As with shouting and screaming, everyone seems afraid of leaving well enough alone, or of leaving a singer alone. It seems a long time since the innocent 1930s, 1940s and 1950s, when many an exemplary backing was fashioned in the studio on the spur of the moment by instrumentalists who could not read music, or who had no music to read. As Pearl Bailey likes to put it: "We used to dance to the tunes of our hearts; now we dance to the tunes of other people's heads."

This may not be Aretha's view. She is a child of her time, which, in music, is increasingly an instrumental time. Personal insecurity may have something to do with it, a reluctance to be left alone with the full responsibility, or it may be just a gospel singer's love of company. A sense of insecurity was evident and troublesome when she was interviewed on television by David Frost in November 1970. She was tense, unforthcoming, chain-smoking, and edgy, volunteering nothing, saying no more than was required to give simple answers to direct questions.

She had started to sing in public when she was ten or twelve, she told Frost, in her father's church in Detroit.

"How did you sing?" Frost asked her.

"Religiously," she replied.

"What sort of gospel?"

"My father's gospel."

"Which father?"

"Both fathers."

"What do you want to get across when you sing?"

"What I feel."

"Do you prefer to sing standing up or playing the piano?"

"Being heard and understood."

So it went. One might have gained an impression of hostility or defiance, but it was almost certainly self-defense. Frost was not the first to find the way barred to Aretha's innermost feelings. Leonard Feather, describing her for *Melody Maker* in May 1968, spoke of "a lady occasionally peeping out from behind her self-imposed curtain." Tony Palmer, in *The Observer*, at about the time of the Frost interview, wrote: "She hates interviews, and has become impenetrable even to her friends." Valerie Wilmer, in *Down Beat*, spoke of her being "plagued with a feeling of insecurity. She comes to life only on the stage."

The Frost show was an example. It was finally time for her to sing, and I noted down "the eagerness, the relief, with which she went to the piano—and to work!" She sang a lot, and she sang well, but it was not until the end of the program, after she and Frost had been joined by her father, and after Frost had failed to get her father to sing, that we viewers were suddenly admitted to the inner sanctum, and were shown what a great singer she can be. She sat at the piano and began: "Precious Lord, take my hand," and I found myself scribbling: "eloquent, elegant, the loveliest thing I have ever heard her do—rhapsodic!"

Aretha has been for me, ever since then, a gospel singer. I suspect that a similar sentiment may have prompted Jerry Wexler, who has guided her recording career at Atlantic, to put her back in church, really, and not just figuratively, with the *Amazing Grace* album. Not only the vocalism here, but also the audible reactions of the congregation, tell more of how she sings, and why, than any other of her records that I have heard. There's a moment in "You'll Never Grow Old" where, after a low, soft beginning, she soars up to an ecstatic, full-voiced B flat, the congregation screaming with amazed delight. The effect is as if they were soaring with her, sharing the thrills of a roller-coaster ride. Aretha, responding, soars up again, sounding as if she would tear her throat out.

In a ten-and-a-half-minute workout on "Amazing Grace," the title hymn, she offers the full range of her resources and devices—first, a cornucopia of melismata (she would call them curlicues) fading out in a long, lovely diminuendo, then, sudden strong, contrasting attacks, to which the congregation reacts as if poked in the ribs, and then the inevitable upward flights, contrasting full voice with falsetto. The voice is always warm and velvety in the middle, but she rarely tarries there. Does she fear that she would lose her listeners if there were too long an interval of true singing between ecstatic screams?

She wouldn't lose this listener. But Aretha knows her idiom. She knows her audience, and, presumably, she knows her voice. She didn't achieve her present eminence singing for the European-schooled, opera-bred, sixtyish likes of me.

20

Ethel Merman

Ethel Merman called her autobiography *Who Could Ask for Anything More?* The title was drawn from the George and Ira Gershwin song "I Got Rhythm." That was the song which, in *Girl Crazy*, in 1930, catapulted her into a Broadway career that would establish her as the Queen of Musical Comedy, a career that may—or may not?—have ended forty years later with her run as the seventh Dolly Gallagher Levi in *Hello, Dolly!* It was she, appropriately, who sang the 2,718th performance, on September 9, 1971, that made *Hello, Dolly!* the longest-running musical in Broadway history.

She was no stranger to long runs. There had been *Anything Goes* (1934) with 420 performances; *Panama Hattie* (1940) with 501; *Annie Get Your Gun* (1946) with 1,147; *Call Me Madam* (1950) with 644, and *Gypsy* (1959) with 702. She always stayed for the run of the show—on Broadway. She had no taste for the road. It was only because of her reluctance to face another probable long run immediately following *Gypsy* that she became the seventh Dolly Levi instead of the first. She had been accorded the right of first refusal, and she refused. Enter Carol Channing, Ginger Rogers, Martha Raye, Betty Grable, Pearl Bailey and Phyllis Diller in that order. Had Ethel Merman chosen to be the first Dolly, she would probably have been the only Dolly—on Broadway.

The success documented in that list of long runs—and it includes only the longest—would seem sufficient to render the question "Who could ask for anything more?" rhetorical. For a Merman it was. Any other singer with a similar vocal endowment could have come up with reasonable additional requests, beginning with a lovelier voice, a wider range, and some elementary vocal schooling. Ethel Merman did not need them. When she auditioned for George Gershwin for *Girl Crazy* he told her: "Don't ever let anyone give you a singing lesson. It'll ruin you." He was almost certainly right. One cannot be sure, for she never put his judgment to the test by taking a lesson. Wise girl.

Assessing, or accepting, Ethel Merman as a singer is a bit like assessing, or accepting, Al Jolson or Hank Williams. The vocal sound, by all traditional and conventional criteria, was godawful. When she was belting, which was most of the time, it was raucous, strident, abrasive, brassy, nasal, open and just plain loud. But, as with Jolson and Williams, if it didn't have beauty, it had character. It was unmistakably, unforgettably hers. As such, it was not a voice that lent itself to any old song. She was fortunate, in the course of her long stage career, in inspiring librettists, lyricists and songwriters to create characters and songs that went with that voice. They rarely went so well with the voices and delivery of other singers.

Her range was hardly more than an octave and a fourth. She herself gives it as extending from G below to C above. She sometimes sang higher, but not much, and when she did, she had to ease off into a thin, tenuous head voice reminiscent of Ethel Waters working beyond her natural range. Merman described her vocal procedure aptly enough in *Who Could Ask for Anything More?*: "I just stand up and holler and hope that my voice holds out."

She remembers hollering like that since she was five. She had probably been doing it almost from the day, in 1909, when she was born, Ethel Agnes Zimmermann, of Scottish-German parentage, in Astoria, Long Island. (She shortened the patronymic to Merman for professional convenience before going into the cast of *Girl Crazy*.) Russel Crouse and Howard Lindsay, who wrote the books for *Anything Goes* and *Call Me Madam*, used to have a little joke: "There was terrific excitement in the Zimmermann home when they discovered that Ethel could talk, too." It is easy to imagine similar

excitement in the Gumm household when they discovered that Frances, the future Judy Garland, could also talk.

Judy and Ethel had a lot in common, vocally. It was not just that both were natural and exuberant belters. It was rather that each carried into a professional singing career a kind of vocal production that had come naturally to them as children. The vocal range was about the same, and similarly limited. They both sang with an unfeigned ardor, with an irrepressible joy in singing, especially when they were belting, that persuaded even sophisticated listeners to countenance and applaud sounds not normally considered becoming to well-behaved females.

It was also true of each of them, I think, that their voices sounded bigger than they actually were. What they had in common, rather than size of voice, was concentration, not in terms of cerebration, but in terms of vocal focus. Their method, or manner, of producing their voices was such that not a particle of breath was wasted as it passed across the vocal cords. They got a 100 percent vocal return for every ounce of breath expended—if breath can be measured in ounces. The sound, when they bore down, was not so much loud, although it could be that, too, as incisive.

Ethel shared with Judy, moreover, what I am tempted to call a second voice. It was almost as if each of them had one voice for belting and another for loving—or for being lovely. When they lightened the weight of breath for gentle utterance, all trace of brashness, abrasiveness, stridency and nasality vanished, giving way to a dark, warm, velvety tone that always reminded me of a viola being played on the D string. The tender sound lost nothing in effect, needless to say, by the startling contrast it offered to the voice used for belting.

There was more to their singing, obviously, than just hollering, and Ethel Merman, speaking for herself, knew what it was.

> As a singer [she related in *Who Could Ask for Anything More?*] I do one basic thing. I project. That means that I belt the lyrics over the footlights like a baseball coach belting flyballs to an outfield. And since I do this one basic thing, I don't have anything that you can analyze and slice thin as "style." A long list of singers have so much "style" that you can imitate them easy, but it's always been hard to imitate me. . . . I don't bother about style, but I do bother about making people under-

stand the lyrics I sing. I honestly don't think there's anyone in the business who can top me at that.

Well, Sinatra could come close, as he demonstrated in his recording of "Anything Goes," written for Merman, and first performed by Merman. Frank did a lovely job with it, a shade slower, more swinging than hard-driving. But it was not really his kind of song. One recalls his comment in rejecting a lyric: "Too goddam many words in this song!" Merman, probably, would have been undismayed. She simply had a thing about words. When she couldn't understand them in another singer's delivery she would describe the result acutely as "concert English."

Other singers have handled words as well as she, but it may be doubted that any other ever handled so many words, or so many tough words. Both Cole Porter and Irving Berlin, especially the former, exploited this facility. With what other singer could he have risked, in "You're the Top" (from *Anything Goes*), "You're my thoist / You're a Drumstick Lipstick / You're da foist / In da Irish svipstick"?

Neither Porter nor Berlin made any secret of his appreciation of Ethel Merman's way with words and of her way with a song. Berlin used to tell other songwriters: "If you're writing for Merman, be sure your lyrics are good, because they'll be heard." And Porter, in an article for *The New York Times*, following the opening of *Red, Hot and Blue*, in 1936, wrote:

> I hope it will not be considered ungracious of me, in the face of the other very talented girls who have sung my songs and helped them along to popularity, to confess that I'd rather write for Ethel Merman than for anyone else in the world. Every composer has his favorite, and she is mine. She has the finest enunciation of any American singer I know. She has a sense of rhythm which few can equal. And her feeling for comedy is so instinctive that she can get every value out of a line without ever overstressing a single inference. And she is so damned apt!

Another admirer was Ira Gershwin. In "Sam and Delilah," another of Merman's hits in *Girl Crazy*, he had assigned the words *hooch* and *kootch* to sustained notes. It was a mistake—or would have been with any other singer. "These words," he wrote, in *Lyrics* on *Several Occasions,* "should be uttered quickly so that the listener hears them as monosyllables, not duo, as 'hoo–ch' and 'koo–tch.' I got away with it, thanks to Merman's ability to sustain any note any human or humane length of time. Few singers could give you *koo* for seven beats (it runs into the next bar, like intermission people) and come through with a terrifically convincing *tch* at the end." It used to be said of Merman that she could hold a note as long as the Chase National Bank.

One can almost hear Ethel Merman going to work on Ira's "terrifically convincing." Cole Porter had given her "terrific'ly" in "I Get a Kick Out of You" (*Anything Goes*), and she has described exactly what she did with it: "I took liberties with that word. I paused in the song after the syllable 'rif.' It was just a way of phrasing, of breaking a word into syllables and holding one syllable longer than I ordinarily would, but for some reason that pause killed the people. I'm not enough of a musician to know why, but I know it had that effect."

Miss Merman, here, has just given an instructive example of *tempo rubato,* the stealing of time. What she did was steal time from *icly* and give it to *rif,* achieving not only emphasis, but also surprise and suspense. The listener instinctively perceived the theft, and was impatient to see how the loss would be made good.

What made a familiar device so telling in this case was her rock-solid rhythm. In order to steal time effectively, a singer must have a clearly established tempo, a momentum, to steal from. Ethel Merman made sure that it was there. When she pulled up on that *rif,* it was like a sudden stop in full career. The audience, for an instant, kept on going, then had to make a quick rhythmic readjustment, waiting for Ethel to rejoin them on *icly.*

It was also this rhythmic drive and solidity that made possible the duets in two-part counterpoint, notably those she did with Russell Nype in *Call Me Madam* and with Bruce Yarnall in the 1966 revival of *Annie Get Your Gun.* Even more spectacular examples were the duets she did with Mary Martin in a television special in 1953, when the two singers combined "Tea for Two" with "You're Not Sick, You're Just in Love" and, improbable as it may seem, "Stormy Weather" with "Indian Love Call."

Speaking of Mary Martin, who, incidentally, would have been the first Annie had Jerome Kern not died, a story is told that reveals

Mary Martin and Ezio Pinza

nicely Ethel Merman's down-to-earth approach to the theater and a wry, trenchant sense of humor. Asked her opinion of Miss Martin, presumably at the time when Mary was making Broadway history with "My Heart Belongs to Daddy," Merman is said to have replied, "Well, if you like talent . . ."

Another of the interpretive devices discussed by Ethel Merman in her autobiography is deliberate flatting:

> Cole Porter likes to tell people that I can deliberately flat a note to get comedy effect. He says he doesn't know whether I'm doing it deliberately or whether I just do it instinctively. I've got a flash for him. If I do it, I do it deliberately. Take the song "Sam and Delilah," more particularly, take the words "Delilah was a floozy." I hit a deliberate blue note in it to emphasize the word "floozy," and it does get an effect in keeping with the character I'm singing about.

Both these devices, *tempo rubato* and deliberate flatting, have been employed by all the singers who have worked in the Afro-American musical idiom. Ethel also employed, skillfully and effectively, both the descending and the ascending *portamento* (some might call it *glissando*, or just plain *swoop*), usually, in her case, covering an interval of a fifth, much as Frank Sinatra has used it. And one detects the influence of black singers in her pronunciation of such words as "never" (nev-ah), "ever" (ev-ah) and "other" (oth-ah). Such idiosyncrasies aside, her singing disclosed fewer Afro-American characteristics than that of any other singer discussed in these pages, except possibly Judy Garland.

Merman was, as I heard her (in *Girl Crazy*, *Call Me Madam* and *Gypsy*), and as I hear her now on records, just a bit old-fashioned. There were echoes of the singing styles of Fanny Brice, Ruth Etting, Al Jolson, Helen Morgan and Sophie Tucker. Again like Judy Garland, she was little given to improvisatory embellishment, beyond the odd modest mordent, nor did she indulge in the melodic deviations that so many of the popular singers have permitted themselves, often to the considerable benefit of the songs.

"I leave the songs the way they come out of the composer's head," she used to say. "If it's a good head they'll be good songs without my editing them." What with Harold Arlen, Irving Berlin, George Gershwin, Ray Henderson, Jerry Herman, Cole Porter,

Arthur Schwartz and Jule Styne, she was not lacking for good heads.

As with Peggy Lee, once Ethel had worked out her way with a song, she stuck to that way. Lyricist Buddy de Sylva once said of her: "Watching Merman in a show after she's got her lines and her songs and her stage business all set is like watching a movie after it's been filmed and edited. After that, no matter how many times you see it and hear it, it's always the same." Ethel would have thought of this as professionalism. "I have no time," she likes to say, "for unprofessionals." Peggy Lee would agree.

Also contributing to a suggestion of old-fashionedness in Ethel Merman's singing was its innocence of any of the refinements and artifices—and dependencies—developed by singers working constantly with microphones. She was not bred to the mike. Indeed, her early successes during a brief apprenticeship in New York, Brooklyn and Long Island clubs, and in vaudeville, in the late 1920s, were due to her ability to make herself heard and understood, and to command attention, in noisy places. Nor was her way with a song compatible with the requirements and the strictures of the microphone. She was never, really, a singer of songs in a conventional sense. She was a projector of character, and she needed the setting to work her special magic. She also needed space for movement and gesticulation within that setting.

This would explain, I think, why she never had the huge success on radio, television and records that she had in the theater.

> I have my specialty [she wrote in *Who Could Ask for Anything More?*] and it isn't pop records. And not playing a character, I had no emotional effect on TV audiences. When I sing merely a love song, or rhythm song, with no motivation or build-up, I have nothing extra going for me. To make people like the thoughts in a song I sing, I have to play a character they like first, as in a play. . . . In nine hit Broadway musicals [that was as of 1955], I had channeled my personality through a story line.

Films might have been expected to provide a more congenial medium, but they did not. Hollywood in the 1930s and 1940s fought shy of the tough characters she played, or at least the tough way she played and sang them. As she expressed it: "I was too brassy, too bouncy, too gutsy. I projected too much." She appeared in many pictures, usually cast, as she put it, as "the other girl." With the exception of *Anything Goes* and *Call Me Madam*, she did not appear in the film versions of the shows she had made famous on Broadway. Betty Hutton played Annie and Rosalind Russell played Gypsy Rose Lee's mother.

Annie Get Your Gun, in 1946, projected a less abrasive Merman. According to her, "It was Irving Berlin's lyrics that made a lady out of me. They showed that I had a softer side. It was about time that I had a softer side, because my hard-boiled Tessie type had become a cliché character." It was probably too late. Those who know Ethel Merman agree with her own description of herself as "a soft-boiled gal." But it was the hard-boiled image and the hard-boiled performance that had made her famous, and they stuck.

What it all comes down to in the end, probably, is that Ethel Merman, like Ethel Waters at about the same time, was a woman of the theater through and through, and of the Broadway theater at that. Her reluctance to tour may have inhibited her fame, and it may have inhibited her film career. For the big musicals, Hollywood presumably felt the need of names that were household words throughout the Americas and abroad. Merman was a household word only at home—on Broadway.

She was a woman of the theater not only in the sense that she had to be playing a part. She could do that in films, too, and did. What she needed was the actual theater itself, and the live audience, eight shows a week. She married four times, and had two children. She even withdrew from the theater to find, or seek, domestic fulfillment, once as far from Broadway as Denver. But the theater prevailed.

It needed her, as one of Broadway's most memorable ovations told her when she joined the cast of *Hello, Dolly!* at the St. James Theater on Saturday evening, March 28, 1970. The theater must have its legends. Ethel Merman, for forty years, has been one of its greatest.

21

Peggy Lee

Here's what it is [wrote Judy Klemesrud in *The New York Times* (April 26, 1970]: Miss Peggy Lee slinks into the living room of her Waldorf Towers suite, wearing a pair of turquoise silk movie star pajamas. Her blonde hair tumbles down past her shoulders now, and her figure is plump—but *womanly*. A youngish Mae West. But then you notice the skin . . . it is as smooth and pink as an Iowa sorority girl's. How can it be true? This sexy, sensuous, seductive woman will be 50 years old come May 26, and she is a grandmother three times! But throughout it all she has endured, grown better with age. And she is still, as Duke Ellington once put it, "The Queen."

In London, two months later, Philip Oakes, interviewing Peggy Lee for the *Sunday Times*, prior to her concert at the Royal Albert Hall, saw "a big buttery blonde with platinum hair and an oddly impassive face which leaps to life when she describes her craft and freezes at the first wink of a camera." Her face leaped to life and stayed there during that interview, for she was telling Oakes how she goes about selecting and preparing a program:

I start by gathering songs, maybe a hundred. I have a standing order with favorite composers—Johnny Mandel and Michel

Legrand, for instance—because anything they write I want to see first. Then I get together with my permanent rhythm section, five or six guys, up at my house [in Beverly Hills], and we go through it all, sorting it into "A" and "B" piles. Then we rehearse some, and my lighting director [Hugo Granata]—who's a former musician—joins us, and we decide on the kind of arrangements, and where to make the light changes.

Then we'll think about clothes—I like soft, flowing things—and start to build the actual program. We rehearse quite a bit, because there are intricate things in the arrangements, and they have to be precise. Then we'll check out the acoustics of the concert hall and the balance of the orchestra. By the time we're ready to go on, I'll have gone through around 120 songs, leaving me with thirty for the show. The odd thing is that my voice seems to be getting stronger all the time. There's no sign of strain. My throat man looks at my cords now and then, and he can't get over how healthy they are.

How this painstaking procedure looks to an outsider was described by a reporter for *The New Yorker* in a "Talk of the Town" item in the issue of March 18, 1972. He had been privileged to attend the final rehearsal before Peggy's opening at the Empire Room of the Waldorf:

Miss Lee entered the room right on the dot at one, wearing a black pants suit with a brown suede vest, and sat down at a table on the bandstand beside the piano. She put a Coke and a small black notebook on the table, and began looking through the notebook. Mr. Levy [Lou Levy, who has been her musical director since 1955] got the band's attention and called up the names of several tunes—"I Love Being Here with You," "Fire and Rain," "Just in Time," "I Felt the Earth Move," and "I Love to Love," among others. We pulled up a chair and sat down in front of the bandstand, about ten feet from Miss Lee. . . .

Throughout the rehearsal, Miss Lee spoke to the musicians in a gentle, friendly way, but she spoke to them often. She stopped "Fire and Rain" several times because a guitar figure didn't sound right, and she hummed what she wanted until she got it. In a new tune called "It Changes" she heard a wrong note from the cellist. Though the cellist was playing what was written, Lou Levy agreed with Miss Lee that it sounded wrong, so it was changed. She stopped the same tune twice more because the French horns were having intonation problems. In another tune she asked the drummer to switch from sticks to brushes, and in another she ordered the elimination of a bass-clarinet passage. . . .

During a rehearsal break, the man from *The New Yorker* asked Miss Lee what was in her black notebook. She replied:

> That's my show book. It has my lyrics, a list of my arrangements, the instrumentation of the orchestra, telephone numbers of people in New York who are pertinent to the show, and notes about the tunes—like I'll mark down something about the bass, or more guitar here, or less of the French horn here—and, uh, it's a very organized little book.

Another who had a look at that black book, Robert Salmaggi, of the *World Journal Tribune*, described it as

> a large, black-leather-bound looseleaf affair, jammed with neatly typed-and-mimeo'd notes and data. Every show she's done for the past two decades, right down to each song she sang and what she wore, is carefully recorded. . . . For any upcoming shows Peggy's book outlines, even to hand gestures, what is to happen on stage for her ninety minutes. She lists what sidemen she'll add to the house orchestra, what numbers she'll do, with detailed side comment on treatment, etc.

The visitor from *The New Yorker* referred to Peggy's reputation as a perfectionist.

> Well, it's true that I'm interested in the whole process of the show. The gowns, the lighting, and especially the music. Now, you don't have an audience of musicians, but the music still has to be just right. Because I think the over-all effect is the result of working on things, ironing out the little creases. I think the audience enjoys it more if it comes off well, simply because I enjoy it more, which gives me a sense of well-being and relaxes me, and enables me to do a better job. I think preparation is the key to the whole thing.

One begs leave to qualify that reference to preparation as "the key to the whole thing," lest it be inferred that painstaking professionalism alone makes a Peggy Lee. It does not. It merely characterizes her. She is not, and never has been, an improvisatory, inspirational artist. Some singers, a Billie Holiday, for example, prefer to be guided by the spirit and mood of the moment and the occasion, shaping a performance somewhat differently each night, or each show. They would feel stifled creatively by strict adherence to routine, once the routine has been set. Other singers have been as painstaking as Peggy without ever evoking the magic of her singing.

Preparation is "the key to the whole thing" in Peggy Lee's case, I believe, because from it she derives the security she needs to do with a song the things that she does. I am thinking of security here not so much in psychological as in physical terms. What distinguishes her interpretive devices from those of other excellent singers is their delicacy, their small scale, their subtlety, their ultimate refinement. They need all the support and reinforcement they can get—the arrangement, the playing of the arrangement by every individual in the band, the dress, the lighting, the gestures, the facial expression, and so on.

It is not merely that negligence or accident could spoil a delicate effect, as indeed they might. It is rather that all these constituent elements are essential to the vocal effect. What she achieves may strike the listener as a vocal miracle, but what makes it seem a miracle is not merely vocal. It is, as she expresses it so well, "over-all." What you get from Peggy Lee is not just a song superlatively well sung. It is a production.

Preparation is probably important to her physically in another sense, too. She has, vocally, very little to work with, and she cannot risk getting less than 100 percent return on every vocal vibration. How wisely and shrewdly she invests her vocal inheritance has been documented over the years in a literature of critical superlatives comparable only to that lavished upon Frank Sinatra and Ella Fitzgerald.

English jazz critic Peter Clayton, at the time of Peggy's Royal Albert Hall concert, called her "quite simply the finest singer in the history of popular music." Leonard Feather has described her as being "about as close to perfection as any singer who ever lovingly fashioned a performance for an audience." Peter Reilly, who has been covering the vocal scene for *Stereo Review* for a decade or more, has said: "Peggy simply has no competition as America's première chanteuse." Rex Reed, also commenting for *Stereo Review*, has written of her as "just about the best singer in the business today, and, like brandy, getting better every year, one of the greatest magicians a good song could ever wish for." And Gene Lees, in *High Fidelity*, has called her "the most mature, the most authoritative, the most sensitive and the most consistently intelligent female singer of popular music in America."

I find it both curious and significant that in the considerable accumulation of hyperbole I have screened, all devoted reasonably enough to Peggy Lee's supremacy among American female popular singers, I have so rarely encountered any reference to the meagreness of her vocal endowment. The explanation, obviously, is that her art has disguised it. Her resourcefulness and good sense have been such that there is never any suggestion of strain, and hence, no betrayal of inadequacy. She seems always to have known just what the voice could give. She has never asked for more, and she has rarely asked even for all. She always gives an impression of having something in reserve.

Hence, too, the healthy vocal cords that so astonish her "throat man." They are, indeed, remarkable in a singer who was born (Norma Doloris Egstrom, in Jamestown, North Dakota) in 1920, and who has sung so many songs so many times over a period of so many years, including the thousands of nights when she has sung two sets of between twenty and thirty songs in smoke-filled rooms. But they surprise me less than they surprise her doctor. Despite all the unremitting hard work to which they have been exposed, there can hardly be another pair of vocal cords in any singer's throat that have been treated so considerately, so affectionately.

I am thinking not of gargles and sprays, the avoidance of iced drinks, drafts and overheated atmosphere, or even of periodic rest, but of the light caressing touch of Peggy's breath upon those cords. Peter Clayton has written of "a voice that has ripened, but from which the early morning mist has miraculously never cleared." The reason is simply that Peggy has never imposed enough weight of breath upon it to blow off the mist.

No other singer in my experience has asked less of a voice while using it so much. No other has done more with what the voice has given her. She has never pushed it beyond its natural compass. I doubt that she has ever sung louder than a *mezzo forte*. And yet, within a precariously narrow range, both of vocal compass and of vocal amplitude, she has mined a wealth and variety of color, inflection, eloquent lyricism and even grandeur hardly matched by any other singer, male or female, not excluding Ella Fitzgerald and Frank Sinatra, both of whom had a lot more voice to start with.

Rossini is supposed to have said that one needs only three things to be a singer: voice, voice, voice. I wish we could have a tape recording of that statement as Rossini made it. The tone of his voice, and the inflection, would, I am confident, leave no room for doubt that Rossini was indulging in a sour joke. Many opera singers in his day, as no one had better reason to know than he, certainly proceeded on that assumption. Many do now, which is why opera produces so many dull singers. Rossini, if he were alive, and if my reading of his famous dictum is correct, would be one of Peggy Lee's most ardent admirers.

Could he return to us and be asked to write for her, he would probably not find the task difficult, but surprising. A range of less than two octaves could be taken in stride. At the outset of her career, as revealed in the records she made with Benny Goodman in 1941–43, it was barely an octave and a fifth, from G below to a C sharp or D flat above, a range similar to that of Judy Garland, Ethel Merman and Ethel Waters, among many others. Another major third has been added to it over the years, but at the lower end of the scale rather than at the top.

It is the pitch, or lie, of the voice that would raise Rossini's bushy eyebrows. Even as a young band singer, Peggy sang easily down to the low G, which would have been low even for Rossini's contraltos. She now sings down to the low E flat without sounding conspicuously low. There are spectacular examples in her *The Man I Love* album, on which Frank Sinatra conducts the Nelson Riddle arrangements. In "Happiness Is a Thing Called Joe," for example, she begins on a low E flat, and in "Something Wonderful," she opens on a low E and stays there as she enunciates a monotone introductory recitative.

The gain at the bottom has been achieved without any corresponding loss at the top. On her recent records she still sings the C sharp, or D flat, which has always seemed to be at, or close to, her ceiling. But it has permitted her to choose lower, more congenial keys. It is instructive to compare the recording of "My Old Flame" she made with Benny Goodman about 1942 with the recording she made of the same song on her *The Man I Love* album nearly thirty years later. The early recording, if my turntable is accurate, was in E flat, the later one in B flat, down a fourth.

In writing for her, I should speculate, the problem would be not a matter of pitch alone, but rather of what may be expected from the voice within that limited range, and where. It has always been thin at the top, and Peggy has not defied nature, as Judy Garland and Ethel Merman did, by hollering. If I hear her early records correctly, she solved the deficiency, or adjusted to it, as Bing Crosby did at a much later stage in his career, by accepting a thin top as a fact of life and easing off when approaching it, thus avoiding the sudden telltale contrast of character and color. She has, by now, so reduced the weight of voice throughout its entire compass that she can even resort to falsetto without its being perceptible to any but an experienced and vigilant ear. Her recording of "I Love Being Here with You" on her *Live at Basin Street East* album offers an example.

With Judy Garland and Ethel Merman, unless they are belting, one is always aware of an approaching register break around D flat and D. The sound suddenly trails off, as if the singer were running out of vocal steam. Where formerly the voice was womanly, warm, rich and confident, it becomes girlish and tenuous. You will find none of that in any record of Peggy Lee's that I have heard. If she couldn't do more at the top, she saved the weakness, or inadequacy, from exposure by doing less in the middle and at the bottom.

There are, if I am not mistaken, other reasons for the low dynamic level of her singing, for the lightness of the breath on the cords. In my notes on a Capitol recording of "I Don't Know Enough About You" made in the late 1940s, I find: "She always seems to be confiding." One doesn't confide in a loud voice. It was, and still is, I am sure, the impression of confiding that has had a lot to do with Peggy's appeal to her listeners, both on records and in supper clubs. It is a flattering sensation, which Frank Sinatra, much like Peggy, has understood, appreciated, and learned to exploit.

A more subtle reason for the quietness of Peggy's singing—it may be not so much a reason as a by-product—is that it gives her greater interpretive scope. This must seem, at first glance, contradictory. Why should a singer impose upon herself, or accept, dynamic limits in order to sing more dynamically? The answer? Because there is a greater interpretive return from a slight variation on next to nothing, or *pianissimo*, than there is from a considerable variation between *mezzo forte* and *forte*, or between *forte* and *fortissimo*.

Peggy Lee works from so nearly next to nothing that anything more, or even anything less, inevitably seems like something. She can give the effect of belting—in "Fever," for example, or "Big Spender" —at a level of sound which, in a Merman or a Streisand, would suggest a stage whisper. This latitude, derived from a low-keyed procedure, is made to order for her essentially theatrical musical and vocal instincts.

My procedure in studying singers has been to listen to them on records, preferably in chronological order, or in person, or both, before pursuing the personal and career history. In Peggy's case, the early record that set lights flashing on my analytical mental switch-board was "Why Don't You Do Right?" This was her first hit with the Benny Goodman band, in 1942. Here, suddenly, was a white girl of Scandinavian origin, and from Jamestown, North Dakota, sound-ing like a sister or girl friend of the Nat King Cole who, a few months earlier, had recorded "That Ain't Right." I noted the "black rhythm-and-blues inflections," and the enunciation of such words as "right" and "money," adding: "She sounds as if she were talking back to Nat Cole." I also noted: "What an ear!"

The next record that called my attention to her histrionic pre-dilections and gift of mimicry was "Mañana," made in 1948 when she emerged from the retirement she had accepted upon her marriage to Benny Goodman's guitarist, Dave Barbour, in 1943. Here was something quite different, not rhythm-and-blues, but a *Latino* thing, a foretaste of the engaging "America" number in *West Side Story*. It was her first big hit as a singer on her own. Like "Why Don't You Do Right?" this was pure characterization. Also like "Why Don't You Do Right?" it was her own song (with Dave Barbour). She knows where her important and distinctive attributes lie. "I regard singing pretty much like acting," she told Philip Oakes. "Each song is like playing a different role. I get very involved with my material."

Other examples of vocal characterization are plentiful in the Lee repertoire. Almost every one of her big hits has been a character song, or a song out of which she had fashioned a character. "Big Spender" is

Jo Stafford   Dinah Shore

a charming example, an exuberant, disarmingly explicit impersonation of a broad on the make. I remember hearing her sing George
Harrison's pop-gospel "My Sweet Lord" at the Waldorf. She was
wearing a flowing, billowy white gown of the type she favors, and
suddenly I thought, Aimee Semple MacPherson!

As her act unfolds [wrote Gene Lees in *High Fidelity*,
covering her season at the Copacabana in New York in the
spring of 1968] you realize that Peggy Lee is a great actress. In
one song she'll be the fragile rejected girl of the Dick Manning-
Luiz Bonfà ballad "Empty Glass." Then, with a wink and a
bawdy wave of the arm, she becomes instantly the frowzy London hooker of "Big Spender." Then, perhaps, she'll become
the mature woman finding love on a new level in "The Second
Time Around." Or the happy, round-heeled jet-setter of "When
in Rome." Or the wistful woman contemplating her vanished
youth in "What Is a Woman?" Toward the end of her act, she
throws dignity to the winds and does her utterly delightfully silly
reading of "Fever."

To see a fine actress build a convincing characterization
in the ninety minutes of a movie is impressive enough. But to
see Peggy Lee build fifteen characterizations in the course of an
hour is one of the most impressive things I've seen in show
business. How does she accomplish these instantaneous trans-
formations? I don't know. It mystifies me.

It may be that her procedure as an actress, *i.e.*, her physical
performance in the presentation of a song, is much like her vocal
procedure. She works from very little, does very little—just what is
right, and no more—and makes everything count. "She has lately
refined her facial and body movements," wrote Peter Reilly in *Stereo
Review*, of an appearance on the Ed Sullivan Show, "to a kind of
minimal art that looks strikingly like total paralysis."

Of her performance on another occasion, Reilly observed: "She
wings into view all of a piece, rather like a fully dressed set on a
turntable stage, and remains all but stationary throughout." The "all
but" is the clue. She knows that when an actor stands stock still,
characterization may begin with the twitch of a pinky, the lowering
of the eyelids or a slight cocking of the head, especially if the lighting
is right. With Peggy Lee the lighting is right.

Many of her admirers have wondered why she has not been

more active as an actress on the stage or in films. She has appeared in two pictures, not counting a short sequence in a Bing Crosby picture. The first was a remake of *The Jazz Singer* with Danny Thomas, in 1953. The second was *Pete Kelly's Blues*, in 1955, in which her performance as an alcoholic blues singer won her an Academy Award nomination for "best supporting actress." She could have had a film career had she wanted it.

My guess would be that she does not need a film to satisfy her histrionic propensities. Most scripts, directors and fellow actors would get in her way. All she needs is the right songs, and she gets them, even if she has to write them herself. She has written more than five hundred, either on her own or in collaboration, at one time or another, with Dave Barbour, Sonny Burke, Cy Coleman, Dave Grusin, Quincy Jones, Johnny Mandel, Victor Young and many more.

Her unique gift of characterization may have had much to do with the fact that she has been more consistently successful than any other singer of her generation in adapting her art to the new song styles that came in with rock in the mid-1950s. If, as Peter Reilly has put it, she is "a survivor in an unfriendly environment," it is because, where most singers shape a song to suit their style, Peggy shapes her style to suit the song. That is why, as Peter Clayton has noted, "she is the one singer who can keep up to date without ever trying."

The vocal technique, the low-keyed approach, the basic interpretive devices remain constant, but the phrasing, the inflection, the pacing, the coloring of the voice, the rhythm and, very importantly, the enunciation all derive from her reading of each song. This adaptability, or perhaps her habit of adapting, made it easier for her than for others to accomplish the leap from, say, Arlen, Berlin, Gershwin and Porter to Carole King, Kris Kristofferson, Randy Newman, Leon Russell and James Taylor.

"Hearing all the great lyrics produced by the Beatles, Burt Bacharach, Donovan, Simon and Garfunkel," she told Leonard Feather (*Melody Maker*, June 1, 1968), "I knew that we were long past the day when you could combine everything in the same bag and put it down as rock 'n' roll. The only suitable term that takes it all in today is 'contemporary.'" Peggy's repertoire, now, aside from the reprises of her old hits, is predominantly contemporary.

Her knack of characterization, her adaptability and her dedica-

June Christy

Doris Day

Chris Connor

tion to her art and craft over a span of thirty years have sufficed to place Peggy Lee in a class by herself among the scores of girl band singers, many of them delightful singers and accomplished musicians and vocalists, who achieved considerable fame and a devoted following during the swing era. There were so many of them, and the best of them were so popular, that I refrain from mentioning a single name lest failure to mention others give offense. George T. Simon, in *The Big Bands*, has given them a knowing and generous tribute in a chapter called "The Vocalists."

Most of them married—many of them married band musicians, and some of them married their bosses—and withdrew from the professional scene. Peggy Lee, following her divorce in 1952 from Dave Barbour, father of her daughter Nikki, her only child, has had three more marriages and three more divorces. She has been felled twice by pneumonia, the first attack, in 1961, leaving her dependent upon a portable oxygen tank, familiarly known as "Charlie," for periodic respiratory assistance. She has always come back.

I find it significant that, sheerly as a band singer, she was not the unique artist of more recent years. She was not the national and international figure with Benny Goodman that Frank Sinatra became with Tommy Dorsey. She may have found the band format inhibiting. I, at least, feel that it was inhibiting when I listen to her Goodman records. She phrased delightfully. She exhibited, even then, an immaculate intonation, and she could swing as few other band singers have ever swung. (Mundell Lowe, the guitarist, speaking from much experience as a member of her later backing groups, says that she is the only singer he has ever worked with who "can swing on quarter notes.")

But the one or two choruses in what was primarily a band number did not give her room to stretch out, to develop a song in her own way and at her own pace. Like Sinatra, she could realize her full potential only when she could work in a format tailored to her measure rather than vice versa, as with a band. There is no doubt, however, that singing with a band was an invaluable experience, as it had been for Sinatra. "I learned more about music from the men I worked with in bands," she has said, "than I've learned anywhere else. They taught me discipline and the value of rehearsing and how to train. Even if the interpretation of a particular song wasn't exactly what we wanted, we had to make the best of it."

As with Sinatra, one can hear in the early records the elements and a foretaste of future greatness. Benny Goodman's sharp ear and intelligence caught the portents when he first heard her in a Chicago club in 1941. He was, as he has told George T. Simon, "struck by her sound and interpretation. After she joined us, she was quite nervous for six months, or we hadn't picked the right material for her at the beginning, and a lot of people were not taken with her singing. But she certainly caught on after that when she came out with 'Somebody Else Is Taking My Place' and 'Why Don't You Do Right?' "

Another who noted something exceptional was Simon, who reported in *Metronome*, December 1941:

> Peggy Lee, who wasn't too impressive till she got over the shock of finding herself with Benny's band, is slowly turning into one of the great singers in the field. The lass has a grand flair for phrasing—listen to her on those last sets at night, when the band's just noodling behind her, and when there aren't any complicated backgrounds to sing against, and you'll get the idea. That she gets a fine beat, that she sings in tune, and that she's awfully good-looking are more self-evident.

This is among the old *Metronome* notices reprinted in Simon's more recent book, *Simon Says*. He appends this comment:

"Lovely lass then, vague and sensitive and very bright. Hasn't changed very much since then, either."

22

Barbra Streisand

When Barbra Streisand sang to 18,000 people at the Forum in Los Angeles on April 15, 1972, in a fund-raiser for the Presidential election campaign of Senator George McGovern, it was her first public concert since that memorable televised outing before a crowd estimated at 135,000 in New York's Central Park in the summer of 1967.

Not that she had otherwise been either out of sight or out of mind. Quite the contrary. She had been making movies, where the bigger money and the bigger exposure are. Her impersonation of Fanny Brice in *Funny Girl* had won her an Oscar in 1969. There had been *Hello, Dolly!* and *On a Clear Day You Can See Forever*, and nonsinging roles in *The Owl and the Pussycat* and *What's Up, Doc?* There had been a long series of record albums, including the soundtracks of her movies and television specials.

Still, there was the suggestion in that Forum concert, if not of a comeback, at least of a *return* or *re-emergence*. For Barbra-watchers —and our number is legion—the ensuing album, *Barbra Streisand— Live at the Forum*, played against the soundtrack album of *A Happening in Central Park*, provided an opportunity to compare the Streisand of 1972 with the Streisand of 1967. The experience recalled to my mind much of what I have read of Angelica Catalani, who

359

lived from 1780 until 1849, and who, in her prime, was always billed as *Prima Cantatrice del Mondo*, or The World's Greatest Singer.

Three contemporary references to Catalani seem to me pertinent to the Barbra Streisand of these two albums. One is attributed to Queen Charlotte, who is reported to have said that she wanted cotton wool in her ears when Catalani sang. Another quotes an unidentified and probably apocryphal London wit as saying, when asked if he were going to York to hear her, that he could hear her well enough where he was. The third comes from the pen of that noble connoisseur of *bel canto*, Lord Mount-Edgcumbe, who, when Catalani returned to London from Paris in 1824 after an absence of nearly a decade, found "her powers undiminished, her taste unimproved."

The Streisand of these two albums calls to mind another parallel from the lore of classical music. I do not now remember the name of the critic who reviewed a recital by the great American Quaker baritone, David Bispham, in Carnegie Hall, in New York, in the early years of the century, but I remember essentially what he said: If Mr. Bispham had been just a bit less emotional, there would not have been a dry eye in the house.

It must seem odd that in discussing one whom I and many others reckon among the great American popular singers, I should begin by drawing unflattering parallels. But with Barbra Streisand the unflattering is not only inescapable; it is also an integral element of her image as a public performer. There are doubtless thousands upon thousands who admire her as a singer without reservation. But I do not know of a single critic who does.

Many of the singers previously discussed in these pages have had their detractors. What distinguishes Barbra Streisand from Bing Crosby, Al Jolson, Elvis Presley and Frank Sinatra is the fact that, in her case, admirer and detractor may so often be united in the same person. I speak from personal experience in remarking how easy it is, in listening to a Streisand album, or a Streisand movie or television soundtrack, to applaud one song and abhor another, sometimes to switch from applause to abhorrence within the span of a single song.

Peter Reilly, in *Stereo Review* (February 1968), expressed as well as anyone the difficulty and, indeed, the necessity, of accepting constant juxtaposition of the delightful and the egregious, of the sublime and, yes, of the ridiculous, in Barbra Streisand's singing. He wrote, reviewing the *Simply Streisand* album:

> Streisand is back in top form, proving again that she is the greatest song stylist of her day, and quite possibly the best singer. These are strong words, I know, and I can already hear the howls of protest from many, but that remains my opinion (yes, she is overly dramatic; yes, she does sound like Aretha Franklin in parts of "Lover Man" and like Mae West in parts of "Stout Hearted Men"; yes, she is more a singing actress than a simon-pure singer-type singer; yes, she is incredibly mannered; yes . . . you fill in your own objections).

This duality in the Streisand public performance, recalling inevitably the little girl with the little curl right in the middle of her forehead, extends, probably characteristically, to her attire. She can dress as well, and as badly, as she can sing. She made the International Best-Dressed list for two years, but was dropped in 1969 because of "a bottom-baring bikini under see-through trousers" that she wore while receiving her Oscar. Rex Reed described what she had on at Central Park as "a perfectly godawful dress that looked like a cut-up parachute dyed in Rit." That same outfit, seen on television, suggested to me a female Batman.

It's as easy to have rhetorical fun with Barbra Streisand's excesses as it is difficult to identify and define all the facets of her vocalism and phrasing that have made her a great singer in spite of them. Or maybe it is simply that what is excessive is so conspicuous that it tends to obscure the lovely things she accomplishes when content to leave well enough alone. That sustained nasal bray on *my* at the close of any of her performances of "Don't Rain on My Parade" is, for example, pretty hard to forget or to forgive.

She has, to begin with, a remarkable voice, remarkable not only in terms of range and volume, but also, and more importantly, in terms of its resources of character, color and nuance. Joseph Morgenstern expressed it well when he observed, in a *Newsweek* article (January 5, 1970), that what matters most about her is "how she's able to make such a lot go such a long way." Few others among the American popular singers—Sarah Vaughan is one—have been so richly endowed.

The voice is a contralto, possibly closer to a mezzo-soprano, of superb quality when not under pressure, with a range of well over two octaves, from a low E to the high G, and probably a bit more than that in either direction. It is, moreover, susceptible of an infinite variety of shade and inflection. Place all this at the disposal and discretion—or indiscretion—of a striking personality who is also a born actress, with powers of personal projection hardly matched by any other singer of her generation, and you have a formidable combination.

The singers Barbra reminds me of most often are Fanny Brice and Ethel Waters, although she never sounds in the least like either. Both Brice and Waters were greater artists, primarily because they understood the communicative magic of understatement. Streisand understands it, too, but the understanding seldom survives the excitement of the moment when she begins to build to the climax of a song, usually shattering an enchanting quiet beginning. If you listen to a lot of Streisand, you begin to hear those quiet beginnings with apprehension, sensing the seductive whisper sheathes a strident yowl.

She is more singer *per se* than Brice was. She has more voice, and she can handle a wider repertoire. Ethel Waters had less voice than Barbra, but she was fully as versatile. What links Barbra so vividly to both Fanny Brice and Ethel Waters is her innate theatrical instinct and her flair for comedy, her sense of fun, and her ability to move back and forth across the thin line which, in great artists, separates, or joins, comedy and tragedy. This important aspect of her art has been insufficiently exploited in her records, although it is what made her Miss Marmelstein in *I Can Get It for You Wholesale* and her Fanny Brice in *Funny Girl* stepping stones to international stardom.

Like Ethel Waters—and like Judy Garland, too—Barbra is a natural mimic, whose mimicry, I would guess, is sometimes unwitting. Despite her pronounced individuality, she often sounds like other singers: Aretha Franklin, Judy Garland, Peggy Lee, Ethel Merman and Joni Mitchell. Her singing of "People," for instance, or of "Don't Rain on My Parade," has always been, to my ears, pure Garland. It all depends on what she is singing. She has many voices, almost, it seems, a voice for every song—except when she is hollering. When the song happens to be identified with another singer, or is conspicuously suited to the style of another singer, Barbra's own singing is likely to recall that singer.

A basic problem is repertoire. So much of what she has sung has been beneath her potential, both as singer and as actress. She is a big artist, and the pop song material with which she has been saddled throughout the better part of a decade, or with which she has saddled herself, has been too slight. She has reacted by blowing up the songs emotionally beyond what a slender subject and a slender musical frame can support or sustain.

Her singing of Jim Webb's "Didn't We?" on the *Live at the Forum* album is a serviceable example among many. The song itself is an endearing, rather wistful account of a love affair that "almost made it." Barbra sings it as if it were Floria Tosca's "Vissi d'arte," or the Immolation Scene from *Götterdämmerung*. Indeed, it has often occurred to me that she should have been an opera singer.

She needs greater, more imposing dramatic substance than most popular songs can give her. A Peggy Lee can take a popular song and make it more dramatic than "Vissi d'arte" simply by mining all that the song contains—and no more. Barbra, instead of scaling her singing to the dimensions of a song, as Peggy does, tends rather to scale the song to her own imposing dimensions and predilections as an actress. Something has to give, and it is not going to be Barbra. She sings about her "precious freedom" in a harmless French trifle, "Free Again," for example, as if she were celebrating an emancipation proclamation for the human race—and sounds silly.

She is not, obviously, going to be an opera singer. Her most recent albums, however, suggest that she may have found a more congenial repertoire in the newer folk, rock and soul idioms—and especially in the latter—than she did in the older mainstream songs with which she began. A departure was suggested with *What About Today?* In *Stoney End* she came closer to a satisfactory identification with the style of today's young troubadours.

It was no accident. Richard Perry, who produced that album, told an interviewer shortly after its release in 1969: "I convinced her that she had gone about as far as she could with the kind of pop stuff she'd been singing up to then. I brought her a pile of new songs, and we sat down and worked them out." Barbra's sensitivity to stylistic subtleties, her ability to match voice and phrasing to the material at hand, were confirmed amusingly when Leonard Feather played "My Man" from the *Stoney End* album for Aretha Franklin in a *Down Beat* Blindfold Test (May 30, 1970). "Was that," asked Miss Franklin, "Diahann Carroll?"

Finally, with *Barbra Joan Streisand*, Barbra would seem to have found her true vocation in a style closer to soul than to folk or folk-rock. John Lennon's "Mother" may not be everyone's idea of a soul song, but Barbra, with expert assistance from Billy Preston, a gospel-based organist, and an ingenious arrangement by Perry and Gene Page, makes a soul song out of it, sounding remarkably like Aretha, only better. Embellishments that sometimes disfigure her treatment of straight pop songs suddenly sound just right. And toward the end she produces three upward *portamenti*, ascending to the high F, that remind me of Mahalia Jackson in her exuberant prime.

Most of the tracks on this album show Barbra moving toward a blacker style than she has explored in the past. The results suggest that she may at last have found the next best thing to opera for the exploitation and satisfaction of her enormous talent. Soul is a style capable of absorbing, accommodating and even benefiting from her habitual excesses. If so, she is uniquely fortunate.

Repertoire has been the despair of most young singers of the past decade, and of many of the older singers, too, as they have tried to keep up with the times. Those younger singers who grew up listening to Ella Fitzgerald, Peggy Lee and Frank Sinatra, listening to the songs they sang and to the way they sang them, and fashioning their own singing accordingly, have been unable to establish rapport with the young listeners, or to efface from the aural memory of an older audience the great singers of the 1940s and 1950s. At the same time, still younger singers who have grown up with the post-Presley sounds of folk and rock and pop, who have written the new songs, and sung them, have not been able to address themselves successfully to listeners of an older generation. Barbra, apparently, can take the blues- and gospel-derived songs of the young, and show how they can be sung well without being made to sound square and old-fashioned.

It is much too early to review the Streisand career as one can review the career of an Ella Fitzgerald, a Billie Holiday, a Peggy Lee or a Frank Sinatra. She is still young. She has, one hopes, many years of singing and maturing ahead of her. The sequence of her record albums suggests an artist still seeking an idiom tailored to her artistic measure. On the evidence of *Barbra Joan Streisand*, she may be getting warm. It is unlikely that she will ever stop hollering. But in a gospel-derived repertoire she may have found a congenial auditorium.

Coda

As I review these chapters, bracketing half a century of American popular singing, I find myself reminded again and again of Alec Wilder's *American Popular Song—The Great Innovators 1900–1950*, published in 1972. Wilder had studied American popular songs much as I have studied the singers who sang them, *i.e.*, as a classically schooled musician finding in the American, or Afro-American, popular idiom a more vital continuity of Western musical evolution than is evident in the so-called *avant-garde* manifestations of "serious" music. I have found myself noting, in the work of the singers, the same cyclical phenomenon of birth, adolescence, maturity and decline that prompted Wilder to select 1950 as a cutoff date.

He feels, obviously, that the first half of the century was a golden age of American songwriting, and I agree. I feel the same way about the singers, although my half-century begins twenty years later; and I feel, as he does, that the golden age, or at least a golden age, has come to an end, that we are as unlikely to have again a Mildred Bailey, a Nat Cole, an Ella Fitzgerald, a Billie Holiday, a Peggy Lee or a Frank Sinatra as we are to find another Harold Arlen, another Irving Berlin, another Jerome Kern. Each of those singers, as was true of Wilder's songwriters, took an inherited, still vital idiom, reworked it in his own fashion, and carried it to a point of perfection and refinement beyond which it was impossible to go.

I have been mindful, too, of other evolutionary parallels that can be drawn from earlier epochs in European music, and especially from the evolution of the vocal art as it can be traced in the history of opera. Contemporary commentary on the state of singing throughout a roughly 350-year span finds older singer after older singer, critic after critic, bewailing the declining standards of the art. The most common complaint was that refinements treasured by one generation were being sacrificed to the vulgar tastes of the generation succeeding—and to the vulgar tastes and habits of its younger singers.

The big sound, the full-voiced high notes, the melodramatic exuberance of the singers of Meyerbeer, Verdi and Wagner would have been thought crude, ill-mannered and inelegant by connoisseurs of the time of Rossini, Donizetti and Bellini, just as those who sang Rossini, Donizetti and Bellini would have been thought uncouth a generation earlier by the admirers of the great *castrati* Pacchierotti and Crescentini. And so it goes, back through the singers of Mozart, Gluck and Handel to those who embodied the poetical and rhetorical precepts of Caccini, Monteverdi and Cavalli.

I find these judgments reflected in my own appraisal of the younger popular singers of the present. I sense a decline from the subtle artistry, the imaginative, ingenious and sure-footed improvisations of the great singers of the 1930s, 1940s and 1950s. I hear them much as older critics of the 1830s heard Gilbert-Louis Duprez when he astonished—and delighted—Parisian opera-goers with a full-voiced high C. Rossini said it sounded like a capon being garrotted. Others thought, less picturesquely, that Duprez was yelling.

I have to remind myself that our younger singers are singing to younger listeners bred to a higher decibel count than I find agreeable or even tolerable. I have to remind myself that they are singing to listeners sympathetic to a kind of exhibitionistic emoting, bordering on hysteria, that I have been conditioned to regard as fustian and ham. It is these younger listeners, not I, who will determine the further course of the vocal art, just as it was the applause of younger, less tradition-conscious listeners that made Duprez' high C and Maria Malibran's theatrical extravagance exemplary for opera singers ever afterward. Every time I hear a tenor reach for those abominable high Cs (unwritten) when singing "Di quella pira" in a performance of *Il Trovatore*, I send a telepathic entreaty to Satan to give Duprez another poke in purgatory. But I am being unfair to Duprez. He was not the cause of the abomination, merely a symptom.

In other words, nothing new. Sheer volume and high notes have always worked their wonders upon human sensibility—or insensibility—whenever the means to achieve them were at hand. The evolution of the symphony orchestra, for example, from Stamitz to Strauss, demonstrates a typical affinity for a rising decibel count, and a typical rise in aural tolerance. Haydn's auditors, or Bach's, if suddenly exposed to Strauss's *Don Juan* or *Ein Heldenleben*, as played by a modern symphony orchestra, would have rushed from the hall in agony, clapping their hands to their ears.

We who relish the racket today simply reflect an aural tolerance raised gradually over a span of two centuries. It is the same with the modern piano. Had Mozart or Beethoven ever hit one of their instruments the way any one of a thousand pianists hits a concert grand, there would have been nothing left but kindling wood and baling wire. What is new today is that electrical amplification has greatly accelerated the rate of increase, both of volume and of tolerance. In the articulation of song, it has similarly assisted and encouraged the ham.

The microphone, one concedes regretfully, has not fulfilled the promise some of us sensed in its use by such artists as Bing Crosby and Frank Sinatra and their contemporaries, male and female. It seemed then that singers had suddenly been relieved of the necessity of raising their voices in order to be heard above an orchestra, or at considerable distances from their listeners. They could beguile us again with the refinements of vocal and rhetorical eloquence so prized by the founders of Italian opera in the seventeenth century. For some thirty years they did. It was not electronic science that put an end to the honeymoon. It was human susceptibility to an assault upon the ear. Singers nowadays holler, as some singers have always hollered, because their listeners like being hollered at. Only now the mischief is compounded by amplification.

I find a further parallel with European musical history in what seems to me a tendency toward overarrangement and overemphasis in the instrumental and choral backings now supplied the popular singer, granting the high level of accomplishment demonstrated by both arrangers and engineers. European singers in the nineteenth

Dionne Warwicke

Diahann Carroll

century were increasingly subordinated to, and inhibited by, the size, activity and importance of the orchestra, which, especially in opera, preempted the singer's former sovereignty.

For the popular singer there is a new factor, especially in recording, in the person of the engineer. He is a problem for the critic, too. Almost all vocal records, today, are the result of "mixing" and adjusting. The microphone cannot improve a singer's sound. Engineering can, especially in the modification of high frequencies to eliminate stridency, and in the exploitation of echo to give body to a voice not so substantially endowed either by nature or by schooling.

What we hear as a performance is, in fact, an amalgam of many performances, musical and engineering, by many individuals in many places. The singer often hears the instrumental backing for the first time in the mixing room. The mixing may be good or bad. When it is good, what we hear is a good performance. But it is not a performance that ever took place. While it may be honorable, it is not honest. Many singers suffer accordingly when required to perform in public concerts under less carefully, less ingeniously, less protectively contrived circumstances.

It would be a rasher—and brasher—man than I who would dare a prediction as to the further course of vocalism in the throats of the popular singers. I would hazard no more than a guess that the influence of the gospel and rhythm-and-blues singers, now manifested in soul, will be felt for some time to come. There is much to be admired in this approach to song and singing, especially the uninhibited and artful use of falsetto by both men and woman. One regrets the predominance of sound over sense, and sometimes the character and quality of the sound itself. But that may be a passing phenomenon. Among the folk singers it has been the other way around. They tend to be poets rather than vocalists, the sense of their communication being more important than the sound. I should not be surprised to see a gradual merger of soul and folk—and to hear some delightful singing.

I do not share Alec Wilder's distaste for the new generation of songwriters, although I do agree that a certain admirable craft and style of songwriting came to an end just as and when he says it did. It may be that the new songwriters merely need the singers who can do justice to their songs, singers who can be to Burt Bacharach, Kris Kristofferson, Randy Newman, Harry Nilsson, Paul Simon, Jim

Webb and Paul Williams what Fred Astaire, Tony Bennett, Ella Fitzgerald, Billie Holiday, Peggy Lee, Ethel Merman and Frank Sinatra were to Wilder's heroes. Indeed, we have already had examples in the way Dionne Warwicke has sung Bacharach, in Johnny Cash's singing of Kristofferson, and in Glen Campbell's of Webb.

Others will be coming along—singing, I hope, not hollering. I commend to them Ethel Waters' reminiscence of her grandmother's advice to Ethel's gospel-shouting mother: "You don't have to holler so. God has very big ears. He can hear you even if you whisper."

So, dear singers, can we!

GLOSSARY

APPOGGIATURA. Derived from *appoggiare*, meaning "to lean," or "support." It is a note inserted between two other notes to assist, support or give emphasis and/or elegance to a melodic or harmonic progression.

ARIOSO. Essentially aria-like, commonly used to identify a melodic episode that falls short of being a self-contained aria or song.

ARPEGGIO. Literally, "harplike," designating a passage in which the voice (or instrument) sounds the successive notes of a chord.

BREATHY. A term used to describe a kind of sound in singing that suggests, or betrays, the emission of breath unapplied to the activation of the vocal cords.

CADENZA. The Italian word for cadence, but designating, in general musical terminology, a brilliant virtuoso episode, written or improvised, preceding the close of a song. The device, although not the term, is frequently employed by popular singers, not for virtuosic but for expressive purposes, and usually improvised from the melodic and harmonic materials of a song.

CODA. Meaning "tail," and used in music to denote an episode added to the end of a song or instrumental piece or movement. As with *cadenza*, popular singers employ the device, but not the term. Frank Sinatra's familiar ending for Harold Arlen's "One for My Baby" is an admirable example.

COMPASS. Used synonymously for range, referring to the range of pitches a singer's voice commands, e.g., two octaves, or an octave and a fifth.

DOMINANT. A term given to the fifth note of the diatonic major and minor scales, or modes, because of the dominant character of its relationship to other notes, or pitches, of the scale, and especially to the tonic, the fundamental note of the scale. In numerical terminology, the tonic is 1, the subdominant (or fourth degree of the scale) is 4 and the dominant 5.

EMBELLISHMENT. Synonymous with ornamentation, referring to notes added to decorate or "embellish" the given melody.

FALSETTO. Literally, false voice, a thin, colorless type of vocal production roughly equivalent to the sound of harmonics on the violin. In the singing voice it usually occurs at the upper end of the range, where the natural voice leaves off unless extended by muscular adjustment (downward) of the larynx. Except as used by countertenors and male altos, it rarely figures nowadays in classical singing. In earlier times it was common to both male and female singers, as it is in American popular singing today, especially in the blues, country, gospel and soul categories.

FOCUS. Synonymous with placement (of the voice), a figurative term covering the coordination of all the muscular factors and functions that contribute to the production of an agreeable, free, resonant and muscularly unconstricted, uninhibited sounding of the voice.

GLOTTIS. The opening between the vocal cords. The *coup de glotte*, or "blow of the glottis," represents a sudden closing of the cords, as in a slight cough. Popular singers use it, although not the term, to give prominence to certain vowels, separating them, in effect, from what has gone before. As they use it, the device has more to do with distinct enunciation than with vocal production.

GRACE NOTE. A general term for a note added for ornamental or decorative purpose.

HEAD VOICE. A type of light vocal production, usually at the upper extreme of a singer's range, distinguished (but not always distinguishable) by the fact that the larynx remains under muscular control, permitting the tone to be augmented or diminished as the weight of breath upon the cords is increased or relaxed. Popular singers, exploiting the auxiliary faculties of the microphone, tend to enter, or employ, head voice at a lower point in their range than do classical singers.

LEGATO. From *legare*, meaning "to bind" or "tie," and referring to a smooth (bound) passage from one note to the other.

MELISMA. Another term for ornamentation or embellishment. As commonly used now, it refers to ornamentation of an especially elaborate or flowery type. It may be applied most aptly to the type of ornamentation widely practiced by gospel singers, and known to them as "curlicues."

MICROTONAL. Refers to an infinity of conceivable pitches between the prescribed pitches of a major or minor diatonic scale. In popular singing these pitches are widely used, as in slurring, although neither notated nor precisely identified.

MIXED VOICE. A kind of vocal production involving the mixture of registers. It is employed most commonly to relieve the weight and tension of "chest voice" by an admixture of "head voice."

MONODY. Or homophony, as opposed to polyphony, referring to a single- as opposed to multiple-voiced music. Not to be confused with *monotone*, referring to sound sustained on a single pitch.

MORDENT. From *mordere*, "to bite," a fast, light shake, involving either an upper or a lower additional note, widely used by popular singers either ornamentally or to produce the effect of a catch in the throat. Almost any record track by Bing Crosby will yield an example.

NOTE VALUE. The length of time allotted to a note within the rhythmic plan of a bar, or measure.

ORNAMENT. See Embellishment.

PARLANDO. In a speaking, or conversational, manner.

PASSAGE. Refers to the area (or areas) in the vocal range where the voice "passes" from one register to another. Vocal technique is largely a matter of achieving the muscular control (primarily of the larynx) required to make the passage not only successful but also imperceptible.

POLYPHONY. See Monody.

PORTAMENTO. From *portare*, meaning "to carry," a device by which the voice is carried from one note to another, especially a distant note, without break, and gliding over the intervening notes.

RANGE. See Compass.

RECITATIVO. In a recitative manner. Less sustained, melodically, than *parlando*.

REGISTER. A term used to designate a certain area of the vocal range, or compass. There are generally assumed to be three such areas: lower, middle and high, or chest, middle and upper (or head).

RIFF. Defined by Gunther Schuller, in *Early Jazz*, as "a relatively short phrase repeated over a changing chord pattern, originally employed as a background device."

ROULADE. A brilliant vocal exercise in which a number of incidental, or passing, notes, usually in a sequential order, are added to the essential notes of a melody.

RUBATO. From *rubare*, meaning "to steal." It is a device, now more widely employed by popular than by classical singers, by which time is stolen from one note and given to another, producing in the listener a sensation of suspense as he waits for restitution to be accomplished.

SCAT. A term given to a kind of singing in which the singer improvises *ad lib* on syllables of no textual significance.

SLUR. A kind of exaggerated *legato*, in which the note of destination is approached in a gliding manner, usually from below, as opposed to "clean" passage from one note to the next.

STACCATO. From *staccare*, meaning "to detach," and referring to notes hit lightly and then instantly released. It is rarely employed by popular singers except in scatting.

TESSITURA. Literally, "texture," but used in vocal music to designate the prevailing, or average, pitch of a song or aria.

TIMBRE. The term refers to the quality, more specifically, to the color image suggested by the sound of a voice.

TONALITY. Synonymous with the more common "key," e.g., C major, C minor, etc.

TONIC. See Dominant.

TREMOLO. The rapid alternation of two notes, usually a third or more apart, as distinct from the adjacent notes of a trill.

TRILL. The rapid alternation of two adjacent notes. It is rarely used by popular singers, and then usually in the form of a slow trill rather than a fast one.

TURN. A four-note embellishment of a given note, employing the note above, the note itself, the note below, and ending on the note itself.

VIBRATO. A more or less rapid, nondetached iteration of a given note, giving the effect of vibration, or throbbing. A fast iteration is usually thought of as a "narrow" vibrato, a slow iteration as "wide." Most voices have a characteristic vibrato. Those in which there seems to be none are thought of as "straight," or "hooty." Billy Eckstine and Sarah Vaughan offer examples of a wide but controlled vibrato. Eckstine likens his to the ripples surging outward from the point of impact when a stone is dropped into a pool of placid water.

YODEL. A kind of vocal production achieved by the rapid alternation of normal voice and falsetto.

INDEX

Completed 6/26/85
Forestville, Ca.